Prostitution and Sex Work

Recent Titles in
Historical Guides to Controversial Issues in America

Prostitution and Sex Work

Melissa Hope Ditmore

Historical Guides to Controversial Issues in America

 GREENWOOD

AN IMPRINT OF ABC-CLIO, LLC
Santa Barbara, California • Denver, Colorado • Oxford, England

Copyright 2011 by Melissa Hope Ditmore

All rights reserved. No part of this publication may be reproduced, stored in a retrieval system, or transmitted, in any form or by any means, electronic, mechanical, photocopying, recording, or otherwise, except for the inclusion of brief quotations in a review, without prior permission in writing from the publisher.

Library of Congress Cataloging-in-Publication Data

Ditmore, Melissa Hope.
    Prostitution and sex work / Melissa Hope Ditmore.
        p. cm. — (Historical guides to controversial issues in America)
    Includes bibliographical references and index.
        ISBN 978–0–313–36289–7 (cloth : alk. paper) — ISBN 978–0–313–36290–3 (ebook)
1. Prostitution—United States. 2. Sex oriented businesses—United States. I. Title.
HQ144.D58   2011
306.74—dc22   2010036300

ISBN: 978–0–313–36289–7
EISBN: 978–0–313–36290–3

15 14 13 12 11   1 2 3 4 5

This book is also available on the World Wide Web as an eBook.
Visit www.abc-clio.com for details.

Greenwood
An Imprint of ABC-CLIO, LLC

ABC-CLIO, LLC
130 Cremona Drive, P.O. Box 1911
Santa Barbara, California 93116-1911

This book is printed on acid-free paper ∞

Manufactured in the United States of America

Portions of chapter 4, "Morality, Money, and Prostitution Prior to the Criminalization of Prostitution," and chapter 7, "Immigration Law and State Legislation of Morality," first appeared in Melissa Ditmore, "Trafficking and Prostitution: A Problematic Conflation" (PhD diss., City University of New York, 2002). They are used here with permission from the author.

*To my mother, Patricia Venditto Ditmore,
and to Sarah Steiner and Evan Steiner.*

"To a Common Prostitute"
By Walt Whitman

Be composed—be at ease with me—I am Walt Whitman, liberal and lusty as Nature;

Not till the sun excludes you, do I exclude you;

Not till the waters refuse to glisten for you, and the leaves to rustle for you, do my words refuse to glisten and rustle for you.

My girl, I appoint with you an appointment—and I charge you that you make preparation to be worthy to meet me,

And I charge that you be patient and perfect till I come.

Till then, I salute you with a significant look, that you do not forget me.

From *Leaves of Grass*. Philadelphia: D. McKay, 1900 (1855)

Contents

List of Tables

Acknowledgments

My friends and family have endured more history lectures over dinner than anyone should have to withstand, much less forgive. Treasured colleagues have encouraged me, and I am deeply indebted to the many people who offered feedback on drafts of these chapters, including, but not limited to, Bob Alford, Melynda Barnhart, Sienna Baskin, Virginia E. Carstens, Patricia Ticineto Clough, Koren Gaines, Deborah Gambs, Belkis Garcia, Jean Halley, Kitten Infinite, He-Jin Kim, Rose M. Kim, Jeffrey Klaehn, William Kornblum, Mickey McGee, Lauren McGuinn, Angus McIntyre, Dina Pinsky, Michael Putnam, Tracy Quan, Barbara Katz Rothman, Tara Sawyer, Ben Singer, Carol Stuart, Juhu Thukral, Amy Elaine Wakeland, Jo Weldon, and Elizabeth Wissinger. Norma Jean Almodovar, Cyndee Clay, Teresa Dulce, Robyn Few, Liz Highleyman, Hawk Kincaid, Carol Leigh, Tracy Quan, Audacia Ray, Tara Sawyer, Jessica Spector, Annie Sprinkle, Margo St. James, Juhu Thukral, and Rachel West took time shared their experiences and offered information about their colleagues. Priscilla Alexander gave me access to her enormous collection of sex work resources along with her experiences. Jesse Ainslie, Scott Ainslie, Naomi Akers, Sean Condron and Billy, Molly Crabapple, Patricia Venditto Ditmore, Judy Dunaway, Nadine Friedman, Roger Giner-Sorolla, Jenny Gutbezahl, Eliyanna Kaiser, Kerwin Kaye, Rose M. Kim, Lia Kudless, John Leavitt, Alix Lutnick, Angus McIntyre, John Mehlberg, John Neilson, Tracy Quan, Suzanne Ramsey, Will Rockwell, Randi Rosenblum, Tara Sawyer, Matthew Weingarden, Jo Weldon, and Rachel West offered marvelous suggestions for primary resources. The resources of the New York Public Library are irreplaceable treasures. The generous hospitality of the McIntyre-Cooper clan afforded me great comfort in a peaceful environment in which to work. My research assistant Rachel Aimee formatted the tables and the bibliography. Vivian Pacheco advised me about useful software features. Greenwood and ABC-CLIO's production coordinator Mark Kane was patient and dedicated throughout the publishing process. My editor at Greenwood and ABC-CLIO, Sandy Towers, deserves all credit for the existence of this book.

Preface

Prostitution is the nexus of two sensitive topics, sex and money. To survey the history of prostitution and sex work in the United States of America is to encounter a dearth of information prior to colonization, salacious tales about voluptuaries told by moralizers and advertisers, anodyne attempts to remove all matters of interest from the topic, and heated political discussions of how to address prostitution. This book attempts to offer an overview of prostitution from the colonial era into the 21st century. Manifestations of the phenomenon of prostitution are addressed throughout. State and federal laws did not directly address prostitution until the 20th century. However, the absence of laws does not mean that prostitution was widely accepted or respected, and so attention is paid to police practices and social mores to highlight the position of prostitutes in society. This book offers a historical overview alongside discussions of recurring themes such as economic motivation for sex work, trafficking in persons, racial and ethnic stratification in sex work, and violence against sex workers.

Space limitations necessitated elaborating on a few themes rather than providing in-depth historical investigation. This could only be accomplished by capitalizing on existing scholarship, synthesized with primary sources, research and advocacy materials from benevolent organizations, private collections of publications by sex workers, and—in a few scintillating instances—conversations with the main characters in the sex workers' rights movement. I have tried to convey the passionate discourse on prostitution and sex work that has occurred since the colonial era and that continues in the United States today.

Introduction

Prostitution and sex work feature prominently in the culture and history of the United States of America. Prostitution simultaneously fascinates and repels, falling as it does at the nexus of two topics rarely discussed openly—sex and money. Prostitution is perennial in history and culture, despite social opprobrium. Prostitutes have been institutionalized, forced out of town, and subjected to mandatory internal physical examinations. Prostitutes who participate in regulated prostitution may be required to cede their right to privacy regarding medical and other personal information. Criminalization of prostitution prevents minimum workplace standards from applying to prostitution. The absence of such standards contributes to variable workplace conditions, ranging from the comfortable and even luxurious to abusive conditions. Prostitutes may be stigmatized for their activities, financially exploited for their presumed access to easy money, or prevented from accessing particular services if they do not renounce their activities. Prostitution persists, despite such opprobrium, for the same reason that prostitution features highly in music, movies, and literature—sex sells.

Prostitution permeates American culture, demonstrated by the evolution of jazz in brothels, clothing styles, and the prominence of prostitution in music, in movies, and in literature. Lyrics about prostitutes are found in every genre of music: folk songs, rap, disco, blues, rock and roll, and more. Prostitutes populate American literature. So many examples of prostitutes in literature exist that they are too numerous to list, crossing genres and media, and appearing in the works of a wide variety of writers and artists: poems by Walt Whitman, F. Scott Fitzgerald's references to the Mann Act, much of John Rechy's oeuvre, and William Gibson's science fiction. Prostitute memoirs are practically a genre of their own, from nearly every era of U.S. history. Radio and television have featured prostitutes, most notably (but not limited to) *Gunsmoke* and Joss Whedon's space opera *Firefly*. Prostitutes' and sex workers' appearances in American cinema range from documentaries to dramas: for example, Elizabeth Taylor in *BUtterfield 8* (1960); exploitation films, such as *Shaft* (1971) and *Sweet Sweetback's Badasssss Song* (1971), featuring African American prostitutes and lionizing "pimps"; myriad documentaries, such as *101 Rent Boys* (2000); and the *Pretty Woman* (1990), who, when rescued by a rich man, "saves him right back." While prostitution and sex work feature prominently in American culture, most such representations of prostitutes and sex workers are not based on the lives of living persons selling sex but instead on the needs of narrative, portraying avatars of social problems, stereotypes of hookers with hearts of gold, or even folk heroes. These cultural aspects are entertaining but are usually more informative about social mores and preoccupations rather than the real lives of people in the milieu of commercial sex. This volume illuminates the fascinating history of sex work and prostitution in the United States.

TERMINOLOGY

The word *prostitution* is used for the most part throughout this book. Many terms have been used as euphemisms, such as "soiled dove," "the fair but frail," "white slave," "woman of easy virtue," "courtesan," "Cyprian," and "fallen woman." Many other terms have been used as slurs, including "whore," "gigolo," "painted woman," "strumpet," "harlot," and "trollop." Words are powerful, and many slurs have been reclaimed and new terms coined. Contemporary readers may be familiar with the term *sex work*, which refers to a wide variety of sexual services exchanged for money or items of value. The focus of this book is prostitution, one form of sex work. *Sex work* may refer to stripping, pornography, and phone sex, for example. While the term *sex work* is preferred in public health and other fields, this book focuses on history, and it would be anachronistic to refer to people who traded sex before the term *sex work* was coined as sex workers. The very useful term *sex work* was coined in 1978 by activist Carol Leigh, about whom there is more in Chapter 9 about the sex workers' rights movement. The terms *prostitute* and *prostitution* are used when referring to people and events prior to 1978. When referring to people and events from 1978 onward, the terms *sex worker* and *sex work* are preferred. However, not all sex workers use the term; it is most popular among sex worker rights activists. Tracy Quan wrote,

As a former sex worker myself, I am skeptical about a trend that puts more picturesque language out of business. During my career in the New York sex trade, the prostitutes I worked with used words like *working girl, call girl, hooker, hustler,* and *pro.*[1]

Definitions of prostitution have changed across time and place. U.S. law does not offer a definition of prostitution until well into the 20th century; and more details are included in the chapter about immigration laws and state laws addressing prostitution. Even when the law is clear about what exactly is prostitution, definitions change from jurisdiction to jurisdiction and in the civil code and criminal code. The general definition of *prostitution* in this work is the exchange of sexual services for goods or money. Prostitution and sex work are income-generating activities, and the neologism *sex work* emphasizes this, rather than emphasizing issues of morality, which neglect the financial motivations of people who sell sex.

The most distressing and emotional term is "sex slave." Slavery in antebellum America included female slaves who were sold for sexual purposes, advertised as "fancy girls."[2] Some of these women were slaves in brothels, others were in less formal prostitution, but all were slaves and without autonomy regarding their work or treatment. There are very few incidents of outright slavery in commercial sex in the United States today, but they are equally heinous. Legally, they are addressed as "human trafficking." This emotional issue recurs in American history, with periodic panics that are not rooted in actual events but which lead to the creation of new legislation. Legal definitions of trafficking hinge upon the use of force, fraud, or coercion, but affect people who sell sex regardless of the presence or absence of coercion. Trafficking panics, anti-trafficking laws, and their effects are discussed in chapters addressing 20th- and 21st-century legal campaigns, and in Appendix 3.

GENDER DIVERSITY

Most terms used to refer to sex workers refer specifically to women, and, sometimes, adolescent girls. However, all gender identities and expressions are represented among sex workers. Differentiating between from normative and non-normative gender identity and expression is important, and particularly so with regard to sex work. "Cisgender" men and women, whose gender identity and sex assigned at birth match, and "transgender" people, whose gender identity and expression does not match their sex assigned at birth, buy and sell sex. A variety of terms are used to refer to diverse gender identities, including but not limited to transgender, transsexual, and genderqueer. *Transgender* is the primary umbrella term used in this book for the range of gender variance.

Cisgender women are the subject of most of the historical record about prostitution, but effort has been made to include diverse gender experiences in this book. Because most legislation about prostitution was primarily used to address women selling sex, and in part because female promiscuity and prostitution were seen as a social problem while male sexuality was not problematized or pathologized in the same way, men and transgender people are less visible in law enforcement records of sex work than women. Male-to-female transgender people who sell sex may be more visible in the historic record than men because of attention from law enforcement, including profiling all transgender women as sex workers.

People whose gender identity and or expression does not fit the dichotomy of "male" and "female" have great difficulty entering the workforce. Workplace discrimination on the bases of age or sex is illegal, but no such protection exists at the national level for transgender people, although scattered local policies do exist. Sex work presents one occupational opportunity available to people who do not fit into the male-female gender binary. The fact that workplace discrimination pushes significant proportions of transgender people into sex work has led to police profiling identifiable transgender women as sex workers. However, male-to-female transgender sex workers are frequently included in police records as "male," rendering some gender variant individuals invisible.

AGE DIVERSITY

Most sex workers in the United States are adults, but the age range of people who sell sex is much broader than most people expect. Some people who trade sex are not of legal age, and some are far beyond the age of stereotypical "girls working their way through college." For example, the Sex Workers Project in New York included interviews with women in their 50s for the 2003 report *Revolving Door: An Analysis of Street Based Prostitution in New York City*.[3] However, the greatest concern is reserved for minors in the sex trade. While the majority of adults in the sex industry are women, a groundbreaking study of adolescents who exchange sex in New York City found that 48 percent were female, 45 percent male, and 8 percent transgender. This study of adolescents found that the average age at which participants started selling sex was 15 years.[4]

The legal and accepted age of consent for sexual activity and accepted ages for undertaking work have changed over time. Until the early 20th century in the United States, children were accepted in the workforce and paid lower wages than those offered to adults. The sale of sex by pre-adolescent children was not always considered shocking, as it is now.[5] The physical onset of adolescence and puberty started later than it does now, in part due to changes in nutrition. At the time when age of consent laws were first established in the United States, the age of consent was much lower. For example, in New York, the age of consent was ten years until 1885. After 1885, age of consent laws changed around the country, reaching 16 in New York in 1889 and 18 in 1895.[6] Prior to these changes, the age of consent in most places in the United States was 10 or 12 years. Gilfoyle describes a level of acceptability of sex with pre-pubescent girls, citing the absence of the risk of pregnancy and the myth that sex with a virgin would cure sexually transmitted infections.[7]

Currently, the onset of puberty may precede the age of consent, and most people in the United States marry well after adolescence. This creates a period of time during which sexual experimentation is normal but also potentially legally vulnerable. This vulnerability is compounded for youth who exchange sex for survival or money, in some unexpected ways. For example, the conflation of children and adolescents as minors under 18 years of age can equate teenagers and infants. At the same time, adolescents who sell sex are frequently arrested and charged with crimes for which they may be treated as an adult, despite statutes intended to protect minors.

Today, advocates and service organizations in the United States that work with youth involved in sexual transactions almost exclusively encounter adolescents, in some cases referred to these organizations through the legal system, typically after arrest. Research shows that law enforcement approaches to minors who sell sex do not empower youth to change their circumstances.[8]

VIOLENCE

Sex workers face greater risk of violence than other people. Sex workers also face difficulty reporting crimes to law enforcement. Legal frameworks and hostile social attitudes contribute to the violence experienced by sex workers. This chapter examines sex workers' experience of violence and factors that contribute to violence against sex workers, including legislative approaches and social attitudes.

Violence has also been documented amongst and committed by sex workers, and violence has been documented in venues for prostitution and sex work among patrons as well as workers.

Brothel Riots

Mobs of people would at irregular intervals descend upon a brothel or another venue and destroy property. In some cases, people were the targets of violence but destruction of property seems to have been the target and result of most early brothel riots in New York City, with physical attacks.[9] Motivations may have varied but seem to have been enforcement of morality combined with intoxication after excessive consumption of alcohol, fueling mob mentality.

A great increase in the numbers of brothel riots was documented New York City in the 1830s, alongside an increase in physical attacks against individual women.[10] This increase in physical attacks was concurrent with an imbalance among the sexes. After initial waves of primarily male immigration, women also migrated to colonial America and the young United States, and gender balance in the city where most immigrants arrived eventually reached parity. Until 1830, numbers of women and men were approximately comparable, but this changed after 1830, so much so that by 1840, there were 125 young women for each 100 men in New York City, in part because men could find work outside the city itself, while women were expected to stay closer to home and family supervision.[11] The rise in brothel attacks and attacks on individual women may have been related to the sheer numbers of women increasing women's public presence, challenging the conventional mores of the time. The women most obviously challenging moral standards were overt prostitutes.

Many brothel riots resulted in court cases in which damages for the value of damaged property. This has changed. Brothels and individual sex workers may be targeted for robbery, sometimes violently, because they are expected to have cash and known to be unlikely to report robbery and even violence to the police because of the criminal status of prostitution.

History of Sex Workers Using the Courts

Helen Jewett was a prostitute in New York City, renowned for her beauty and her use of the court system. She went to court in one case to sue for damages to her wardrobe, which had been cut up by a patron.[12] Jewett's presence in the courts exceeded her life. She was murdered in 1836 and her murder was reported by the media. A suspect was tried and acquitted. The trial was covered by the tabloid papers, including protests against the acquittal.[13] Prostitutes used the courts to regain property or compensation for damages to property during brothel riots.[14] Historian Anne Butler offers examples of prostitutes using the courts in cases involving police, customers, and other prostitutes with examples from various locations including Cheyenne, Wyoming; Clear Creek, Colorado; San Antonio, Texas; and Tucson, Arizona.[15]

Prostitutes were also witnesses in cases involving their clients or their places of work,[16] including brothel riots, demonstrating that prostitutes were seen as credible witnesses. These examples contrast with more recent events in which sex workers were not able to register complaints with the police.

Legal Frameworks Can Contribute to Violence

The previous historical examples demonstrate that sex workers have used the court system when they have not feared arrest or imprisonment or abuse by police officers. Unfortunately, in the United States today, sex workers are discouraged from reporting violence and crime to the police by their criminal status in most places. The fear of arrest deters many sex workers from reporting crimes, including violent crimes, committed against them. Sex workers have described difficulty in reporting crimes to the police, police not taking their complaints, and not investigating their complaints.[17]

Examples of police neglect contributing to deaths of sex workers include serial killers. Gary Ridgway, the Green River killer of the Pacific Northwest, and Anthony Sowell, in a recent example from Cleveland, were both suspects and had been visited by police based on complaints that were abandoned, perhaps because the people who complained to the police about violent assault and attempted murder were not deemed worthy of attention.[18] The fact that police do not adequately address violence against sex workers conveys the impression that sex workers are appropriate targets for violence. In effect, lack of police attention to crimes against sex workers makes sex workers targets for violence. Ridgway, who confessed to killing 48 women, said,

I also picked prostitutes as victims because they were easy to pick up without being noticed. I knew they would not be reported missing right away and might never be reported missing. I picked prostitutes because I thought I could kill as many of them as I wanted without getting caught.

Indeed, prostitutes are more likely to be murdered than other people.[19] Sex workers are also targeted for robberies. Additionally, sex workers are targets of violence by police, further alienating sex workers from people who in other circumstances would be expected to assist victims of violence.[20]

Interpersonal Violence

Prostitutes and sex workers have been subjected to violence by people presenting themselves as clients and by other predators. In some cases, physical violence is the motivation, but other motives include money gained from robbing or mugging sex workers. Women interviewed by the Sex Workers Project of the Urban Justice Center described robbery, often accompanied by assault, and robberies that were chaotic and frightening because of the threat of violence in addition to any losses.[21] People interviewed described their fears reporting these crimes to the police and even speaking about these experiences to other people associated with their work. The fact that sex workers hesitate to report robbery and violence due to fear of arrest contributes to the ways in which they are preyed upon by others.

Some perpetrators of violence against sex workers may see themselves as vigilantes. Brothel riots described above could be considered vigilante violence if and when morality is the motivation. Some murderers may justify their actions to themselves by presenting themselves as vigilantes.

Residents' associations have sometimes targeted sex workers in their neighborhoods, particularly street-based sex work. Actions have included harassment, photographing sex workers, photographing cars and their drivers in order to intimidate clients of sex workers, and calling the police.[22] Some of these activities have been included online in efforts to shame people involved in sex work, and to publicize their dislike of the presence of sexual activities in their neighborhoods. Rare incidents have escalated to violence but when residents associations combat prostitution in particular neighborhoods it contributes to hostility towards sex workers.

Homophobic and Transphobic Violence

Sex workers face other causes of violence, including homophobia and transphobia. In the lead up to the 2009 Transgender Day of Remembrance, commemorating transgender people killed because of who they were, there was speculation among organizers that all transgender people murdered in the United States in the previous year had been sex workers. Tara Sawyer, a member of the board of directors of the Diversity Center in Santa Cruz, said, "We believe all the transgendered murders this year in the United States were sex workers."[23]

Cyndee Clay, director of Helping Individual Prostitutes Survive, an organization that promotes harm reduction for sex workers in Washington, D.C., said,

Violence against transgender women and violence against sex workers in our country is epidemic, ignored, and sadly deemed acceptable by many communities. Both communities are seen as outlaws, gender or otherwise and somehow deserving of blame. If a woman is both transgender and a sex worker, she is doubly at risk for violence from those who would commit violence against those that society chooses not to protect.[24]

Police Abuse

Violence and harassment from law enforcement has been documented in the United States.[25] Police violence is related to abuse of authority. Documented examples include sexual and physical violence, including rape, sexual assault, and battery. Abuses by law enforcement agents are particularly difficult to address for any member of society, for multiple reasons including difficulty reporting and difficulty resisting an assailant who is an officer of the law; these obstacles are even harder for sex workers.

Effects of Violence

Violence has direct physical effects including injury and death. Violence also has psychological effects. In 1998, a study linked prostitution to post-traumatic stress disorder (PTSD),[26] which has symptoms very much like those associated with surviving rape.[27] Research methods of this study have been critiqued for substantial flaws,[28] but after the publication of this study, many sex workers reported that therapists were diagnosing them with PTSD.[29] While many sex workers who have suffered traumatic experiences such as rape and assault, those who have not endured such experiences are unlikely to exhibit symptoms originating from such traumatic experiences. A staff member with an organization that offered health services and referrals to sex workers said that many callers asked for referrals to therapists and explained that they sought new therapists because their current therapists wanted to diagnose them with PTSD. She told me that one caller explained, "I know I have a lot of problems, but PTSD isn't one of them."[30] Over-diagnosis of PTSD may contribute to and be symptomatic of pathologization of sex work.

Strategies against Violence

Sex workers have developed responses to violence to try to limit their exposure to violence. Some sex worker organizations have organized self-defense classes and workshops for their members. Another attempt to avoid violence is the sharing of information about known attackers, including by word-of-mouth, on paper in "bad date lists," and now, using online forums. Some sex workers use the Internet to learn more about their clients in order to verify their identities and intentions. In 2009, Julissa Brisman, an escort who advertised on Craigslist, was killed in a hotel. Her computer was used to discover with whom she had scheduled appointments, and eventually to identify a suspect. More information about strategies implemented by sex workers to protect themselves is included in Chapter 9 on the sex workers' rights movement.

December 17 was named International Day to End Violence Against Sex Workers in 2003. The remembrance was conceived of by Annie Sprinkle and popularized by Robyn Few of Sex Workers Outreach Project.[31] The Transgender Day of Remembrance offered a model to be emulated, with events and vigils held around the world to commemorate people killed because of who they were.[32] However, it is clear that violence against sex workers will not be mitigated without greater community outrage at and attention to violence committed against sex workers.

ORGANIZATION OF THIS BOOK

Most phenomena related to prostitution recur over time and are not associated with a single period of time. Therefore, the next chapters offer an overview of the places in which prostitution has historically occurred in the United States and the people involved, not limited to prostitutes, sex workers, and their patrons but also including personnel ancillary to the sex industry such as musicians and management. The following chapters address events and phenomena that are more bounded chronologically, such as the passage of legislation and its effects in enforcement, or geographically and chronologically specific, such as western migration by people of European descent and prostitution in these contexts, and prostitution tolerated or regulated in specific locations, and the sex workers' rights movement. However, each of these phenomena overlaps chronologically and in some cases geographically. For example, tolerated red light areas existed at different times in different parts of the country, while moral panics have recurred and lead to the creation of legislation addressing trafficking in persons at different times. Within each chapter, events are described in chronological order; however, across chapters there is significant chronological overlap. The timeline clarifies the periods in which phenomena overlapped and the specific dates of legislation passed.

NOTES

1. Tracy Quan, "The Name of the Pose: A Sex Worker by Any Other Name," in *Prostitution and Pornography: Philosophical Debate about the Sex Industry*, edited by Jessica Spector (Stanford, CA: Stanford University Press, 2006), 343.

2. Alecia P. Long, *The Great Southern Babylon: Sex, Race, and Respectability in New Orleans 1865–1920* (Baton Rouge, LA: Louisiana State University Press, 2004), 10.

3. Juhu Thukral and Melissa Ditmore, *Revolving Door: An Analysis of Street-Based Prostitution in New York City* (New York: Sex Workers Project at the Urban Justice Center, 2003), http://www.sexworkersproject.org/publications/reports/revolving -door (accessed November 14, 2009).

4. Ric Curtis, Karen Terry, Meredith Dank, Kirk Dombrowski, and Bilal Khan, *The Commercial Sexual Exploitation in New York City Executive Summary* (New York: The Center for Court Innovation, 2008), 4, http://www.ncjrs.gov/App/publications/ Abstract.aspx?id=247061 (accessed November 14, 2009).

5. Timothy Gilfoyle, *City of Eros: New York City Prostitution and the Commercialization of Sex, 1790–1920* (New York: Norton, 1994), 69; Anne M. Butler, *Daughters of Joy, Sisters of Misery: Prostitutes in the American West 1865–90* (Urbana and Chicago: University of Illinois Press, 1985), 16.

6. Gilfoyle, 1994, 69.

7. Gilfoyle, 1994, 69.

8. Young Women's Empowerment Project. *Girls Do What They Have to Do to Survive: Illuminating Methods Used by Girls in the Sex Trade and Street Economy to Fight Back and Heal* (Chicago: Young Women's Empowerment Project, 2009), http://youarepriceless.org/node/190 (accessed November 14, 2009).

9. Timothy Gilfoyle, *City of Eros* (New York and London: Norton, 1994), 76–91, 321–29.

10. Gilfoyle, 1994, 78.

11. Christine Stansell, *City of Women: Sex and Class in New York, 1789–1860* (Urbana and Chicago, IL: University of Illinois Press, 1987), 83.

12. Patricia Cline Cohen, *The Murder of Helen Jewett* (New York: Random House, 1998), 96–100.

13. Cohen, 1998.

14. Gilfoyle, 1994, 83.

15. Butler, 1985, 112–13.

16. Butler, 1985, 110–14.

17. Thukral and Ditmore, 2003; Juhu Thukral, Melissa Ditmore, and Alexandra K. Murphy, *Behind Closed Doors: An Analysis of Indoor Prostitution in New York City* (New York: Sex Workers Project at the Urban Justice Center, 2005), http://sexworkers project.org/publications/reports/behind-closed-doors/ (accessed December 12, 2009).

18. Associated Press, "Suspect in Ohio Killings Was Arrested Last Year," *ABC News*, November 13, 2009, http://abcnews.go.com/US/wireStory?id=9073002 (accessed November 20, 2009); Silja J. A. Talji, "The Truth about the Green River Killer," *Alternet*, November 12, 2003, http://www.alternet.org/story/17171/ (accessed November 20, 2009).

19. John J. Potterat, Devon D. Brewer, Stephen Q. Muth, Richard B. Rothenberg, Donald E. Woodhouse, John B. Muth, Heather K. Stites, and Stuart Brody, "Mortality in a Long-term Open Cohort of Prostitute Women," *American Journal of Epidemiology*

159 (2004): 778–85, http://aje.oxfordjournals.org/cgi/content/full/159/8/778 (accessed November 19, 2009).

20. Thukral and Ditmore, 2003.

21. Thukral, Ditmore, and Murphy, 2005, 50–52.

22. Ronald John Weitzer, "Community Groups vs. Prostitutes," *Gauntlet* 1, no. 7 (1994): 121–24.

23. Personal correspondence, 2009.

24. Personal correspondence, 2009.

25. Thukral and Ditmore, 2003; Amnesty International, *Stonewalled: Police Abuse and Misconduct against Lesbian, Gay and Transgender People in the U.S.* (New York: Amnesty International, 2005), http://www.amnestyusa.org/lgbt-human -rights/stonewalled-a-report/page.do?id=1106610 (accessed November 2, 2009).

26. Melissa Farley, Isin Baral, Merab Kiremire, and Ufuk Sezgin, "Prostitution in Five Countries," *Feminism & Psychology* 8, no. 4 (1998): 405–26.

27. Ann Wolbert Burgess and Linda Lytle Holmstrom, "Rape Trauma Syndrome," *American Journal of Psychiatry* 131 (1974): 981–86.

28. Ronald Weitzer, "Flawed Theory and Method in Studies of Prostitution," *Violence against Women* 11, no. 7 (July 2005): 934–49, http://www.gwu.edu/~soc/ faculty/weitzer.cfm (accessed December 12, 2009).

29. Communication with Prostitutes of New York, 1999.

30. Personal communication with Kate Larkin of FROSTD in New York City, 2000 and 2009.

31. Annie Sprinkle, "Stopping the Terror: A Day to End Violence against Prostitutes," *On the Issues* (Fall 2008), http://www.ontheissuesmagazine.com/cafe2.php ?id=21 (accessed November 20, 2009).

32. Transgender Day of Remembrance, http://www.transgenderdor.org (accessed November 14, 2009).

1

Venues

Variations abound in venues for prostitution and sex work. This overview is intended to contribute to understanding particular workplaces and contexts that are featured later on in this book, as well as a general understanding of some of the venues and working conditions in sex work and prostitution. This chapter describes various venues that have existed and currently exist in the United States. Understanding particulars of venues for sex work and prostitution, such as what is meant by "crib" and that some theaters have been sites of prostitution, will be helpful when reading later chapters addressing regulated prostitution, westward movement by settlers of European descent, and moral panics.

Varied venues exist for prostitution and sex work by people of all genders. Many sex workers and prostitutes work in a variety of venues during their careers. Some venues are fairly straightforward and visible, while others are hidden and only recognizable to people looking for them. Work across venues may overlap. There could be some upward mobility, sometimes associated with greater control of working conditions, but also downward mobility, as youth and attractiveness remain valued assets in sex work. However, beauty is not the only desirable trait. Conversational wit and the ability to put another person at ease are skills that some sex workers cultivate. Just as workers may move between venues, venues may have characteristics associated with more than one sort of venue. For example, a 19th-century brothel that served food and had music and dancing resembled a dancehall or nightclub in some ways, and a dancehall or a saloon with rooms to rent resembled a hotel or brothel.

STRATIFICATION

Venues for prostitution and sex work are stratified and within each level, there is further stratification, and then still another layer of stratification at the individual level. Race, class, and gender also figure in stratification. Stratification across venues is typically perceived in relation to the amounts charged in each venue, the number of customers seeking the services of a person, and, in some cases, how many clients seeking services are turned down. Street-based prostitution typically costs less than services in a brothel, which in turn may cost less than an appointment with an escort. Therefore, the perception is that the escort is the elite. However, these strata do not necessarily align with income. An independent escort may earn more per client than someone who works on the street, but most escorts have fewer clients than some workers in some other venues, and someone working a higher-end stroll or in a brothel may generate more income overall. The brothel worker who keeps only part of the money generated may earn less than someone on the street or who sees fewer people overall but who retains all the money generated.

There is stratification within each rank, such that massage parlors or brothels where charges are lower than at others may be viewed by some as lower class. Other factors include market and image. Race, class, and gender all affect income and reflect stratification in sex work. Prostitution and sex work typically replicate and thereby reinforce conventional standards of beauty and gender roles. Such standards also offer specialization, which may have a particular place in the stratification of sex work. For example, interracial sex was a specialization and also a subject of scandal, sometimes leading to protests from neighbors of brothels and prostitutes.[1] Some accounts describe white women catering to Chinese men as "the most wretched, degraded and vile."[2] However, working across race was not always frowned upon and was a feature of prostitution in New Orleans,[3] to be described in a later chapter.

Class, in the form of education and table manners, is another factor in stratification. Prostitutes and sex workers who specialize in multiple-hour engagements that may include social outings to restaurants may find table manners and similar etiquette to be useful. Such niceties may be of less import to prostitutes whose clientele proceeds more rapidly.

At the individual level, age, attractiveness, and earnings are the indicators of stratification. However, this may play out counter-intuitively. Prostitutes who have learned the skills of their trade, particularly the interpersonal skills of brilliant conversation and putting others at ease, may learn these skills over time. Sex workers who look younger than they are may have the longest career. Attractiveness is an asset for attracting clients but social skills that may not be typical of the youngest sex workers may be the most critical asset for those seeking regular clientele.

Stratification across venues may be replicated in interactions between people employed in different workplaces. A woman from an expensive brothel described her visit to another sort of venue for prostitution this way:

In one place where the woman was at least forty my heart was so filled with pity that I urged the man to buy and buy, and when he would no longer order drinks I bought them myself, though I was not in the habit of spending money for booze. But this poor old creature, offering her body for sale, wrung my very heart-strings, and I was determined she should have at least one profitable night. But if my life had depended on it, I could not have fraternized with her, and when we left her place she came to the door and poured forth a stream of filth because I was a "stuck-up parlor-house tart." I did not blame her.[4]

THE STREET

Streetwalking may be the most democratic venue for prostitution. It is open to all. However, street-based sex work today is linked to high rates of violence against sex workers from vigilantes and predators. Residents in some areas where street-based prostitution takes place have created associations geared at eliminating street-based prostitution in their neighborhoods, claiming that it leads to reduced property values and increased noise and traffic.

In the past, people who worked in other venues used the street as a visible place to advertise themselves and their colleagues, both on foot and in vehicles. Helen Jewett, a brothel prostitute in New York City in the 19th century, used her frequent trips to the post office as an opportunity to advertise herself.[5] *Madeleine: An Autobiography* includes this description of one of Madeleine's colleagues:

I succeeded in inducing her to discard her flamboyant hats and leave off her make-up when we went into the street. She reluctantly consented to do this, for she believed in advertising, but I refused to go out with her while she wore the badges of her profession.[6]

There are descriptions of women sitting in carriages and other vehicles as they drove through town, particularly on Sundays, which offer insight into another realm of advertising. The liveliest example includes a woman waving her foot from a carriage in the prostitutes' parade commemorating the creation of New Orleans's Storyville (red light district).[7] This is not to say that everyone working on the streets enjoyed such a situation, and street prostitution is not legal anywhere in the United States today.

The street is stratified. "The stroll" is one phrase for places where people seek clients on the street. People of all genders, races, and appearances work the stroll. However, street-based sex work is frequently compartmentalized, with men offering sex in one location, women offering sex in another, and male-to-female transgender people in yet another. Further categorization plays out as well, for example, according to race. Higher-end "strolls" exist where sex workers charge more per transaction than people in survival sex situations. There are also accounts of women trading sex for entertainment, in part because women's wages are generally lower than men's and so women could not afford particular entertainments such as the theater. Some overtures to "charity girls"[8] were made on the streets, and many toward girls employed at the counters of stores and shops while they were working. Charity girls may have been opportunists accepting unsolicited offers rather than advertising sexual exchange.

The Internet has created a new "stroll" where many people advertise rather than being visible on the streets. However, many people who work or have worked the streets have done so out of extreme financial need, sometimes for survival. No investment is required for trading sex on the streets. In the United States, survival sex on the streets has been associated with addiction, homelessness,[9] and runaways. A recent study found that approximately half of the youth engaging in transactional sex who participated in the study in Brooklyn were male, counter to most stereotypes of runaway girls trading sex.[10]

CRIBS

Cribs were stalls or rooms that a prostitute could rent in which to work. In the urban east, cribs were typically found in multi-story buildings where people did not live. Moving west toward less crowded areas, cribs were one-story buildings that faced the street, where one person lived and worked. Many prostitutes lived and worked in cribs, particularly in frontier and mining towns in the 19th century. They were considered low dwellings and were simple buildings erected quickly, not much more than a hut, requiring limited investment in materials and design. Although cribs were not luxurious, they could be very expensive in 19th-century boomtowns, frontier and military towns, and other emerging markets where they might be some of the first housing produced.[11] Some were squalid closets while others contained multiple rooms. Streets along the cribs were one place for the local residents to advertise availability and for visitors to find people who might entertain for a short time or an entire night.

Madeleine: An Autobiography describes visiting cribs in Butte, Montana, when it was a thriving mining camp town, and the contrast between the "parlor house" brothels where the author worked and the decrepit cribs. The visible nature of the cribs and the fact that many clients were laborers repelled her: "think of sitting with your face in a window and having them pass along leering and peering, as if you were part of a live-stock exhibition; and then think of receiving a dollar for entertaining the beasts."[12] An acquaintance of the author explains that the money was not in selling sex but rather alcohol with a 300 percent markup in price, demonstrating overlap with saloons and parlor houses.

THEATERS

In cities and places with established entertainment venues, theaters were another place where prostitutes and their clients congregated. The upper tiers of theaters were noted for the presence of prostitution and other unsanctioned sexual activity. Upper tiers are higher up and further from the stage, and priced accordingly. Theaters in New York and other cities, including San Francisco when theaters were built in the 1850s, were notorious places for working-class entertainment including prostitution. The association of prostitution and theater preceded the United States: Nell Gwyn started as an orange seller in a theater before becoming the mistress of King Charles II in London.[13]

Until the mid-20th century, it was a common perception that women who appeared on the stage as well as people in the upper tiers were available for hire for sex.[14] Some theaters, called "concert saloons" across the southern United States, offered titillating performances, snacks, and alcoholic drinks, and patrons were not expected to devote their attention to the performance but instead could converse with companions and order drinks and snacks during performances. The waitresses who served drinks and snacks wore revealing clothing and were believed to sell sex in addition to food and drink.[15] Theaters were not only entertainment venue that offered multiple attractions. Other music venues also offered additional options.

DANCEHALLS, SALOONS, AND NIGHTCLUBS

Urbanization led to the creation of more entertainment venues including dancehalls, saloons, nightclubs, and other gathering places. Not every place that offered music and alcohol was sure to offer access to sexual services, but, particularly as settlers of European descent crossed the country with large numbers of men and military locations, sexual services for hire were a feature at numbers significant enough to merit mention here. In 19th-century frontier garrisons and mining towns, women were a minority in the first years and so entertainers, including sex workers, were sometimes able to earn significant amounts of money. As the gender balance evened out, financial opportunities in these venues declined.

Urbanization led to the creation of more and more entertainment venues. Some dancehalls in the east and west hired women who would dance with the patrons for a small fee. Some of these women were amenable to arrangements for sexual services as well. June Miller, the wife of author Henry Miller, was a taxi dancer and the basis for Mara, the taxi dancer who marries a character remarkably similar to him, in Miller's novel *Sexus*.[16] Such venues continue to exist today, most notably but not exclusively in Latino immigrant communities.[17] This is also similar to contemporary gentlemen's clubs, discussed later. Some dancehalls and saloons also had rooms for rent. These rooms were where the women working in the saloons and dancehalls lived and received visitors. Some also rented rooms to visitors. In this way, the dancehalls and saloons overlapped with brothels.

Karaoke Parlors

Karaoke parlors in some places are a niche market for some sex workers. Karaoke is Japanese for "empty orchestra." Karaoke offers music, typically popular songs, without a singer, in order for a live person to sing. Many karaoke machines function as a teleprompter, displaying the lyrics for the singer. Most Americans are probably more familiar with the karaoke machine in a restaurant or bar. However, rather than being in a large room with a public audience, karaoke parlors typically feature small rooms, often containing a karaoke machine and a sofa. Patrons can buy alcohol or drinks to take into or be delivered to the rooms. These are more commonly viewed as venues for prostitution and sex work in Asia but also figure in some Asian communities in the United States Not all karaoke parlors or piano bars are places for prostitution or other sex work. However, the private, sound-proof karaoke rooms with locking doors offer an environment in which sexual activity is possible. Karaoke parlors featuring private rooms and a staff of people to sing with are sometimes locations for sex work.[18]

Strip Clubs, Gentlemen's Clubs, Lap Dancing, and Exotic Dance Venues

The overwhelming majority of strippers and exotic dancers do not sell sex. However, strippers and exotic dancers have been the object of police scrutiny and many have been charged with prostitution-related offenses, or similar charges as are often leveled against sex workers. And some exotic dancers do sell sex in addition to the visual tease of the dance performance.

In some places, women receive individual payments for table dances, literally standing over her patron, or lap dances, sitting astride or on the knee of the patron. These payments are reminiscent of the ways dancehall girls, who would dance close to their paying partners, worked. Lap dancing is also referred to as contact dancing, and some customers may ejaculate from the friction generated, and some men wear condoms under their clothes to prevent soiling their clothing. Women interviewed in a documentary about lesbians working in strip clubs and lap dancing clubs in San Francisco refer repeatedly to avoiding men's ejaculate at work.[19] Such activities render it difficult to discern between the performance of dance and prostitution, and lap dancing has not been permitted or has been addressed as prostitution in some locations.[20]

BROTHELS

At their most basic, brothels are places where clients meet prostitutes and sex workers of all genders for sexual services, specifically including activities geared toward orgasm, including sexual intercourse, oral sex, and manual manipulation. However, just as music and theater venues were also in some cases places to meet people selling sexual services, brothels have also offered other entertainment, including music and meals. Some brothels, particular in the 19th century, offered striptease shows. For its workers, a brothel typically offers a place to work in which advertising and the maintenance of the physical space is undertaken by someone else. Some brothels are rather regimented, with fixed shifts and regular schedules. Brothels may employ cleaners and someone to handle telephone calls. Some retain attorneys. Some retained medical doctors to examine the workers, even into the late 20th century, but now that house calls by doctors are rare, referrals to doctors are sometimes made. Xaviera Hollander, madam and author of *The Happy Hooker*, wrote of her doctor,

The man I found is the "trade" specialist, a groovy man with a practice near fashionable Fifth Avenue in the Seventies. This man is to prostitutes what a trainer is to professional football players. He keeps in good playing condition all the muscles and tissues and tubes that in our trade get overworked and sometimes abused.[21]

Medical checks were a feature of regulated prostitution, which now exists only in rural Nevada, and will be addressed later.

Brothels range from basic to luxurious. In cities, some brothels are apartments. Fancier and larger establishments include 19th-century "parlor houses" which featured at least one parlor in which visitors might meet the brothel denizens. Women who worked in these brothels typically lived there and were often charged for room and board. Hollander wrote,

Some of the girls live in my apartment for a week or a month at a time. For this, they pay me $125 a week, and, of course, they get first choice of the johns who come in, especially the nooners . . . at lunchtime. So the girls don't object to this rent arrangement, and it helps me, because my apartments always run five hundred to $1,000 a month.[22]

Parlor houses were publicly known. In more clandestine places, women might visit the apartment or house during a shift or specifically for assignations. Brothels catered to many economic brackets and desires. As they do today, brothels of the 18th and 19th centuries offered sex with men, women, and people who did not easily fit into either category, including cross-dressers. Some brothels were racially segregated, featuring women of particular ethnicities or races. Some brothels were specialized, offering people of particular shapes or sizes, or particular sex acts including special activities such as bondage and domination. Some catered to people seeking sexual interactions across color lines,[23] which was socially unacceptable and even illegal in some locations. Some brothels, such as Paresis Hall in New York, offered sex with pre-adolescent and adolescent boys.[24] Most brothels strive to have people of a variety of physical appearances at any given time and cater to men seeking straightforward sex acts including oral and vaginal sex and manual manipulation.

Massage Parlors

Massage parlors and body rub parlors and spas frequently charge a flat rate for a half-hour or one-hour massage or rubdown, and the people who perform the massage or body rub may offer sexual services for additional charges. In some places, there may be a standard menu for "extras" including partial or full nudity, physical contact or specific sexual acts.

Massage parlors are not new in the United States. Chicago instituted a licensing scheme for massage parlors in 1893,[25] not without opposition, as documented in the *Chicago Daily Tribune* headline "Fight against Massage Parlors" from 1895.[26] By 1921, the *Chicago Daily Tribune* reported "Massage Parlor Owners Rounded Up in Vice Drive."[27] License fees were one way for some municipalities to generate income[28] but as licenses were and continue to be administered by the local police, they also brought massage parlors under police regulation. Practicing massage without a license is a felony in the United States.

Some contemporary massage parlors in the United States are the dominion of Asian women, and many massage parlors are still managed and staffed predominantly by Asian women, most typically Chinese, Korean, and Vietnamese immigrants. Many of the owners and workers came to the United States from Asia with men they married, men who had been stationed in Asia during the Korean and Vietnam wars, and some capitalized on local advertising and foreign connections to hire staff.[29]

In recent years, Asian-owned and operated spas and massage parlors have been targets of vice, immigration, and anti-trafficking raids across the United States, using the Trafficking Victims Protection Act passed in 2000 and immigration and vice statutes with varying effects,[30] to be discussed in Chapter 8. There is confusion about traditional spas, where prostitution is not a feature, and some traditional spas have been raided by police and all workers arrested for prostitution.

ESCORT AGENCIES AND INDEPENDENT CALL GIRLS

Agencies are similar to brothels in some ways, because they may offer the services of a number of individuals and arrange appointments for paid trysts, and take a cut of the money generated in any transaction. However, agencies typically (but not exclusively) operate remotely, sending sex workers to clients, and clients to sex workers, while brothels typically receive visitors at a fixed location. Traveling to the client is referred to as "outcall." If the client comes to the sex worker, this is "in call," and may be at a brothel as described previously or another location, sometimes at the home of the sex worker. Some agencies have staff on call at a fixed location, and accept visitors as well as send out staff in response to calls. It may be more common today for sex workers who travel to their clients to be contacted by telephone to be given their assignments. Prior to the advent of mobile telephones, escorts might stay close to a fixed landline in order not to miss a call from an agency or a client. An agency location may be attractive because calls could not be missed if a worker was on the premises. Mobile phones have changed the working conditions of escorts and call girls and rent boys, affording them great mobility while awaiting calls.

The person who handles the calls for the agency and makes appointments can wield significant power because this person ultimately decides who is sent on calls. Escorts may tip the person who makes their appointments in order to influence these decisions in their favor.[31]

Escorts, some called "call girls" or "rent boys," may also work independently of an agency and place their own advertisements, sometimes screen their own clients and may travel to see their clients or accept clients' visits to them. Agencies and brothels may be preferred by people who may not be willing or able to undertake the management aspects of their business, such as advertising and screening callers, while others prefer the level of control held by an independent sex worker. Some people place their own advertisements and simultaneously work for an agency.

HOTELS

Hotels are venues where prostitutes and sex workers may visit clients who are staying in hotels and also venues where sex workers and prostitutes may seek to meet clients in hotel restaurants, lobbies, and bars. Hotels are a preferred venue for many because clean linens are usually expected and hotel staff will clean up afterward. Hotels are not without risk, however, because hotels have been used by police in efforts to arrest prostitutes, and hotel staff may not always be cooperative with regard to prostitution. Some hotels are venues where street-based prostitutes go with their clients, and some hotel staff have cooperated with hotel patrons and sex workers even to the extent of facilitating appointments with prostitutes.[32] Some prostitutes may live in hotels permanently or for extended periods, at far greater expense than a permanent residence.

DUNGEONS AND CLUBS GEARED TOWARD SADOMASOCHISTIC PLAY

In some but not all places in the United States, sadomasochistic role-playing is considered prostitution if money changes hands. Many prostitution and sex work venues accommodate a range of fantasies and role-playing scenarios. Workplaces that specialize this way are sometimes referred to as dungeons. The word "fetish" is applied very widely, to any fantasy or equipment requested. In this context, fetishes can include parts of people, such as feet, for the most well documented example; or clothing such as rubber, latex, leather, or fur garments; or activities, such as spanking. Sexual fetishes are psychologically defined as something depended upon or necessary for sexual gratification; however, most customers do not meet the psychological definition of a fetishist, but pursue interests rather than depend upon particular items for their gratification.

The most stereotypical fantasy scenarios may involve a flirtatious secretary, a teacher punishing a student, or spankings from parents and other disciplinarians. Customers can pursue any imaginable fantasy, from smothering to infantilism to rape fantasies. Some sex workers specialize in "kink," while others may accommodate such requests. Not all sex professionals accept such requests. Role playing may involve a fair amount of special equipment and clothing. Restraints and paddles and other gear may represent a significant financial investment.

BEING "KEPT"

Some prostitutes and sex workers make arrangements to be supported exclusively by one person, who typically becomes their sole client for the duration of the arrangement, which may be a few weeks or even years. Such arrangements are overt and negotiated rather than some more informal relationships. Madeleine describes one such offer, "he was going to rent a flat and keep me all for himself."[33] Such arrangements do not suit everyone.

Some hustlers refuse sugar daddy clients. John in Philadelphia said, "They're not the type of people I want to be involved with. They say they're looking for someone to keep, and they say they want to try me out first to see if I'm worth keeping for awhile. I tell them to get lost."[34]

THE INTERNET

The Internet, like all new technology, is used by sex workers and their clients to advertise, to seek and to meet sex workers of all genders and clients, and to find out information about potential clients and sex workers. Online advertising caters to all markets, including discussions of on-the-street strolls, advertising for quick encounters, and higher-end markets, including websites of individual escorts. The Internet has enabled sex workers of all genders to gain more control over their working conditions. However, gendered patterns remain discernable. Men seem more likely to work independently, using their own individual websites to attract clients or using advertising sites specifically for sex work, while escort agencies offering women's services remain a large presence despite the increasing numbers of women who work independently.[35]

The Internet may have created opportunities for two kinds of interactions at previously unseen levels. The first is the use of the Internet by sex workers to vet their clients, to ensure their own security, and to confirm the identities and past behavior of potential clients. The second is the emergence of a community of the invisible men in sexual transactions, clients, who refer to each other as "hobbyists." A large number of online message boards and review boards have arisen where sex workers and clients interact among themselves and with each other. Print reviews and directories had existed but the Internet permits far more immediate contact and conversation than any print form of advertising, with layout, printing, and distribution contributing to the lag time.

Message boards and other websites provide forums where clients compare notes about their experiences with sex workers, and also where sex workers share information, including about violence. However, they have not gone unnoticed by law enforcement and advertising sites and message boards have received scrutiny. Some message boards have been shut down, some of those have reappeared. The Internet is a venue that uses old and new slang and promotes the creation of neologisms in order to communicate wishes and possibly avoid creating evidence of solicitation or intent to commit prostitution.

The greatest amount of coverage of the use of the Internet to make assignations occurred after Julissa Brisman was found murdered in a Boston hotel room in April 2009. She had made a massage appointment with a client, apparently using the popular advertising website Craigslist (which in September 2010 removed the category "adult services" under governmental pressure). Her computer recorded her correspondence, and Philip Markoff was arrested based on this evidence and recently committed suicide in his jail cell while awaiting trial. The media storm after the murder lead to greater monitoring of users and the implementation of charges for the use of Craigslist by people seeking "adult services" on the website.

The Internet has led to changes not only in sex work but also in activism by sex workers. This will be addressed in Chapter 9 on the sex workers' rights movement.

CONCLUSION

Prostitution and sex work venues have myriad manifestations throughout American history. Each workplace is uniquely affected by legal frameworks, local contexts, immigration, social trends, and economic phenomena, to be addressed in later chapters.

NOTES

1. Timothy J. Gilfoyle, *City of Eros: New York City, Prostitution, and the Commercialization of Sex 1790–1920* (New York and London: W. W. Norton, 1994).

2. William McAdoo, *Guarding a Great City* (New York: Harper and Brothers, 1906), 170–71, quoted in Gilfoyle, 1994, 219.

3. Alecia P. Long, *The Great Southern Babylon: Sex, Race, and Respectability in New Orleans 1865–1920* (Baton Rouge, LA: Louisiana State University Press, 2004).

4. Anonymous, *Madeleine: An Autobiography* (New York: Persea Books, 1986 [1919]), 212.

5. Patricia Cline Cohen, *The Murder of Helen Jewett* (New York: Vintage, 1998).

6. Anonymous, 1986, 151.

7. Judith Kelleher Schafer, *Brothels, Depravity, and Abandoned Women: Illegal Sex in Antebellum New Orleans* (Baton Rouge, LA: Louisiana State University Press, 2009).

8. Kathy Peiss, " 'Charity Girls' and City Pleasures: Historical Notes on Working-Class Sexuality, 1880–1920," in *Powers of Desire*, edited by Ann Snitow, Christine Stansell, and Sharon Thompson (New York: Monthly Review Press, 1983), 74–87.

9. Juhu Thukral and Melissa Ditmore, *Revolving Door: An Analysis of Street-based Sex Work in New York City* (New York: Sex Workers Project at the Urban Justice Center, 2003), http://www.sexworkersproject.org/publications/reports/revolving -door (accessed November 24, 2009).

10. Ric Curtis, Karen Terry, Meredith Dank, Kirk Dombrowski, and Bilal Khan, *The Commercial Sexual Exploitation in New York City Executive Summary* (New York: The Center for Court Innovation, 2008), 4, http://www.ncjrs.gov/App/publications/ Abstract.aspx?id=247061 (accessed November 14, 2009).

11. Anne M. Butler, *Daughters of Joy, Sisters of Misery: Prostitutes in the American West 1865–90* (Urbana and Chicago, IL: University of Illinois Press, 1985), 60.

12. Anonymous, 1986, 216.

13. Margaret Sankey, "Nell Gwyn," in *Encyclopedia of Prostitution and Sex Work*, edited by Melissa Hope Ditmore (Westport, CT: Greenwood Press, 2006), 1: 192–93.

14. Kirsten Pullen, "Actresses," in *Encyclopedia of Prostitution and Sex Work*, edited by Melissa Hope Ditmore (Westport, CT: Greenwood Press, 2006), 1: 9–11.

15. Long, 2004, 73–77.

16. Henry Miller, *Sexus* (Paris: Obelisk Press, 1949).

17. Melissa Ditmore, *The Use of Raids to Fight Trafficking in Persons* (New York: Sex Workers Project, 2009), http://www.sexworkersproject.org/publications/ reports/raids-and-trafficking/ (accessed November 2, 2009).

18. Rose Kim, "Alleging Brutality," *New York Newsday*, March 23, 1998, A3.

19. *Straight for the Money: Interviews with Queer Sex Workers*, documentary, directed by B. Hima (San Francisco: Independent film, 1994).

20. Katherine Frank, "Stripping," in *Encyclopedia of Prostitution and Sex Work*, edited by Melissa Hope Ditmore (Westport, CT: Greenwood Press, 2006), 2: 466–67.

21. Xaviera Hollander with Robin Moore and Yvonne Dunleavy, *The Happy Hooker* (New York: Dell, 1972), 186.

22. Hollander, Moore, and Dunleavy, 1972, 253.

23. Alecia P. Long uses this term rather than "interracial sex" because it more eloquently addresses people of mixed race and the constant changes in conceptions of ethnicity and race. See Long, 2004, 6.

24. Joseph Jeffers, "Paresis Hall," in *Encyclopedia of Prostitution and Sex Work*, edited by Melissa Hope Ditmore (Westport, CT: Greenwood Press, 2006), 2: 343–44.

25. William T. Stead, *If Christ Came to Chicago* (Chicago: Laird & Lee, 1894), 253.

26. "Fight against Massage Parlors," *Chicago Daily Tribune*, May 21, 1895, 7.

27. "Massage Parlor Owners Rounded up in Vice Drive," *Chicago Daily Tribune*, December 31, 1921, 5.

28. "$534,195 Goes to City on Licenses in 1927; Quigley Reports Gross Revenues of $758,258—Most Permits Issued to Pool Rooms," *The New York Times*, December 27, 1928, 28.

29. Grace M. Cho, *Haunting the Korean Diaspora: Shame, Secrecy, and the Forgotten War* (Minneapolis, MN: University of Minnesota Press, 2008).

30. Ditmore, 2009.

31. Sora Chung, "Escort Agencies," in *Encyclopedia of Prostitution and Sex Work*, edited by Melissa Hope Ditmore (Westport, CT: Greenwood Press, 2006), 1: 146.

32. Robert C. Prus and Stalliano Irini, *Hookers, Rounders and Desk Clerks: The Social Organization of the Hotel Community* (Salem, WI: Sheffield Publishing Company, 1988).

33. Anonymous, 1986, 191.

34. Michael Anderson, "Gay Hustlers," *Gay Community News*, January 24, 1981, 9.

35. Juline A. Koken, "Internet," in *Encyclopedia of Prostitution and Sex Work*, edited by Melissa Hope Ditmore (Westport, CT: Greenwood Press, 2006), 1: 227.

2

Personnel

Prostitution supports far more people than prostitutes alone. Many ancillary positions are involved in sex work. This chapter describes many of the roles within the ecology of prostitution, including people who cook and clean in brothels, receptionists and people to answer telephones, management, musicians, and others. All of these people are supported by prostitutes and their clients. Most of the people involved in prostitution and sex work either directly or in an ancillary role live otherwise unexceptional lives, with families and friends and the vagaries of these relationships. An entire industry has grown to support sex work as an industry. Therefore, prostitution affects far more people than sex workers and their clients. This chapter offers an overview of the personnel involved in and ancillary to prostitution and sex work.

PROSTITUTES AND SEX WORKERS

Prostitutes and sex workers are people who offer sexual services in exchange for money of something else of value. Prostitution and sex work provide income for people who sell sex. Money is the motivating factor for most prostitutes and sex workers. Most lead relatively "normal" lives; in other words, most sex workers are "deviant" only in their occupation. Consider the fact that most sex workers have families and friendships, including workplace friendships. Sex workers inhabit the same social roles as most people, child, parent, neighbor, worker, and so on. Insofar as sex workers can conceal their work, they may be able to avoid stigma and discrimination related to their work.

Disclosure of a sex worker's occupation can affect all aspects of life. Family dynamics may be affected. For example, in divorce proceedings, child custody decisions may be influenced against a person who sells sex. Housing situations may be affected. Someone arrested at home may be forced to move. Work situations may be affected. A record of arrest or conviction for a prostitution-related offense may present an obstacle to keeping or securing other employment. For these reasons, sex workers and prostitutes are vulnerable to extortion.

Xaviera Hollander wrote about how she dealt with being threatened with exposure by someone who had incriminating photos of her. She received a threatening telephone call, saying,

We want you to have $5,000 ready for us. . . . We can give the pictures to the people where you work, and you'll be fired and be in big trouble with immigration. Think about it. We'll be back to you tomorrow at seven in the evening.[1]

CLIENTS

Clients are the customers of sex workers, people who seek out prostitutes and sex workers and hire them and pay them for their services. They are sometimes referred to as "johns," or, among those who communicate on websites created for clients, "hobbyists." Clients are overwhelmingly men but include women and transgender people. Performer Mirha-Soleil Ross offered this comparison between stereotypes of the patrons of sex workers and her experience with her own clients:

Sexist hypocrites cheating on their wives . . . Horny brutes willing to buy women's bodies . . . Ugly boogey-men in trench coats objectifying women . . .

In my book: a bunch of mostly nice guys whose invisibility is perhaps the political missing link to the obtainment of prostitutes' rights.[2]

Clients may come from any profession and any religious or socioeconomic background. An 1850 description of the clientele at a New York oyster cellar and brothel described a cross-section of society among the male patrons.

among the men you would find, if you looked curiously, reverend judges and juvenile delinquents, pious and devout hypocrites, and undisguised libertines and debauchees. Gamblers and fancy men, high flyers and spoonies, genteel pickpockets and burglars, even, sometimes mingle in the detestable orgies of these detestable caverns; and the shivering policeman who crawls sleepily by at the dead of night, and mechanically raps his bludgeon upon the pavement as hears the boisterous mirth below, may be reminding a grave functionary of the city that it is time to go home to his wife and children after a discharge of his "arduous public duties."[3]

Like sex workers, clients may also face consequences related to arrest and disclosure. Some cities have instituted fines and fees associated with diversion programs for men arrested as clients of sex workers. These programs are discussed in more detail in Chapter 3 addressing legal approaches to prostitution. As with sex workers, the personal lives of clients may be affected by disclosure.

MANAGEMENT

Many sex workers do not want to undertake or may not be competent at the tasks necessary to run a business. Those sex workers who do not expect to be long in the business may not see any value in investing time in managing a business and so may opt to work for another. These people are management, and typically handle advertising, seeking clients, setting prices, arranging locations and schedules, and bearing the costs of these many tasks, in exchange for a percentage of the money taken in by an individual worker. The gendered terms "madam" and "pimp" are used, respectively, to refer to a woman or man who manages a venue or workers in the sex industry. Both may be used pejoratively or as workplace argot, but the word pimp is particularly associated with stereotypes of violence and manipulation, and in some cases, cars.

Driving about in a carriage, before the predominance of the automobile, or a car was one form of advertising. One prostitute said,

I saw some pimps today—two black guys with Texas plates—I'll say they had guts. There they were with those Texas plates on a 1970 Cadillac with a blue-flowered convertible top. Man, those guys had class. Ever seen a Cadillac with a flowered top? Nothing but a pimp or possibly a rock'n'roll star would ever sport that.[4]

Other examples of advertising include print, but even though similar recollections from establishments run by women exist, fancy cars are indelibly associated with pimps.

Madams and Pimps

Stereotypes of madams and pimps do not usually incorporate the role of business manager or owner. However, these terms are used to describe people who profit from the prostitution of others, which is a felony offense in the United States outside Nevada's licensed brothels. Management styles vary in sex work as in other workplaces. Some managers operate equitably while others operate exploitatively.

Outreach conducted by Judson Church in New York revealed that stereotypes of pimps were not true of most pimps:

What the women have told us—namely, that their entry into the profession was not at the behest of some man looking to make a buck off a woman's body. In fact, it is the circumstances of women's lives and the narrowness of choices open to them, not some all-powerful pimp that motivates them. Once in the life, many choose to be with a man society labels a pimp because, like the rest of us, prostitutes need someone to love and be loved by, and pimps are the only men they know who do not judge and reject them because of their profession.[5]

Judson Church's outreach focused on people selling sex on the streets, primarily in New York City's midtown area. They found most people called pimps to be boyfriends, some of whom shared the earnings of their partners. They recognized most violence in these relationships as domestic violence. The Sex Workers Project in New York City has documented a small number of shockingly abusive relationships and marriages that meet the definition of trafficking in persons, in which women were romantically attached to men who forced them into prostitution, supporting the men's other families this way.[6] These situations are rare and shocking to people familiar with the milieu of prostitution. One 19th-century prostitute and madam wrote,

The one girl I have never met in all these years and in all the cities and the countries that I visited was the pure girl who had been trapped and violated and sold into slavery, and held prisoner unable to effect her escape—the so-called "white slave."[7]

Xaviera Hollander, author of *The Happy Hooker*, described the skills required of a madam:

I believed I had the qualities it takes to be a successful madam: aggressive leadership, a head for figures, and a matchless stamina. . . . But above all I had what I call "madam instinct": the ability to know when to be bitchy or soft, the diplomacy to handle difficult clients, good hostess skills, and a sense of humor.[8]

One aspect of management is education about sexual technique and hygiene.[9] In addition to physical matters, behavior and etiquette were sometimes instilled in newcomers to a workplace. The Everleigh sisters, proprietors of a famous and exclusive brothel in Chicago which opened in 1900, recognized that most of their workers had come from the lower classes and so spent great effort to educate the women in their employ about comportment among the upper-class men they cultivated as their clientele.[10]

SUPPORT STAFF

A wide variety of staff beyond sex workers may be employed at brothels, by escort agencies, and by independent sex workers. Certain types of establishments employed musicians, and cooks are still employed at licensed brothels in Nevada where staff live on-site. Some people rely on drivers to ensure that they get to their appointments. Businesses where clients come to a specific location, such as a brothel, need to be cleaned, and their linens to be changed and washed. Someone might be employed to answer telephones, take messages, and make appointments. These responsibilities may overlap.

Receptionists and Telephones

Some establishments hire staff specifically to answer telephones and make appointments for clients and sex workers. A large business may have multiple telephone lines, and the telephone receptionist may have a busy job. Prior to widespread use of the telephone, answering the door for a large establishment and taking coats could have required a great deal of attention. One 19th-century prostitute described a Japanese butler whose responsibilities were "answering the door-bell and in serving wine."[11]

The person who makes the appointments for others wields a certain level of power over how others are described, appointments given, and introductions made. In some establishments, it is standard to tip the person who makes appointments, and tipping may influence decisions about who will see clients.

Security

Elaborate security procedures, including employing dedicated personnel, may be associated with large businesses, particularly those with rowdy clientele or handling large amounts of cash. Brothels, massage parlors, and independent sex workers have been targeted for robbery because they are cash businesses that are not likely to report crimes to the police.[12] Some establishments employ men akin to bouncers whose job is to defuse conflicts and eject unruly patrons if they cannot be intimidated into behaving well. Some establishments employ men in other roles, but they may be called upon to carry out security-related tasks if necessary. Some independent escorts hire bodyguards, who may double as drivers. Security precautions in licensed brothels in Nevada include electrically operated gates, controlled by a person inside the premises, who may also be responsible for making appointments and handling money or other tasks.

Drivers

Some escort services employ drivers to take sex workers from one appointment to another. Some independent escorts employ drivers for the same purpose. Some may rely on car services or drive themselves. Some brothels in rural Nevada offer travel services to the nearest city or airport. Drivers may also be employed as security and be expected to follow-up and intervene if necessary should problems arise.

Musicians

Many prostitution venues featured in-house entertainment. Nightclubs, dancehalls, saloons, some bars, some hotels, and some brothels, particularly parlor houses, offered musical entertainment and in some cases, choreographed or impromptu dancing. A number of famous musicians, particularly those associated with jazz, started their careers in brothels, including Jelly Roll Morton, James Brown, and others.

One parlor house resident wrote,

I knew it was against the rules in any first-class house to talk to the pianist. This is a rule which is never observed, but landladies make it, because in every society there must be someone who is lower on the social scale. . . .

This particular man was a harassed-looking middle-aged man who had a family of four children to support, and who wanted to be home with them at night instead of thumping out syncopated trash for people who did not give a rap what he played, so long as it was something that did not make them think. The present-day craze for ragtime has floated up from the brothel.[13]

Musicians were typically the only support staff who interacted with patrons at the brothels.

Cooks

Some brothels had or have cooks. This is most common among brothels in which prostitutes and perhaps other staff live. Parlor houses and other brothels sometimes offered meals in addition to entertainment. Cooks were necessary employees in brothels that offered meals.

In some establishments, the roles of the support staff may have been multiple. For example, Peter Sewally, also known as Mary Jones, was a transgender woman, born male but who lived as a woman in a female brothel, where she worked as the cook and cleaner. Sewally may have sold sex in the house and was arrested for stealing from a client met in the street.[14] None of her roles were exclusive of other work in the brothel where she lived.

Cleaners

Many brothels employ staff to clean rooms, change sheets, and wash laundry. Rooms are cleaned after use. A "houseboy," who described working in a brothel where all the workers were women and all the cleaners were gay men, wrote,

When I went into a room to clean after a session, I would notice how empty and soulless it was. As if any trace of life or personality had been sucked out of it, which was amplified by the vapid '80s décor. Lots of grays and mauves. I'd vacuum or dust and just feel sad and lonely. Maybe it was because of the fake plants and artificial light. The rooms were set up to resemble a sort of high-end bedroom or hotel. You know, *Penthouse Forum* material. They weren't supposed to look like anyone lived there or did anything that gave it an air of permanency. They were temporary spaces for temporary activities like sex. I preferred to stay in the more populated areas, like the living room or office, and chat with the girls and [the manager]. That turned out to be what I did the best and the most of.[15]

This person describes cleaning as a lonely job in a very social work environment because the rooms being cleaned are inherently empty of others.

Runners

In some venues, workers are not able to leave during their shifts. In licensed brothels in Nevada, people whose job it is to run errands such as shopping for things needed by brothel residents are called "runners." They run errands and are typically paid in tips and a fee for the service, currently approximately 10 dollars.

HOTEL STAFF

Hotels can be places where sex workers meet their clients, as in the case of an escort meeting a traveling businessman, places where they seek clients, perhaps in the bar, and places where they bring clients, as some people who work the streets go to particular hotels near their "strolls." In some cases, hotel staff may arrange assignations and are paid for doing so.[16] However, hotel staff can also be hostile to prostitution and sex work either to control and profit from arrangements they make or to attempt to prevent prostitution on hotel premises. A publication by a group of sex workers included this item: "Girlcott! Stay out of the Hotel Intercontinental. Many girls have been running into overly aggressive security staff. If you go, be prepared for handcuffs and cameras!"[17]

ADVERTISING

Advertising is necessary to attract clients, and creates another layer of employment associated with prostitution and sex work. Perhaps the most direct advertising was chapbooks, akin to online advertising now.

Taxi Drivers

Taxi drivers may be asked to take a person to a place where sex is sold. Taxi drivers may know where to find brothels and places where sex workers are found on the street. In some cases, drivers received kickbacks for bringing people to a specific business.[18]

Printers and Touts

Advertising was not limited to those who could bring people to venues for sexual commerce. Printed materials were sold or passed out on the street. This required printers, and people who distributed printed matter, now sometimes called flyer guys. "Blue books" offered listings of addresses where prostitutes worked, sometimes with descriptions of the people employed there.[19] Prostitutes advertised in these local guidebooks like the *Storyville 400*.[20] Some were described using terms reflecting race and appearance, such as octoroon and quadroon, as well as French, terms signaling eroticism and sexual activities as much as or more than heritage.[21]

Website Hosts and Webmasters

A website requires someone to create the site and a location for it. These are managed by site hosts, Internet service providers, and webmasters or people who design and maintain websites for others. There are sites dedicated to hosting paid advertisements for sex workers. Some sex workers have their own individual sites to advertise their services. Some sites host message boards and other communication between sex workers and clients, groups of clients, or groups of sex workers.

LOOKOUTS

Street-based sex work has its own support staff. Some people work with others, and may look out for each other, trying to remember license plate numbers of clients' cars in order to be able to trace a person who goes missing. Gary Ridgway, who confessed to killing 48 female sex workers, was first contacted by police after his car was followed by the boyfriend of one of his victims.[22] Unfortunately, Ridgway was not a suspect until two decades later.

POLICE

The role of law enforcement has changed dramatically over time, from protector to prosecutor. This is not to imply that police championed the rights of prostitutes, but rather that prostitutes were able to report crimes committed against them, including violence and theft or damage to property, to police and to use the court system to pursue redress. Examples exist from large urban centers like New York[23] and frontier towns.[24] Some such cases arose in the aftermath of brothel riots[25] in which damage to property could be extensive and disproportionately affected the owner of the establishment.

Prostitutes may have been arrested for chastity offenses such as "lewdness" and adultery before the criminalization of prostitution across the nation in the early 20th century, to be discussed in more detail in a later chapter. The criminalization of prostitution created a cat-and-mouse dynamic, with police essentially hunting prostitutes for arrest. The Federal Bureau of Investigation (FBI) was the first national law enforcement agency, and it focused on prostitution during its early years.[26] Criminalization of prostitution has also contributed to corruption in the form of graft by police taking protection money from sex establishments in exchange for warning about arrests or avoiding arrests. One prostitute said,

She finally took me to this whorehouse in Trenton, New Jersey. This place was too much to believe. The police, the detectives used to come every day for their payoff. They used to talk to the madam of the house; they'd pick up their money and leave.[27]

Sex workers are less likely to turn to the police for assistance because they fear arrest and persecution by the police. An sex worker in New York City said, "I got beat up twice, both times by a cop. . . . If I call them, they don't come."[28]

Many sex workers describe taking great pains to avoid interactions with the police[29] including not reporting crimes committed against them. Others report police refusing to accept complaints from sex workers. A street-based sex worker in New York said, "If I have a situation in the street, forget it. 'Nobody told you to be in the street.' After a girl was gang raped, they said 'Forget it, she works in the street.' "[30] Considering these situations, many contemporary sex workers retain attorneys or take other precautions related to the law.

ATTORNEYS

Prostitution has been a criminal act throughout most of the country for most of the time since World War I. Prior to World War I, prostitutes may have been arrested for adultery, homosexual activity, and other charges related to chastity or lewdness. The risk of arrest created prostitutes' need for criminal defense attorneys. Some attorneys have specialized in defending prostitutes. An attorney with a not-for-profit institution said,

There's one lawyer I've seen do all the expensive prostitution grabs, an old, gray-haired, greasy, pin-stripe-suited guy, making all his money off women. But he's always the one they want. I don't know whether his offices are in the court and he just sits there and waits, or whether he goes into the pens and pick [sic] up cases, or whether he's known to all, or what the situation is, but he deals with all the prostitution cases where a lawyer is hired, all the cases that Legal Aid doesn't get, all the cases where a woman wants to get out quickly.[31]

Other attorneys may be appointed by the court to defend prostitutes and sex workers, and the district attorney may prosecute those who do not plead guilty.

Charges related to prostitution are not the only legal difficulties that attorneys for sex workers may address. The Sex Workers Project at the Urban Justice Center is the sole not-for-profit dedicated to offering legal services to sex workers in the United States. Founded in 2001, the Sex Workers Project has addressed a wide variety of legal concerns from assisting trafficked persons to obtain legal residence permits, securing legal immigration status, protecting legal rights in family court, clearing criminal records, assisting with name changes, housing court situations, and fighting police misconduct in addition to assistance beyond legal services. Open Society Institute described the Sex Workers Project, saying,

The Sex Workers Project offers legal advocacy and assistance to sex workers in New York City to defend their rights, whether they are immigrants or born in the United States, whether they are men, women, or transgender, whether they are doing sex work out of choice, circumstance, or coercion. . . . The Sex Workers Project collaborates with defense lawyers and prosecutors to ensure sex workers get the best possible legal outcomes. Staff also work with case managers and social workers to help sex workers obtain other forms of support.[32]

Attorneys cannot address all law or court-related issues related to arrest, such as posting bond or bail after an arrest.

BONDSMEN

When a person is arrested in the United States, bail or bond may be a condition of release. People who do not have the money available to do this may turn to a bondsman, a person who specializes in posting bail or bonds for the release of someone who has been required to post bail or bond for their release. These situations arise only rarely in relation to prostitution and sex work, typically in situations involving more serious charges than misdemeanor prostitution, such as those of people charged with profiting from the prostitution of others, situations involving force or coercion, or very young people.

REFORMERS

Reformers seek to take people from the milieu of prostitution and sex work and see them established in other employment. Reformers are a strong part of American history that continues to this day. Some reformers have relied on religious motivation, such as Reverend Charles Pankhurst who denounced the sex trade in New York from 1890 on.[33] Stories of "white slavery," which referred initially to wage labor (as opposed to outright slavery) and later referred to forced prostitution, were constant fodder for reform. Many stories of white slavery were told in titillating terms in order to generate sales of penny newspapers.[34] William Stead, who published stories of the purchase of children for sexual indenture from poor parents in Victorian London, later visited the United States and wrote *If Christ Came to Chicago!*,[35] offering addresses and owners of brothels on a red, black and white map. It is clear to reformers, whatever their motivations that sex sells. The emergence of social work institutionalized reform and created philanthropic and government funding bases for reform of prostitutes.[36]

Emma Goldman pointed out that sexual commerce would continue despite efforts to improve morality among women because most young women were paid extremely low wages.[37] Her point was that economic motivations can be combated successfully only with economic rather than moral strategies.

Most prostitutes do not believe that reformers know much about what they seek to change. One woman, a successful 19th-century prostitute and then madam wrote,

Not long since a woman who devotes much time to social uplift—and whose activities are as wide as her ignorance is deep—wasted a perfectly good evening in trying to enlist my aid in a social-purity campaign in which she is gaining fame and earning a comfortable living. . . . After endeavoring to impart my benighted mind some understanding of the roots and ramifications of the white-slave traffic, the ravages made by drink, and the general feeble-mindedness and incorrigibility of the children of the poor, she advised me to wake up, acquire a first-hand knowledge of these conditions (taking her as a teacher and guide), and then assume my share of the world's work.[38]

This same woman wrote, "I do not know anything about the so-called white-slave trade, for the simple reason that no such thing exists. I know all there is to be known about prostitution."[39] More information about reformers and their campaigns is in Chapter 4, addressing prostitution prior to criminalization; Chapter 5, addressing regulated and tolerated prostitution; and chapter 8, addressing 21st-century campaigns.

OUTREACH WORKERS

Outreach workers are associated with programs that want to help sex workers. Many visit places where sex workers and prostitutes can be found. Most visit street-based sex workers, but some outreach projects take steps to reach sex workers who do not work on the street. Most outreach efforts offer condoms and something warm to eat or drink when it is cold outside. Some are affiliated with medical programs and offer health services. Most distribute condoms, sometimes with personal lubricant, and in some cases, materials like safe injecting kits or kits for smoking crack safely, particularly in urban areas where street-based prostitution is associated with drug use or substance dependence. Judson Church in New York City began an outreach program in the 1970s:

For the next year, several nights a week would be spent on Eighth Avenue by members of the Judson congregation. . . . They were people with a multitude of skills: A nurse would come along and discuss health matters with the women; a beautician would trim their hair; someone would help with housing and child care problems; and all of them, through their presence, let the women know that a congregation of people who made no judgment about their profession cared about them as human beings.[40]

The greatest asset of some outreach may be that outreach can inform service organization professionals to understand the lives of the people they seek to assist, to recognize that sex workers are not very different from others around them except in the fact that they sell sex, and to understand what kind of help would be genuinely helpful. Outreach workers with Judson Church described this process, writing,

Learning about herself through this exchange, she found her prejudices and preconceptions, her acceptance of the media-created mythology about prostitution and prostitutes, being eroded by firsthand experience. Though she had considered herself free of prejudice in the beginning, it was only when she acknowledged with surprise that the women were in most ways not dissimilar to girls she had known in her lower-middle-class Bronx high school that Arlene realized her unconscious expectation that they would be.[41]

Arlene Carmen is not the only outreach worker who has discovered that sex workers were more like her than she initially knew. Outreach workers are typically the most well-informed people within any organizational staff because of their direct contact with the people being assisted.

CONCLUSION

The sex industry employs far more people than sex workers. This chapter has described a few of the positions related to prostitution. Some that have been omitted due to limitations of space include seamstresses and tailors, who made many of the garments worn by the residents of parlor houses before the widespread availability of ready-to-wear garments, and hairdressers and aestheticians who tend to the hair and nails and other grooming of prostitutes (sometimes at the workplace), and the grocers and suppliers of alcohol and other items consumed in a brothel, or the manufacturers of condoms and personal lubricant and other necessities for the trade. The economics of prostitution and sex work reach far beyond those immediately involved. Every person involved in prostitution has or came from a family, and these families may be strongly affected by prostitution, not merely in terms of the income generated but also in social stigma and loss of social status, or fear of this stigma and loss of status; loss of income related to arrest or violence; and the threat of the loss of employment in an unstable workplace due to criminalization.

NOTES

1. Xaviera Hollander, Robin Moore, and Yvonne Dunleavy, *The Happy Hooker* (New York: Dell, 1972), 97.

2. Mirha-Soleil Ross, "Dear John" performance piece excerpted from "Yapping Out Loud: Contagious Thoughts from an Unrepentant Whore." 2002. Published in *eXXXpressions: Forum XXX Proceedings*, Stella, April 2006, http://cybersolidaires.typepad.com/ameriques/2006/05/dear_john.html (accessed December 6, 2009).

3. George G. Foster, *New York by Gaslight with Here and There a Streak of Sunshine* (New York: Dewitt & Davenport, 1850), 9.

4. Kate Millett, *The Prostitution Papers: A Quartet for Female Voice* (New York: Ballantine Books, 1971), 78.

5. Arlene Carmen and Howard Moody, *Working Women: The Subterranean World of Street Prostitution* (New York: Harper & Row, 1985), 42.

6. Melissa Ditmore, *The Use of Raids to Fight Trafficking in Persons* (New York: Sex Workers Project, 2009), http://www.sexworkersproject.org/publications/reports/raids-and-trafficking/ (accessed November 2, 2009).

7. Anonymous, *Madeleine: An Autobiography* (New York: Persea Books, 1986 [1919]), 238.

8. Hollander, Moore, and Dunleavy, 1972, 147–48.

9. Hollander, Moore, and Dunleavy, 1972, 181.

10. Karen Abbott, *Sin in the Second City: Madams, Ministers, Playboys, and the Battle for America's Soul* (New York: Random House, 2007), 18–19.

11. Anonymous, 1986, 124.

12. Juhu Thukral, Melissa Ditmore, and Alexandra Murphy, *Behind Closed Doors: An Analysis of Indoor Sex Work in New York City* (New York: Sex Workers Project at the Urban Justice Center, 2005), 50–52, http://sexworkersproject.org/publications/BehindClosedDoors.html (accessed November 2, 2009).

13. Anonymous, 1986, 148.

14. Timothy J Gilfoyle, *City of Eros: New York City, Prostitution, and the Commercialization of Sex 1790–1920* (New York and London: Norton, 1994), 136–37.

15. Sam Formo, "New Job," in *Hos, Hookers, Call Girls and Rent Boys: Professionals Writing on Life, Love, Money, and Sex*, edited by David Henry Sterry (Brooklyn, NY: Soft Skull Press, 2009), 23.

16. Robert Prus and Styllianoss Irini, *Hookers, Rounders, and Desk Clerks* (Salem, WI: Sheffield, 1980).

17. "Prostitutes of New York," *PONY X-Press*, no. 2, 1991, 29.

18. Gilfoyle, 1994, 176.

19. Alecia P. Long, *The Great Southern Babylon: Sex, Race, and Respectability in New Orleans 1865–1920* (Baton Rouge, LA: Louisiana State University Press, 2004), 165.

20. Long, 2004, 163.

21. Long, 2004, 168, 206–9, 212.

22. Peggy Andersen, The Associated Press, "Sister's 1983 murder still fuels brother's rage at Ridgway," *The News Tribune*, December 24, 2003, http://www.thenewstribune.com/news/projects/gary_ridgway/story/366375.html (accessed December 8, 2009).

23. Patricia Cline Cohen, *The Murder of Helen Jewett* (New York: Random House, 1998), 96–100.

24. Anne M. Butler, *Daughters of Joy, Sisters of Misery: Prostitutes in the American West 1865–90* (Urbana and Chicago: University of Illinois Press, 1985), 112–13.

25. Gilfoyle, 1994, 83.

26. Jeff Shantz, "Hoover, J. Edgar," in *Encyclopedia of Prostitution and Sex Work*, edited by Melissa Hope Ditmore (Westport, CT: Greenwood, 2006), 1: 216–17.

27. Millett, 1971, 122.

28. Thukral, Ditmore, and Murphy, 2005, 49.

29. Thukral, Ditmore, and Murphy, 2005, 48.

30. Juhu Thukral and Melissa Ditmore, *Revolving Door: An Analysis of Street-based Prostitution in New York City* (New York: Sex Workers Project at the Urban Justice Center, 2003), 47, http://sexworkersproject.org/publications/reports/revolving-door/ (accessed November 2, 2009).

31. Millett, 1971, 138–39.

32. Anna-Louise Crago, *Our Lives Matter Sex Workers United for Health and Rights* (New York: Open Society Institute Public Health Program, 2008), 57–58.

33. Gilfoyle, 1994, 177.

34. Gilfoyle, 1994, 176.

35. William T. Stead, *If Christ Came to Chicago! A Plea for the Union of All Who Love in Service of All Who Suffer* (London: Laird & Lee, 1894).

36. Laura María Agustín, *Sex at the Margins: Migration, Labour Markets and the Rescue Industry* (London: Zed Books, 2007), 105–27.

37. Emma Goldman, "The Traffic in Women," in *Anarchism and Other Essays*, 2nd ed. (New York & London: Mother Earth Publishing Association, 1911), 183–200. Reproduced in Appendix 1.

38. Anonymous, 1986, 320.

39. Anonymous, 1986, 321.

40. Carmen and Moody, 1985, 37–38.

41. Carmen and Moody, 1985, 39.

3

Legal Frameworks

Legal frameworks applied to prostitution and sex work contribute to the context and conditions of prostitution and sex work. This chapter offers an overview of legal frameworks used to address prostitution and sex work in the United States. This information will contribute to greater understanding of Chapters 7 and 8 addressing specific laws, such as immigration acts, the Mann Act, and the Trafficking Victims Protection Act.

Prostitution is considered a moral issue in the law. In the United States, moral issues have typically been addressed by state and local laws. This has contributed to a variety of different laws being passed at different times across the nation to address prostitution. Therefore, the minutiae and particulars of any legal context may differ from state to state, city to city, and county to county. However, there are three basic approaches to prostitution and sex work and most state and local laws fall into these categories. The legal approaches are decriminalization, in which prostitution and/or sex work are not included in the criminal code but may be addressed in the civil code; legalization and regulation, which may impose restrictions via the civil code, sometimes rendering those out of compliance to be addressed by the criminal code; and prohibition, under which prostitution and sex work are addressed by the criminal code. Statutes have primarily been used to address women in prostitution, although men who sell sex have never been free from legal scrutiny when prostitution is addressed by criminal law. Legislative and punitive efforts to address men as clients have been implemented in some parts of the United States.

It is important to recognize the difference between the civil and criminal codes in American law. Criminal law addresses injuries or harms that violate social norms of civility and non-violence and so are prosecuted by the government standing in for the community as a whole. Crimes are separated into felonies and misdemeanors, and can be punished with imprisonment, fines, or, in exceptional cases, execution. Civil law, primarily tort law, addresses monetary or physical injuries caused to one individual or organization by another individual or organization. Civil judgments result in monetary payment such as reimbursement of expenses incurred, or, more rarely, punitive damages. Civil law includes all aspects of the law outside the criminal system.

DECRIMINALIZATION

Decriminalization of prostitution means that the criminal code is not used to address prostitution. However, sex work may be addressed using the civil code. In the United States, prostitution was not criminalized until after 1910. (These specific legal changes are addressed in greater detail in Chapter 7.) Prior to widespread criminalization of prostitution during the Progressive Era, prostitution was not addressed in the criminal code. This does not mean, however, that prostitution was not addressed by the law prior to widespread criminalization during an unfounded moral panic about forced prostitution. Local laws addressing adultery and fornication were sometimes used against prostitutes and their clients.

In 1980, Rhode Island decriminalized indoor prostitution. At first, arrests remained standard but this changed with arrests declining over time. The most visible manifestation of indoor prostitution permitted under law was in massage parlors, immortalized in the 2009 documentary *Happy Endings*. In 2009, with pressure from a coalition of feminist and religious leaders, the state re-introduced criminalization of indoor prostitution. Decriminalization is not used in the United States now but is used most notably in parts of Australia, New Zealand, and the Netherlands. Australia and New Zealand have occupational safety and health policies for sex work venues. These policies address, for example, the storage conditions of safe sex materials and what to do if a condom breaks during intercourse.

Decriminalization is the legal framework most frequently recommended by sex worker rights organizations and advocates because arrest is not helpful to those arrested and can limit future occupational and other opportunities. However, as implemented in New Zealand and the Netherlands, legal obstacles prevent foreign sex workers from working in venues where sex work is decriminalized, contributing to the creation of some situations that may be addressed by criminal law.

LEGALIZATION AND REGULATION

Legalization of prostitution is typically accompanied by regulations, primarily requiring female prostitutes to undergo gynecological exams and blood tests at regular intervals. Regulatory frameworks have not been imposed upon men who sell sex, and men who sell sex are typically ignored by such policies. For example, men are not permitted to work at licensed brothels in Nevada. These exams are meant to prevent any woman with Chlamydia, gonorrhea, syphilis, or HIV from doing sex work. However, these regulations do not include the clients of sex workers and so leave the burden of protection, disease, and blame upon the regulated sex worker, rather than protecting her (and it is always her) from infection. Furthermore, this sexist regulation limited any public health benefits. Since 1988, condoms are mandated in licensed brothels in Nevada, and the mandatory use of condoms is partly responsible for the lack of transmission of sexually transmitted infections in the brothels.

Regulated prostitution, usually in brothels, has been implemented in a few places in the United States. The most well known is New Orleans's Storyville. New Orleans's and similar regulatory regimes implemented in the United States are addressed in a later chapter. Currently, only rural counties in Nevada permit licensed brothels. Licensed prostitution in Nevada is discussed in a later chapter.

There have been numerous instances in the United States, in which prostitution was in fact regulated but not recognized under the law, including prostitution in a number of military areas and situations. Chapter 6 on the Wild West includes examples of military outposts and garrison towns where "hog ranches" were de facto regulated but not acknowledged by military supervisors. Laws such as the Chamberlain-Kahn Act, passed as the United States entered World War I, and the May Act, passed as the United States entered World War II, were intended to close regulated brothels and other venues for commercial sex near military bases. A conflict between local municipalities and military governors over local police actions and who would administer the regulated but unacknowledged brothels for servicemen in Hawaii contributed to the conditions that led up to the strike by prostitutes in Honolulu during World War II. The strike is discussed at greater length in Chapter 9 on the sex workers' rights movement.

PROHIBITION

Prohibition is a legal framework that criminalizes most or all manifestations of prostitution, and, in some cases, sex work more generally. In most systems that prohibit prostitution and other forms of sex work, the sex worker is more likely to be arrested than the client. The more visible the sex worker, the more likely arrest or other attention from law enforcement becomes. Hence, people who work on the street have more run-ins with police than people who work in other venues. People who make fewer appointments are less likely to be caught up in law enforcement operations targeting sex work. People who earn less for each interaction are more likely to see more clients and therefore more likely to experience arrest or other interactions with law enforcement. Women of color have been found to earn less from sex work than their white counterparts.[1] This may render sex workers of color more vulnerable to arrest than sex workers of European descent, because they may need to see more clients to earn the same amount of money.

Criminalization of Clients

Most law enforcement efforts target sex workers themselves. However, some law enforcement initiatives target the clients of sex workers. Police stings have been set up with police posing as prostitutes on the street in order to arrest would-be clients of prostitutes.

Additional law enforcement efforts focusing on clients include diversion programs colloquially called "John Schools." The first such program in the United States was implemented in San Francisco in 1993 and was known as the First Offenders of Prostitution Program (FOPP).[2] Men arrested for the first time for trying to meet with prostitutes paid a fine and attended a day or two of classes intended to discourage further efforts to seek out sex workers. If the person arrested is not arrested again after a specified period of time, the arrest record may be cleared.

"End Demand" has been promoted as a tag line to accompany law enforcement initiatives like "John Schools" that target clients of sex workers. One such provision was included in the Trafficking Victims Protection Reauthorization Act of 2005, diverting money for social services to policing efforts. While "end demand" has been promoted by feminists and religious conservatives, it does not help sex workers out of bad situations and may make it more difficult for clients, who are among the most likely people to help sex workers in coercive situations,[3] to assist them. "End demand" presumes that sex work is per se coercive and therefore advocates for the criminalization of the clients (the demand) for sex work. A coalition of organizations that advocate on behalf of or provide services to trafficked persons pointed out that the End Demand for Sex Trafficking Act of 2005 focused on "unlawful commercial sex rather than trafficking per se,"[4] demonstrating a focus on prostitution rather than trafficking for sex or labor. There is a persistent conflation of trafficking in persons including force, fraud, and coercion and sex work. This conflation contributed to the passage of End Demand in 2005, despite the Act's not addressing trafficking at all. This conflation is discussed in more detail in Chapter 8 on recent legislation addressing trafficking in persons.

ALTERNATIVES TO INCARCERATION AND DIVERSION PROGRAMS

John Schools are a kind of diversion program because they permit people to undertake an activity in order to clear their arrest record. Diversion programs also address sex workers themselves in addition to their clients. This is a welcome opportunity to avoid time in jail and alternatives to incarceration save money. Imprisonment and jail are more expensive to implement than are diversion programs. Salt Lake City's Prostitution Diversion Program involved both Criminal Justice Services and the Harm Reduction Project, and did indeed provide an alternative to incarceration by presenting an avenue for participants to stay out of jail. However, participants were treated inconsistently, with those sex workers more likely to be perceived as victims afforded more opportunities to capitalize upon alternatives to incarceration than were sex workers who were not perceived as victims. People who seemed to have more resources to avoid sex work were effectively punished for this by receiving fewer diversion opportunities.[5]

A NOTE ABOUT ENTRAPMENT

Entrapment in American law is widely misunderstood by laypeople. Entrapment refers to situations in which a person is arrested for something that they would not have done or attempted to do if they had not been encouraged by law enforcement personnel. An example of entrapment would be if a person was approached by a stranger and offered a significant amount of money for sex. If that person refuses the offer, but a second or even a third offer for more and more money is made, and then the person accepts, that might be entrapment because he or she was not offering services and presumably would not have attempted to offer such services. However, it is nearly impossible to use entrapment as a defense against a prostitution-related charge if a person has a prior arrest record related to prostitution. A person who has any record of any involvement in prostitution or has ever been arrested for a prostitution-related charge is likely to be viewed as someone who would have offered sexual services or accepted a financial offer for sexual services. This is why entrapment is not usually an effective defense.

CONCLUSION

Legal frameworks used to address prostitution in the United States have changed over time and place. At different times, prostitution was not criminalized at all in one location, while regulations were applied in other locations, and still other places regulated prostitution despite criminal status. This description of legal approaches used with regard to prostitution and sex work is intended to clarify what is meant by the terms legalization, regulation, decriminalization, and prohibition as they are used in the following chapters.

NOTES

1. Juline A. Koken, Blair W. Morris, Kevicha H. Echols, and Jeffrey T. Parsons, "My Fair Lady of the Evening: Cultural Capital among Independent Escorts," paper presented at the Annual meeting of the Society for the Scientific Study of Sexuality, San Juan, PR, November 2008.

2. Stephanie Wahab, "Diversion Programs," in *Encyclopedia of Prostitution and Sex Work*, edited by Melissa Ditmore (Westport, CT: Greenwood Press, 2006), 1: 137–40.

3. Melissa Ditmore, *The Use of Raids to Fight Trafficking in Persons* (New York: Sex Workers Project at the Urban Justice Center, 2009), http://www.sexworkersproject .org/publications/reports/raids-and-trafficking/ (accessed November 2, 2009).

4. Global Rights, International Organization for Adolescents, Lawyers Committee for Civil Rights, The Door, Urban Justice Center, "Comments on Bill to End Demand for Sex Trafficking Act of 2005," April 22, 2005, 2.

5. Wahab, 2006, 139.

4

Morality, Money, and Prostitution Prior to the Criminalization of Prostitution

Prior to the 20th century, prostitution was not usually addressed overtly by law. This does not mean, however, that prostitution was allowed to grow unchecked. Social mores against prostitution were periodically enforced by vigilante mobs that vandalized, attacked, and looted brothels and red light areas. Men and boys who sold sex were likely to be subject to charges related to lewd behavior and homosexual acts, referred to as "buggery" or "crimes against nature," but often without reference to monetary compensation. While prostitution was not counter to the law, four men were executed for sodomy and 19 were prosecuted between the years 1610 and 1740.[1] Women were treated slightly differently, typically with laws against promiscuity, in addition to laws against lewd behavior.

COLONIAL-ERA PROSTITUTION

Prostitution was visible once Puritan colonists arrived. The ship that carried John Smith and others to Jamestown in 1607 carried no women.[2] The settlers arrived in Virginia lacking provisions, and sailors from the ships that would return to England sold provisions to these early colonists in exchange for "money, saxafras, furs, or love."[3] This was not the last reference to sexual exchange between men during the colonial era. In 1677, Nicholas Sension went to court for sodomizing an indentured servant. Witnesses included a townsman who said that Sension "proffered me a bushel of corn if I would

put down my breeches," and another who said, that "[Sension] told me if
I would let him have on bloo at my breech he would give me a charge
of powder."[4]

POPULAR EFFORTS TO ADDRESS THE SALE OF SEX
Brothel Riots

Mobs rioted against brothels in 19th century Boston, Cincinnati, New
York, Portland (Maine), and Saint Louis.[5] Riots were not limited to prostitution, but were a visceral outlet for popular offense at a variety of issues. The
1830s are called New York's "decade of riots" because there were riots against
abolition, riots during elections, and riots over commodities, as well as
brothel riots.[6]

In Boston, mayoral efforts to address prostitution were concentrated in
one neighborhood, the West End. This pushed prostitution to other neighborhoods. People who were anxious about their social status and the value
of their property in the North End included artisans and craftsmen, who
seem to have encouraged and participated in riots that systematically attacked
brothels in this neighborhood. In 1927, as many as 300 men in blackface carrying pitchforks and whistles tore open featherbeds and ransacked brothels,
which were home almost exclusively to women.[7] It is ironic that people concerned about their own property justified their destruction of the property of
others, much of belonging to and/or used by women.

Initially, most such riots attacked property and violence against persons
was rare.[8] After 1820, however, violence against prostitutes increased.[9] In
some cases, the aim seems to have been to demonstrate community opposition
to a brothel, in cases in which complaints to local authorities did not have
the desired effect. Historian Timothy Gilfoyle describes such a situation at
Catherine Brown's King Street brothel in 1833, after which she did not
return to the house.[10] However, some attacks were random or spontaneous
and seem less driven by outright goals. Nonetheless, some patterns emerge.

Historian Barbara Meil Hobson explains that vigilante brothel riots in
Cincinnati, Portland, and Saint Louis shared specific characteristics. These
cities did not have established zones for prostitution or clear policies about
prostitution (although at the time prostitution would not likely have been
stated outright). These factors meant that existing law enforcement may
have had little or no jurisdiction over brothels. Rioters were local people. In
Cincinnati, St. Louis, and Boston, riots were not violent; destruction focused
upon property rather than hurting people.[11] But this does not mean that

prostitution was of no interest to law enforcement. Statutes against promiscuity and vagrancy appear to have been used to address prostitution.

THE EARLIEST FORM OF WELFARE AND PUBLIC RESPONSES

Hobson describes colonial towns "warning" out strangers whom they feared would become dependent on the community, "officially giving them notice that they would not be supported and expelling them."[12] Note that this was predicated upon the town not supporting people who did not have the means to support themselves, people who might be sent to a poorhouse; a person who offered skills or had the financial means to support themselves—people who would not be a burden in a poorhouse and who would not have children that would be a burden—were not subject to such attention. Women who might have children out of wedlock were frequently warned out of town, in order to prevent unwed mothers and their offspring from becoming dependent upon the community. Some unwed mothers found themselves facing the choice between the workhouse and the brothel.

Statutes against vagrancy and lewdness were used to charge prostitutes and, sometimes, their patrons. Hobson also describes that after the Revolution, laws were enacted that enabled communities to ship vagrants to their home communities,[13] much the way homelessness is dealt with in some contemporary American communities and with the same motivations.

Proprietors and managers in brothels and boarding houses where some women may have sold sex were subject to being charged with "keeping a bawdy house." Brothel keepers were sometimes accused of abduction by husbands and fathers of their employees. Stories of abduction and "white slavery" narratives were typical fodder for reformist publications, with stories featuring women offering work or lodging to a naïve newcomer who did not realize that she would become the inmate of a brothel. These situations were outnumbered by those of women seeking ways to generate income, for whom formal or informal prostitution may have presented one among a limited range of choices. Exchanging sexual favors may have offered solutions to some problems, but brought risks in that it made women vulnerable to social opprobrium and punishment, not only from individuals but also by the state.

Men also worked in brothels. Many houses employed boys who ran errands, transported messages, and even answered doors and showed in visitors, ascertaining their interests and introducing visitors to the appropriate residents.[14] In some brothels, people who would today be referred to as transsexual or transgender worked, sometimes receiving clients and sometimes in other roles. The men and transgender people present could also have been charged with keeping a bawdy house or other offenses.

PUNISHMENT AND REFORM OF INDIVIDUALS BY THE STATE

Attention from law enforcement, charges and punishments were influenced and affected by sex, gender, race, and class. For example, in the 18th century, male offenders who attracted the interest of law enforcement—clients of prostitutes—were fined but women were lashed for selling sex.[15] Morals charges such as lewd behavior were brought against women with greater frequency than against men. The gender disparities in crimes of chastity increased in the 19th century. This category of crimes against public order included lewdness, stubbornness, disorderly conduct, drunkenness, in addition to fornication and adultery, were much more frequently used against women than men.[16] With regard to prostitution outright, women were charged, while their clients and people who arranged their assignations were typically treated more leniently.[17] To this day, women who sell sex are more likely to face arrest than their clients or men who sell sex. Women's prisons and houses of reform were created partly as a result of this gendered enforcement of morality.

Venues to purchase sex included the street, brothels, and the homes of women who sold sex, who may have paralleled independent sex workers today. All genders were represented, and these venues were stratified along race and class lines. The street offered the most democratic availability of sex with lower prices than other venues but also, because of the inherent visibility of the street, the greatest amount of attention from law enforcement. Arrests of women for lewd behavior in 19th-century Boston affected all races, but women who were not of European descent were disproportionately represented.[18]

Most chastity offenders were not professional prostitutes but were more frequently young women who were not engaged in criminal activity or prostitution.[19] Prisons meant to reform women focused on morality rather than addressing the difficult economic issues that contributed to prostitution being a reasonable option among limited choices to earn a living or supplement an inadequate income. The Women's Prison Association highlighted the economic roots of women's incarceration in reform and penal institutions in 1870.[20] The lack of viable economic options offering women a livable wage was acknowledged, but reform did not extend to addressing expanding workplace options and addressing discrimination along the lines of class, gender, and race.[21]

The treatment of "fallen women" in the prisons was especially harsh, and also gendered. Because the goal of imprisonment was reform, those deemed beyond reform were pariahs within the prison system. Many women in prison became pregnant in prison and births in prison are commonly read in the records. However, the most egregious example of abuse during this era within prison was forced prostitution of female inmates for prison guards in an Indiana state prison.[22]

At first glance, "reform" may appear less harsh or punishing than punishment. However, reform institutions were typically operated punitively and were not perceived differently from imprisonment by their inmates. Furthermore, because reform is not sentence-based but meant to effect personal change in the individual, reform institutions held inmates for years while punitive sentences might have been months.[23] Residence within Boston's Penitent Females' Refuge was stated to be voluntary, but only six women seemed to petition to enter, and the most frequent way women left the institution was to "escape."[24]

Criminology

In 1895, Cesare Lombroso published his descriptions of the physiognomy of criminals.[25] In the next decade, measures of intelligence were used to promote arguments correlating lesser intelligence with criminal tendencies. These now-disproven hereditary indicators were used to promote expansion of the population by people of northern European descent, to justify oppression of African Americans in the migration northward after the Civil War, and to justify restrictions on immigration from southern Europe. Eugenics proposed that crime could be controlled by limiting births among those perceived as inferior or of criminal types and encouraging births among people of Anglo-Saxon descent. These beliefs promoted the view that some people were inherently irredeemable and were not capable of reform, because they were inherently criminal. Such beliefs were challenged by people familiar with the inmates of penal and reform institutions, such as the Women's Prison Association mentioned previously and Progressive Era reformers, who emphasized economic motivations for prostitution,[26] based upon their interactions with inmates and the pioneering work of early 20th-century female criminologists such as Frances Kellor, who found no justification for Lombroso's theories, and Katherine Bement Davis, who revamped reform-era institutions to offer economic and life skills to inmates.[27]

URBANIZATION: LABOR AND LEISURE

Women's being "warned out of town" during the colonial era lest they become dependent on a town[28] contributed to the movement of unattached women from rural areas to cities, where the size of the community rendered such efforts to monitor the status or even the arrival of all newcomers impossible. Even during the colonial era, the returns from farming were not usually substantial enough to support all the people in a family without significant holdings of land. Sons and daughters who did not inherit land, and children of hired help or farmhands who were no longer needed, were likely to move to places where they believed opportunities were greater. Emigration from rural areas and farming communities encouraged the growth of cities and eventually, western expansion.

Changes in earnings and employment were affected by immigration to the United States, which swelled cities, and by rural emigration to cities as farm earnings declined. An additional factor was industrialization, and the creation of factories that required wage labor. Recent arrivals in cities required lodging and employment. Men typically roomed in boarding houses. Female boarding houses were presumed, usually accurately, to be brothels. Women who were not involved in prostitution typically sought lodging with a family, for which references were usually required. A woman without references may have found herself with few options for lodging.

Industrialization and wage labor also led to a decline in the level of skills needed, and therefore also for wages paid. For example, the sewing machine lead to demands for seamstresses to produce more garments within a specific timeframe, but the change in compensation per piece declined precipitously, so much so that seamstresses could need to work very long hours every day to earn only a subsistence wage. This lead to economic pressures upon women, pressures that in some cases were lessened by additional income from prostitution. Nearly three-quarters of women in the Philadelphia city register worked in a trade or as servants while selling sex.[29] This was true of registered prostitutes in one city but this would not have included "charity girls" who exchanged sex for outings to restaurants, amusement parks, and theaters.[30] Women had many economic pressures that could encourage them to accept opportunities for the most lucrative work available to them or other informal economic support from men. Reliance on men, in a recognized exchange like prostitution or less formal dating and treating situations were the only way some women would have been able to afford leisure activities.[31] Women's wages were lower than men's because men were expected to support families; however, women contributed to their family incomes and many were the breadwinners, especially in cases in which a father had died or left a family under other circumstances. Women who were downwardly mobile—for example, seamstresses who saw a decline in their wages after the introduction of the sewing machine—may have turned to selling sex in order to maintain their expectations and standards of living.

Domestic service had previously been seen as the ideal sort of work for working class women, but industrialization led to changes in the stratification of work. Factory workers believed themselves to be above domestic workers in the hierarchy of occupations. Domestic workers may have earned more and their housing and board were included in their wages, but domestic workers endured longer hours and were isolated within the homes where they worked. Factory employees may have had to pay for room and board out of lower wages, but they had more leisure time and the society of their work-mates. These factors may have contributed to the fact that former domestic workers were extremely common among prostitutes.[32] Some may have sold sex on their days off, while others left domestic work for brothels and other venues in which sex was sold.

While the sale of sex was part of the pursuit of money and leisure for many (of all genders), the *purchase* of sex was always a leisure pursuit. Laws against vagrancy and lewd behavior were ineffective against the popular pursuit of sex for sale. Acknowledged red light areas were established by law or tolerated in cities across the country. New Orleans had Storyville, named from the legis-lator who created the district. New York and Chicago had "tenderloins." San Francisco had the "Barbary Coast," and San Bernardino had "D" Street. In mining areas, "camp followers" set up shop to cook, clothe, launder, and also to sell sex.

Prostitution flourished almost without inhibition in the late 19th century as urbanization and waves of immigration swelled the nation's cities. Prior to the 20th century, prostitutes were able to pursue damages in the courts when their garments were harmed or when they experienced theft of services. How-ever, mob raids on brothels also happened in the United States prior to the criminalization of prostitution in the 20th century. In these cases, mobs of working class men would storm and loot brothels.[33] The context for these sit-uations involved urbanization and industrialization, with men and women relocating to cities from the countryside, and with increasing waves of immi-gration throughout the 19th century.

Urbanization led to families relocating to cities and to women moving to live apart from their families in cities. Women followed westward migration, and as mining camps grew, some, like San Francisco and Denver, eventually becoming cities. Some young women in cities lived apart from their families, and were thus "unsupervised." To survive, many were seamstresses, laun-dresses, and prostitutes. "Seamstress," "laundress," and other acceptable female occupations were frequently euphemisms for prostitute, the only occupation other than wife that offered women a livable wage.

Cities offered luxuries and amusements that were less available elsewhere, including amusement parks, theaters, and restaurants, all of which required cash in exchange for enjoyment and which existed only in places with the density of population to support them. Working women and children earned less than men and were less able to afford such entertainments. The first part of the 20th century featured "treating,"[34] which looks to modern eyes like dating, but was the subject of many articles about wayward women.

Girls and women were not the only people who migrated to cities or who were not likely to be able to afford the pleasures of city life without supplementing incomes from mainstream jobs or venturing full-time into underground commerce including the sex trades. Boys also received lower wages than adult men, and some were associated with sexual exchanges as errand runners, people who delivered messages, and eventually recruited clients for people who sold sex.[35] Newspaper boys and messenger boys were particularly associated with prostitution.[36] Some boys also sold sex.

Red light areas and tenderloin districts emerged in cities throughout the United States, most notoriously New Orleans's Storyville, but also areas in San Francisco and New York City, and in Chicago's Levee district. These were places where young women, men, and transgender people who worked by entertaining "sporting men" could legally earn a livable wage and thereby enjoy the entertainments offered by these cities. Tolerated and regulated prostitution in red light districts is the topic of the following chapter.

NOTES

1. Mack Friedman, *Strapped for Cash: A History of American Hustler Culture* (Los Angeles: Alyson Publications, 2003), 2.

2. Friedman, 2003.

3. John Smith et al., *A Map of Virginia*. Oxford, 1612. Section 2, chapter 2, 9, quoted in Mack Friedman, *Strapped for Cash: A History of American Hustler Culture* (Los Angeles: Alyson Publications, 2003), 2.

4. Connecticut State Archives, Connecticut State Library, Hartford. Reprinted in Jonathan Ned Katz, *Gay/Lesbian Almanac* (New York: Harper and Row, 1983), 111–18, 678. Quoted in Mack Friedman, *Strapped for Cash: A History of American Hustler Culture* (Los Angeles: Alyson Publications, 2003), 3.

5. Barbara Meil Hobson, *Uneasy Virtue: The Politics of Prostitution and the American Reform Tradition* (New York: Basic Books, 1987), 24.

6. Timothy J. Gilfoyle, *City of Eros: New York City, Prostitution, and the Criminalization of Sex, 1790–1920* (New York: Norton, 1994), 76.

7. Hobson, 1987, 23–24.

8. Gilfoyle, 1994, 77.

9. Gilfoyle, 1994, 78.

10. Gilfoyle, 1994, 79.

11. Hobson, 1987, 24.

12. Hobson, 1987, 16.

13. Hobson, 1987, 16.

14. Friedman, 2003, 43.

15. Hobson, 1987, 33.

16. Estelle B. Freedman, *Their Sisters' Keepers: Women's Prison Reform in America, 1830–1930* (Ann Arbor, MI: University of Michigan Press, 1981), 14.

17. Freedman, 1981, 146.

18. Hobson, 1987, 35–36.

19. Freedman, 1981, 85.

20. Freedman, 1981, 42.

21. Freedman, 1981, 125.

22. Freedman, 1981, 16, 59–60.

23. Freedman, 1981.

24. Hobson, 1987, 119.

25. Cesare Lombroso and William Ferrero, *The Female Offender* (New York: D. Appleton, 1895).

26. Freedman, 1981, 111.

27. Freedman, 1981, 114–18.

28. Hobson, 1987, 16.

29. Hobson, 1987, 106.

30. Kathy Peiss, " 'Charity Girls' and City Pleasures: Historical Notes on Working-Class Sexuality, 1880–1920," in *Powers of Desire*, edited by Ann Snitow, Christine Stansell, and Sharon Thompson (New York: Monthly Review Press, 1983), 74–87.

31. Freedman, 1981, 124.

32. Hobson, 1987; Freedman, 1981.

33. Gilfoyle, 1994; Hobson, 1987.

34. Peiss, 1983.

35. Friedman, 2003, 43.

36. Friedman, 2003, 43–44.

5

Red Light, Green Light

Most American towns and cities responded to prostitution, whether by ignoring it or regulating it. With or without official sanction, the treatment of prostitution is an important feature of American history. This chapter describes some of the ways prostitution and sex work have been addressed in various municipalities at different times in U.S. history.

THE ESTABLISHMENT OF RED-LIGHT DISTRICTS

Working class and immigrant neighborhoods were 17th- to 20th-century locuses of prostitution, although obviously not all people who lived in these areas offered sex for sale. Nineteenth-century vigilante riots against brothels and law enforcement efforts against lewdness increased when prostitution became visible in wealthier areas and when families moved to frontier areas. These forces effectively pushed prostitution outside primarily residential areas and outside central business districts. Some red light areas, such as New Orleans's Storyville, were overtly recognized and created by elected officials, while others emerged in response to pressure exerted by neighbors, politicians, and law enforcement. Red light areas are neighborhoods in which people who sell sex and the places where they work are clustered and concentrated. Some red light areas emerged as places where prostitution was not acknowledged by the authorities, others were regulated by official or unofficial policies, and some were overtly recognized and regimented.[1] Some red light areas, including San Bernardino's "D" Street, were so recognized by local authorities that they required regular gynecological examinations of prostitutes.[2] However, most such regulations and requirements were informal, tacitly accepted but not overtly condoned. The only truly regulated brothels, in which the system has been recognized by all levels of government, emerged in St. Louis between 1870 and 1874 and in licensed prostitution in Nevada, since 1971. However, lack of official recognition did not prevent the creation of red light areas or systems within them.

Most attempts to regulate commercial sex place limits on where prostitution may occur. Acknowledging or tolerating prostitution in a geographic location or a type of venue implicitly marked other places as locations or venues in which prostitution would not be tolerated. Places in which sex was sold included the street, brothels, and the homes of women who sold sex. Selling sex on the street may have been tolerated in some places at some times, but because of its inherent visibility, the street may be the least likely location for regulated commercial sex. However, the streets functioned as a place for prostitutes who did not work on the street to advertise their wares. For example, illustrations of Helen Jewett, a 19th-century New York prostitute noted for her beauty and for having been violently murdered, walking to the post office were included in chapbooks and journalistic accounts of her murder and the subsequent trial.[3] Being seen on the street may also strike against someone. Simply being on the streets of particular neighborhoods—in known or recognized red light districts, or places where female boarding houses were found—was enough to mark a woman as a prostitute.

All genders and ethnicities were (and are to this day) represented in sex work and prostitution. In some brothels, men sold sex alongside women.[4] However, regulation of prostitution and prostitutes in the United States has until very recently, in early 2010, addressed only female prostitution. Reasons for this may include social mores and norms enforcing heteronormativity and homophobia, although early American sexual mores were relatively accepting of sex between men,[5] but female sexuality and sexual activity historically have been more supervised and regulated than male sexuality and sexual activity.

Toleration and Regulation

One of the arguments for the establishment of known areas for sexual commerce was to ensure the ability to distinguish "respectable women" from women who might be amenable to or available for sexual transactions. It would have been unconscionable for ladies of elite society to be mistaken for or treated similarly to "common" women. This became more critical as urbanization progressed. Shopping districts and restaurants came to be frequented by women of leisure, including women from long-established and well-respected families,[6] the equivalent of local nobility, such as those families listed in the social register. Such concerns date to the emergence of shopping districts, but also changes in fashion. Many fashions have moved from the working classes and from prostitutes to wealthier strata including people of higher social standing. This meant that appearance alone did and does not indicate social status.[7] Additional concerns included not only treatment but also interactions. While it might be conceivable that a wife and a mistress could frequent the same establishments, it would be unheard of for them to interact with each other or with women of lower social classes. Women who associated with prostitutes or women of low social stature, no matter the reason, risked their social reputations. Women who were seen in or in proximity to venues associated with sexual commerce, such as theaters and concert saloons, were guilty by association, due to proximity to promiscuity, no matter their actions.[8] However, concert saloons and theaters, where waitresses wore scanty dresses and many were or were presumed to be available for commercial sex, opened on commercial thoroughfares in many cities, including New Orleans's Royal Street.[9] The men who profited from the business of sex and those who paid for sexual services typically did not suffer similar stigma or social opprobrium. Most residents and brothel workers of red light areas were also concerned with their own respectability.

Prostitutes might dress similarly to other people outside their workplaces, but at work, their clothing was very specific to their trade. Fancy gowns were standard in some brothels while "short clothes" (dresses that would be inappropriate everywhere else, usually short, exposing more skin than street clothing) were worn in concert saloons.[10]

New Orleans, Beyond Storyville

Storyville is the most famous, most researched, and most written about recognized red light area in the United States. However, it was the smallest of five such areas, among which it was the last to be created, in New Orleans.[11] Storyville is famous, but four other red light districts were well established when it was created. As early as 1857, New Orleans used regulations as part of the "Lorette Ordinance" in order to eliminate street-level establishments for prostitution, moving prostitution to higher, less visible floors; to impose a licensing structure for prostitutes and their landlords; and to create four red light districts within New Orleans in which prostitution was tolerated.[12] The districts were large and in four different areas of the city. Over the years that followed, more ordinances were created that attempted to regulate the behavior of prostitutes and the locations where they could conduct business. New Orleans therefore has perhaps the longest and most well chronicled history of attempts to regulate prostitution in the United States.

Storyville and Segregation

Storyville was created within a particular social context that took shape right after the U.S. Supreme Court ruled in favor of segregation in *Plessy v. Ferguson*. "Separate but equal" did not necessarily apply exclusively to race, and in the creation of Storyville, segregation applied not only to race but also gender, social class, and standing. The district was sarcastically named Storyville for Alderman Sidney Story, who proposed the creation of the district.[13] The creation of this particular district reflected and enforced social mores that segregated some women from other, more "respectable" women specifically. Prostitutes and African Americans were both associated with the spread of disease, particularly sexually transmitted infections, and the segregation of both groups of people was intended to limit their interactions with "respectable" people.[14] Prostitutes and African Americans were both considered undesirable associates by the creators of the district.[15] The neighborhood, like most neighborhoods in New Orleans, was not racially homogenous, but it was definitely considered an African American neighborhood, with "Negro Dance Halls," a "Negro Chop House," and a "Negro Club Room" within the demarcations of the district.[16] African American families were not able to pay the new rents demanded of the prostitutes moving into the district, and so many families moved out.[17] On one hand, the creation of the district emphasized segregation of families and others with higher social standing from "lewd and abandoned women." At the same time, given this equation of prostitutes and African Americans as people separate from those with greater social clout, the creation of the district further segregated the African American residents who could no longer afford to live in their neighborhood.

Storyville, like New Orleans generally, was associated with socializing across color lines, particularly sexual activity.[18] Mixed-race women were eroticized as Octoroons and quadroons, with lighter skin than many people of African descent but seen as retaining the stereotyped sexuality associated with blacks.[19]

Not everyone was pleased by the creation of the district. Storyville's creation was concurrent with a conservative social and political movement called the Citizens' League, which consisted mostly of businessmen. Many of its members were party to a lawsuit that was filed contesting the creation of the district on the grounds that property values could decline, that women who lived nearby would lose their social standing, and that local businesses and establishments would suffer.[20] One church—a primarily black church that foresaw the loss of its parishioners—was party to the lawsuit.[21] However, property values increased substantially with the proposal to create the district. Astute brothel owners immediately sought to buy property within the district upon the demarcation of its boundaries.[22] Indeed, for those who rented housing to prostitutes outside the district, the forced relocation of prostitutes to another area was perceived as confiscation of assets in the form of the income from the rents paid by prostitutes.[23] This was accompanied by the displacement of residents who could not afford the newly increased rents charged of prostitutes. The neighborhood was low-lying, with a high water table, and inhabited by people with low social standing, typically associated with race and lack of wealth.[24] They did not have the social clout to influence the location of the vice district. Many people favored the ordinance on the grounds that it would remove brothels and prostitutes from the rest of the city.[25] The ordinance that created Storyville specified that known prostitutes could not live outside the delineated red light districts. Therefore, large numbers of women who worked in the red light areas were forced to move into the districts because they were no longer permitted to live in their homes outside the districts.[26] No such restrictions were applied to the visitors to the districts, who patronized the resident prostitutes.

The most famous establishments within Storyville, such as Lulu White's Mahogany Hall, were known for their opulent environs. However, Storyville included low cribs alongside such posh establishments.

Social and sexual interactions across races were not always tolerated in Storyville's 20-year tenure. In 1908, Louisiana prohibited sex across color lines.[27] This did not immediately affect the district, but increasing attention was brought to bear, with the gradual enforcement of a racial dichotomy of white and non-white rather than the varied palette acknowledging people of mixed heritages and many backgrounds. This binary racial categorization threatened mixed-race proprietors. In 1917, the New Orleans City Council instituted residential segregation by race in Storyville, with Canal Street as the dividing line.[28] The residents of the district contested this new restriction. Willie Piazza, a mixed-race woman who ran a brothel on the side of Canal Street suddenly redistricted for white prostitution only, challenged the city to evict her from the property, which she owned.[29] She prevailed, and a new ordinance restricted only where white prostitutes could live and work in Storyville.[30] Nevertheless, wartime legislation led to the demise of the district soon after.

Storyville's creation did not include one hallmark of regulated prostitution, the physical examination of prostitutes, in part because of the actions of feminist campaigners.[31] Internal physical examination using a speculum has been called "instrumental rape"[32] and contested in the United Kingdom in the Victorian Era, and eventually removed from regulation of prostitution.[33] An outspoken campaign was undertaken by feminists and former abolitionists who opposed similar requirements for physical examination of prostitutes in the United States, with success in New Orleans due in part to the participation of local women.[34]

The Jazz Age: Prohibition and Brothels

Prostitution was associated with alcohol and with the birth of jazz. Urban whorehouses were sites of entertainment, including music, food, and drink, and rural bars offered similar delights, some with upstairs rooms to which to retreat for private pursuits. Other entertainment venues such as concert saloons were associated with both prostitution and alcohol. Some of the early jazz greats, including Louis Armstrong, Earl "Fatha" Hines, and "Jelly Roll" Morton, got their starts playing in New Orleans brothels.[35] Later, James Brown started as an entertainer in a bordello in Georgia.

The United States prohibited the sale of alcohol in 1919. Prior to that date, Louisiana enacted the Gay-Shattuck Law that prohibited the sale of alcohol in places that did not also serve food, and also prohibited the sale of alcohol in places where people socialized across races.[36] This meant that restaurants—where men went with their wives—could serve alcohol, but that concert saloons and the clubs and brothels of racially unsegregated Storyville could not. Some establishments immediately offered food, such as Ada Hayes' tamale stand, while others adopted policies to cater to specific races and therefore be able to continue to serve liquor.[37]

The Volstead Act of 1919 (also promoted by coalitions of feminist and religious moralizers) prohibited the consumption of alcohol, transforming one of the social arenas in which prostitution occurred. Bars and taverns were not typically frequented by "respectable" women prior to Prohibition. Many saloons rented rooms above for short stays or to prostitutes who lived there. However, during Prohibition, speakeasies became places where all women could and did go. Prohibition coincided with the criminalization of bawdy houses in the United States, and whorehouses, many of which offered food and drink as well as company, therefore became doubly criminalized. Prohibition linked prostitution and alcohol in brothels as places where leisure activities that shared criminal status occurred. Prohibition changed the landscape, and ambiguity ensued as places that served alcohol became the site of some dating rather than places where most women present would have been suspected or expected to engage in sexual exchanges. Brothels continued to serve alcohol and offer music as well as sexual services without the concern over who was and who was not on the game.

Public Health and the Military

The Chamberlain-Kahn Act

The Chamberlain Kahn Act of 1918 was enacted as the United States entered World War I, to prevent U.S. soldiers from fraternizing with prostitutes and promiscuous women.[38] It effectively closed regulated and recognized red light areas throughout the United States. Although the Act led to results that reformers had long sought, passage of the Act was prompted less by moralizing than the fact that at any given time typically one-third of active soldiers were laid low by sexually transmitted infections (STIs). Today, many such infections are easily treated with antibiotics, but prior to the development of effective treatments, infections, including gonorrhea and syphilis, were rampant among the military. The same motivation promoted sanctioned brothels at which workers were examined and presumably were free of sexually transmitted infections.

The Chamberlain-Kahn Act of 1918 was passed ostensibly to prevent STIs among the troops. In reality, any women near military bases in the United States without escorts were suspected of prostitution and subject to arrest, gynecological examination, and detention for as long as it took to determine their physical health with regard to STIs. The irony was that this institutionalized sexism, combined with poor sanitary practices, led to medical exams promulgating infections among arrested women. Most women were quarantined for a few months, but minors were detained for longer, sometimes years.[39]

The May Act

The May Act was passed in 1941, just as the United States entered World War II. Like the Chamberlain-Kahn Act, it was intended to prevent instances of STIs among military personnel. The May Act increased penalties for prostitution in military areas, upgrading the charge to a federal offense. The May Act was rigorously enforced but ironically contributed to situations in which prostitution was prohibited by law but regulated in practice. Prostitution was generally prohibited around the country by the time the May Act was passed. However, as demonstrated by the previous examples, prostitution was officially and unofficially tolerated in different places at different times. In some instances, the control of the regulation of prostitution was lucrative and sought after by competing interests. Hawaii during World War II offers an especially interesting example of a dispute between the military and local police about the unofficial administration of prostitution. The three-week strike by Honolulu's prostitutes, in protest of the conditions of such unofficial regulation, is discussed in Chapter 9.

The military is still associated with brothels and unofficial policies intended to prevent STIs among troops. To this day, some U.S. military bases in the Philippines are in proximity to licensed brothels. Licensed brothels were closed in South Korea in the early years of the 21st century; however, as late as 2008, soldiers were given warning about police activity near brothels,[40] indicating that soldiers and sex workers continue to fraternize, despite official policies.

LICENSED PROSTITUTION IN NEVADA

Nevada's system of legal, regulated prostitution is unique in the United States. Rhode Island law decriminalized indoor prostitution in 1980 and recriminalized sex work in any venue in 2009.[41] Like many states, Nevada passed laws against prostitution after the passage of the federal Mann Act (see Chapter 7). In 1971, the state legislature of Nevada passed a statute stating that "the license board shall not license anyone to operate a house of ill fame or repute for the purpose of prostitution in a county of 250,000 or more" residents.[42] The state Supreme Court ruled in 1978 that this statute permitted licensed brothels,[43] called "ranches," just as they have been since brothels were established alongside mining operations and military garrisons.

Licensed prostitution affects the tax base of rural counties in Nevada, supporting schools and generating income in rural areas. Storey County charged $35,000 per year for a brothel license in 1994.[44] The license fee system favors large brothels. The licensing fees structure removes the possibility of a woman legally working independently; one or two women working together would not likely be able to support themselves and the license fee. The brothels themselves are not usually luxurious. Some are simply trailers in the desert. Others are buildings, some with landscaped grounds and pools that are used by the resident workers. High fences are standard, typically requiring that the gate be electronically opened for anyone entering and often for anyone leaving.

Regulated prostitution is heavily regimented. Until very recently, only female prostitutes were allowed to work in licensed brothels in Nevada. Applicants pay for and undergo physical examinations and testing for Chlamydia, gonorrhea, syphilis, and HIV as part of the registration process to work as a prostitute in a licensed brothel. Fingerprints are taken and background checks are conducted. After the initial tests and the background check, people who do not have any sexually transmitted infections are permitted to work in the licensed brothels. Working prostitutes are required to undergo weekly testing for Chlamydia and gonorrhea and monthly testing for syphilis and HIV. All related costs are borne by the sex workers. Condoms are required for all penetrative sex acts. No evidence of transmission of HIV within a licensed Nevada brothel has been documented.[45] However, these precautions are implemented in such a way that indicates that the intention is to protect customers from prostitutes rather than to safeguard the health of all parties.

Prostitution is treated as an exceptional sort of employment in which brothel workers are subject to restrictions that would be seen as untenable restrictions of liberty in other occupations. Some of these restrictions seem to be intended to prevent socializing in the areas where they work, enforcing separation from residents. Local police and brothel management can impose regulations in addition to the medical examinations imposed upon brothel workers. For example, in some cases, management sets brothel policy about when employees are allowed to leave and their work schedules. In some localities, prostitutes are not allowed the same freedom of movement as other people. Winnemucca requires brothel prostitutes to be at their workplace by 5 p.m. Additionally, prostitutes must register their cars, because the use of their cars and where they are allowed to drive is restricted. Ely distributes regulations specifying where brothel prostitutes may go (for example, to the movies) and where they may not (bars).[46] Other women's mobility is also restricted in some areas. Winnemucca forbids women who do not work in the brothels to visit them or drive to them.[47] In early 2010, men were permitted to work as licensed prostitutes in the brothels, and only a handful of men have been employed in the licensed brothels. It remains to be seen whether men will accept similar restrictions at work or prefer to work in less restrictive locations.

Brothel management is allowed to charge for room and board for the duration of the prostitute's stay. Some brothels do not permit resident workers to leave during their stint, instead employing others who run errands and shop for the brothel prostitutes, typically for a service charge. To some outsiders, these practices appear exploitative.[48] Conditions vary; not all brothels implement such restrictions on their workers. Storey County brothels, which are close to the city of Reno, impose fewer such restrictions than some others.

In Nevada, as in the earlier examples, many women find that brothel prostitution suits them despite the regulations and restrictions. Some of the women who work in the licensed brothels include porn stars and people who advertise on their own behalf. CB radio is used in some brothels to communicate with truckers and to encourage them to visit the brothels. Technology has advanced but the purposes for which it is used have stayed the same: Many brothel workers use the Internet to promote themselves, encouraging online reviews, and participating in online forums and message boards.

NOTES

1. Alecia P. Long, *The Great Southern Babylon: Sex, Race, and Respectability in New Orleans 1865–1920* (Baton Rouge, LA: Louisiana State University Press, 2004), 105–7.
2. Karen K. Swope, "D" Street in *Encyclopedia Prostitution and Sex Work*, edited by Melissa Hope Ditmore (Westport, CT: Greenwood, 2006), 1: 126–27.
3. Patricia Cline Cohen, *The Murder of Helen Jewett* (New York: Knopf, 1988).
4. Timothy Gilfoyle, *City of Eros: New York City Prostitution and the Commercialization of Sex, 1790–1920* (New York: Norton, 1994), 135–9.
5. Gilfoyle, 1994, 135–36.
6. Long, 2004, 83–84.
7. Long, 2004, 68.
8. Long, 2004, 68–9, 96, 104.
9. Long, 2004, 89.
10. Long, 2004, 77.
11. Long, 2004, 3–4.
12. Long, 2004, 3.
13. Long, 2004, 103.
14. Long, 2004, 114.
15. Long, 2004, 137–38.
16. Long, 2004, 131.
17. Long, 2004, 132–33.
18. Long, 2004, 192.
19. Long, 2004, 205–6.
20. Long, 2004, 104, 119.
21. Long, 2004, 133–37.
22. Long, 2004, 156.
23. Long, 2004, 119.
24. Long, 2004, 116.
25. Long, 2004, 121.
26. Long, 2004, 117.
27. Long, 2004, 209.
28. Long, 2004, 192.
29. Long, 2004, 192–93.
30. Long, 2004, 214–20.
31. Long, 2004, 113.

32. Judith Walkowitz, *Prostitution in Victorian Society: Women, Class and State* (New York: Cambridge University Press, 1980), 90.

33. Walkowitz, 1980.

34. Long, 2004, 113.

35. Emily Landau Epstein, " 'Spectacular Wickedness': New Orleans, Prostitution, and the Politics of Sex, 1897–1917" (PhD diss., Yale University, 2005); Long, 2004, 105, 196.

36. Long, 2004, 181.

37. Long, 2004, 181.

38. Barbara Meil Hobson. *Uneasy Virtue: The Politics of Prostitution and the American Reform Tradition* (New York: Basic Books, 1987), 176–78.

39. Hobson, 1987, 176–81; Kate Kramer, "Chamberlain-Kahn Act," in *Encyclopedia of Prostitution and Sex Work*, edited by Melissa Hope Ditmore (Westport, CT: Greenwood Press, 2006), 1: 93–94.

40. Katherine Moon, *Sex among Allies: Military Prostitution in US-Korea Relations* (New York: Columbia University Press, 1997); Jimmy Norris and Hwang Hae-rym, "Soldiers Warned about Prostitution Crackdown Near Yongsan Garrison," *Stars and Stripes*, Pacific ed., Thursday, September 11, 2008, http://www.stripes.com/news/soldiers-warned-about-prostitution-crackdown-near-yongsan-garrison-1.82898 (accessed November 24, 2008).

41. CNN AMFix, "RI closes loopholes on minors stripping, indoor prostitution," http://amfix.blogs.cnn.com/2009/11/02/ri-closes-loopholes-on-minors-stripping-indoor-prostitution/ (accessed November 2, 2009).

42. NRS 244.342, quoted in Lenore Kuo, "Licensed Prostitution, Nevada," in *Encyclopedia of Prostitution and Sex Work*, edited by Melissa Hope Ditmore (Westport, CT: Greenwood, 2006), 1: 253.

43. *Nye County v. Plankinton 94 Nev. 739*, 1978, quoted in Lenore Kuo, "Licensed Prostitution, Nevada," in *Encyclopedia of Prostitution and Sex Work*, edited by Melissa H. Ditmore (Westport, CT: Greenwood, 2006), 1: 253.

44. Lenore Kuo, "Licensed Prostitution, Nevada," in *Encyclopedia of Prostitution and Sex Work*, edited by Melissa Hope Ditmore (Westport, CT: Greenwood, 2006), 1: 253.

45. Alexa E. Albert, *Brothel* (New York: Random House, 2001).

46. Kuo, 2006, 253.

47. Kuo, 2006, 253.

48. Lenore Kuo, *Prostitution Policy, Revolutionizing Practice through a Gendered Perspective* (New York: New York University Press, 2002).

6

The Wild West

The American West is wildly romanticized, and the women there, perhaps especially the prostitutes, are especially so. These women include the colorfully named Calamity Jane and Timberline Kate, notorious Ah Toy of San Francisco, and generous Julie Bulette. The opportunity for self-invention led to transformations from harlots to *filles de joie* and the adoption of popular names like Kate and Fannie instead of Hattie.[1] Memory has transformed plain women into beauties and plain homes into mansions. Historian Marion Goldman offers the example of Julie Bulette of Virginia City, Nevada, as a legend of an extraordinarily successful madam who single-handedly funded civic life in this boomtown, but who in reality was an Englishwoman who lived in a two-room cottage and was generous within her modest means.[2] Despite this reduction of fortune, the lives behind the legends gain in fascination with the stories of hardship, boomtown business, travel, violence, and the evolution of social mores on the frontier.

War and speculation contributed to westward expansion during the 19th century. The U.S.-Mexican war ended with the United States gaining control of the American southwest, including what are now the states of Texas, New Mexico, Arizona, and California, just as gold was discovered in California, sparking the migration of treasure seekers. Settlers of European descent moved across the United States for opportunities to own land and to mine for precious metals. Consider the conditions in mining camps and frontier outposts, with a primarily male population detached from familial community. "Camp followers," women who followed soldiers, miners, and others in primarily male occupations, performed tasks traditionally regarded as women's work, including washing laundry, preparing meals, and sewing clothing. Many also sold sex.

RACE AND ETHNICITY ON THE FRONTIER

A racial hierarchy emerged reflecting the origins of the ethnicities present in the American West. Historian Anne M. Butler describes a frontier culture in which settlers of European descent dominated economic activities, and the way this was replicated in prostitution. The "Indian Wars" culminated in the creation of reservations and forced migration of Native Americans westward to inferior land to which they had negligible, if any cultural ties, contributing to multitudes of deaths and extreme poverty unalleviated to this day. Prior to the arrival of European- and American-born settlers, fortune favored one tribe or another depending on their relations and resources. Within 300 years of the arrival of the Spanish in what is now Florida and 200 years of the arrival of the Dutch, English, and French further north, all tribes were dominated militarily, geographically, and economically by descendents of European colonizers. Some indigenous women from western reservations exchanged sex for money or goods in one of the few ways available to them to generate income.[3]

Many male settlers were veterans of the war in which Mexico had been defeated. Animosity toward Mexican people did not recede at the war's end, affecting the status of Mexican people in the United States, including prostitutes. Mexico was populated primarily by peasants who performed agricultural and ranching work for the numerically smaller but more powerful landed gentry. Mexican prostitutes in the American west were primarily of peasant stock, and their relative powerlessness and low status did not change. Many Mexican women were in situations in which they had little control, having indentured themselves to be brought to California, and many subsequently were essentially sold to the lowest class of brothels. They worked in situations in which they had little control or self-determination.[4]

After the end of the Civil War, the numbers of African American prostitutes in the American west increased.[5] Psychologist Howard B. Woolston eloquently described the way slavery afforded physical access to slave women:

A woman whose body is the actual property of a man, in the same way as is that of a horse or a cow, to be disposed of as he sees fit, finds any physical attractiveness she may possess a distinct bar to virtue. In a society which accepts as a matter of course a double standard of sex morality and a belief in the physical necessity of the sex act for men, it is to be expected that the presence in its midst of a group of women without legal right to their own persons would make prostitution in its accepted sense almost unnecessary.[6]

Opportunities for education and to gain skills that could contribute to employability were nearly entirely absent for people who had been enslaved, and such opportunities did not substantially increase with freedom.

Prostitution afforded a source of income for unskilled people, including many freed from slavery.[7]

Not everyone arrived in the West from the eastern United States or Mexico. San Francisco Bay offered a harbor for ships that traveled through the Panama Canal, along the Pacific coast between North and South America, and from Australia and Asia. Chinese populations came to California primarily as indentured labor. Very few Chinese women were present. The Chinese Exclusion Act prohibited Chinese people from entering the United States and its western territories. This change led to longer periods of indenture, including for Chinese women. Some of these women were prostitutes, some of whom were treated no better than slaves.[8] Smaller numbers of Japanese women were also present in brothels.[9] Asian immigrant communities were shunned by white society and so remained in many ways impenetrable due to differences in language and lack of interest in knowing each other. This did not preclude the desire to do business and earn money. Historian Benson Tong demonstrates that many Chinese prostitutes in the West were "unsubmissive women" who defied stereotypes and successfully negotiated business, marriage, and more.[10] Tong offers detailed descriptions of girls effectively sold by their families,[11] eventually unwillingly traveling to the American west.[12] Some of the Chinese prostitutes in California worked in sweatshops by day and sold sex at night.[13] Most, like Cum Choy, turned over their earnings to their "owner" or the proprietor of the brothel where they worked. Ah Woo retained some of her earnings, and "Selina" was enviable because she worked independently.[14]

Women with the least control over their working conditions suffered the greatest discrimination, earning the least money in the most *déclassé* workplaces.[15] Latin Americans suffered similar discrimination, and those who could pass for Spanish benefited. Many of the small number of Chinese women endured similar situations, and great discrimination.[16] It is not coincidental that the groups of women who had the least control over their work and earned the lowest wages were visibly ethnically distinct from arrivals descended from northern Europeans. White women were more esteemed than women of color, and those with the closest ties to Europe were the most revered. A ship carrying professional prostitutes from France arrived in San Francisco shortly after the gold rush began, and these women were regaled as the epitome of feminine grace and beauty. They were not indentured and worked in more luxurious establishments where they earned larger sums of money. American-born women were regarded in a similar light, but were ranked as less elegant than their French peers.[17] However, all prostitutes on the frontier, no matter their origins, were socially affected by the dominant morality of the Victorian era.

Men and women came to the Pacific coast from Mexico, Australia, Ireland, Germany, Spain, France, and England. It seems that many women of European descent, no matter their occupation, were afforded status and respect in San Francisco and other frontier posts during the brief interval while there were very few women in these outposts. However, once relatively equitable numbers were established and families started, married women enforced mores including social boundaries separating prostitutes and mistresses from wives and families.[18] Jacqueline Baker Barnhart tells the stories of San Francisco madam Irene McReady being shunned by family women at a gala in 1850 and of Bella Cora's refusal to leave a theater in that city at the request of a married woman who did not want to be associated or seen with a mistress.[19]

For all residents of the American west, perceptions of race and their manifestations permeated and informed all facets of life, but especially policing, hiring, and interactions with people of other ethnicities and races.

WORKPLACES

Venues and working conditions varied widely. Venues for prostitution included canvas tents in mining camps, the one- or two-room wooden shacks called "cribs," saloons and gambling houses, rural ranches, and well-appointed parlor houses. Gambling halls, saloons, brothels, and parlor houses offered entertainment including music and, particularly in parlor houses, meals in addition to sexual entertainment. Most venues served alcohol.

"Cat" wagons[20] carried prostitutes from one small outpost to another and eventually back to town after such a tour of duty, camping in their wagons. In mining camps and very new frontier outposts, nearly everyone lived in canvas tents prior to the erection of more stable structures. Some prostitutes in towns and cities walked the streets. They were afforded the lowest status in the hierarchy among prostitutes. Women who lived and worked in cribs, which were single-story homes frequently lining an alley or a less desirable block, paid high rents for sub-standard housing, but they charged relatively little for their services. They endured economic hardship and did not share in the boomtown prosperity that all aspired to cash in on. Prostitutes who worked in saloons and gambling houses were afforded status according to the status of the venue in which they worked. Some saloons and gambling houses had rooms for rent to prostitutes and their patrons. These were not typically considered elite establishments.

As already noted, in rural areas in the American west, brothels were called "ranches." This terminology is still used to refer to legal brothels in rural

Nevada. Brothels established near military bases were known as "hog ranches" and primarily catered to low-ranking military men.

Many people on the frontier lived in boarding houses. Female boarding houses were frequently brothels in which the residents may have been afforded some level of independence or developed relationships with others who brought in clients. Some buildings were stand-alone brothels managed by a madam. Parlor houses were the most elegant brothels and were found primarily in cities that could support more chic and costly pursuits of leisure. Such establishments sometimes advertised their wares by driving women workers through town in an open carriage, enabling passersby to admire the women in their best outfits.

Prostitutes' balls were another form of advertising. These could be small parties at parlor houses, brothels, saloons, or ranches, but some were large events held in theaters.[21] The theater itself was another avenue to advertise, and some prostitutes performed on the stage. The purchase of tickets and drinks, and in some cases food, supported these events. The public nature of large balls and the presence of some respectable women (who would typically leave early) prevented the disclosure of the identities of the patrons of prostitutes.[22]

The status afforded different venues affected interactions with law enforcement and levels of protection from violence, but this status did not necessarily reflect the income individuals derived from prostitution. Boarding-house, hotel, brothel, and parlor-house residents each paid rent, and prostitutes were charged higher rents than others. Residents may also have been charged for meals. The people who most benefitted financially were those who earned money from the prostitutes in these venues: madams, managers, and owners.[23] In this way, prostitution is not different from other kinds of work; the owner of the mine earned more than the employee of a mining company.

FAMILY LIFE AND LESS TRADITIONAL RELATIONSHIPS

Frontier family life was not serene. The historical record consists of newspaper items that record violence, murder, and abandonment, alongside arrest and theft.

Many of the women in prostitution married on the frontier, and many more had children. Most women who married continued working as prostitutes to support their families, especially when they married people associated with their milieu, such as proprietors of brothels and gambling houses. Not all marriages were formal, and not all marriages endured the harsh conditions on the frontier. Divorce, abandonment, and informal separation encouraged some married women's entry into prostitution.[24] Butler cites birth records of women delivering children as they crossed the frontier, first in one city, followed by a child born in another city further west.[25] Many of the children born were lost to disease, particularly typhoid and cholera.[26] Female children often followed their mother's occupation.[27]

Not all families adhered to the gender norms of the time and today. While many men may have sought male companionship at the frontier, the historical record of male prostitution on the frontier is scant.[28] However, one Mrs. Nash, a laundress, was involved with one enlisted man after another in serial relationships with a number of men stationed at Fort Meade in the Dakota Territory. Mrs. Nash died in 1878, and upon preparing the body for burial, it was discovered that Mrs. Nash was actually physically male.[29] This may be the most well documented example of transgender or homosexual activity in the context of the military presence on the American frontier. Non-traditional families may have quietly settled on the frontier but would only enter the historical record upon discovery and scandal, as in the case of Mrs. Nash. Same-sex relationships among women were also noted, including "the night that Calamity Jane was ejected from a brothel in Bozeman, Montana, because she was corrupting the other inmates."[30] Prostitution and same-sex attachments were not illegal, and some records indicate that some women dressed as men and may have had lesbian relationships with women who dressed as women. Cross-dressing was subject to fines in some places, and one man in the audience of theater/saloon/brothel was discovered to be female and "chased away."[31]

POLICING

Formal municipal police departments were rare on the frontier. Rather than salaries, sheriffs and justices of the peace were paid through a fee structure and fines, creating an incentive to create and enforce a fine schedule for gain rather than municipal interest.[32] Prostitutes were not typically fined for prostitution, which was more likely to be subject to fees and protection money, but for using foul language, drunkenness, and other charges related to what now comes under the rubric of "disorderly conduct."[33] Other charges included "lewdness" and adultery, and "keeping a bawdy house."[34] Municipalities passed ordinances against brothel keeping and keeping a gambling den, in line with English common law.[35] The fines imposed were significant for many people on the frontier, demonstrated by the number of women who served jail time because they could not pay the fines.[36] Tong describes

Chinese prostitutes paying fees or protection money to "police" hired by Chinese citizens.[37] These fees and fines constituted an improvised form of taxation that supported the justice of the peace and efforts to address crime.[38] Butler cites the example of Canadian, Texas, where "the court permitted prostitutes to pay a deposit on the fine and then return to the streets to earn the rest of the money. This was not allowed all prostitutes before the court and may have been based on the woman's record of dependability for paying off her outstanding debts."[39] Not all charges merely formed the basis for the payment of municipal authorities by incurring debts. Some addressed existing debts. Taxation of property and falling behind in rent were two more reasons prostitutes appeared in court records, again addressing debts.

Race and ethnicity affected interactions with local law enforcement. Tong describes the disproportionate numbers of arrests and raids on Chinese brothels.[40] People of Mexican, Native American, and Asian descent suffered upon arrest because until 1873, they were not permitted to testify in court against white defendants. They could, however, testify against non-whites.[41]

Charges addressing violence and theft were serious offenses. It is easy to understand the temptation or appeal of theft for people unable to pay frequent court fines. People working in places where alcohol flowed and many were armed saw a great deal of violence and also offered alibis in court for people suspected of violent crimes. Prostitutes appeared in the court records as both victims and perpetrators, and also as witnesses. In murder cases, law enforcement typically sought the murderer of a prostitute, but convictions were more rare and sentences related to violence against prostitutes were light.[42] However, when the victim was not white, violence was treated less seriously, although if the perpetrator of violence was not white, sentences were harsher. Butler offers the example of the ten-year sentences delivered to Mattie Lemmon, an African American prostitute and Belle Warden, an African American madam, convicted of murder in Denver.[43]

REFORM

There were no sustained campaigns against prostitution because, in the words of Goldman, "Any attempt to eradicate the vice districts would have been foolhardy, for prostitution was very important to the Lode's economic life."[44] This was true not only of Comstock Lode but also of the mining and garrison towns throughout the American West.

Reform efforts around the frontier were sporadic and typically church-driven. Most offered no replacement for the income derived from prostitution and so failed to attract any long-term converts. The exception was the

St. Paul chapter of the Sisters of the Good Shepherd, which offered room and board in an all-female environment. Butler points out that this was not very different from the brothels many of the women lived in prior to coming to the convent.[45]

MILITARY GARRISONS

Military garrisons proliferated across the frontier as American settlements multiplied in number and expanded in size. Official statements offered no acknowledgment of prostitution related to the military, a policy that continues to this day, but it is clear that the frontier garrisons offered a specific venue for prostitution. Camp followers, including laundresses and seamstresses, typically sold sex or offered situations akin to serial marriage at the garrisons. Hog ranches catered to enlisted men and officers. Some arrangements seem to have been facilitated by garrison shopkeepers.[46] Many colorful anecdotes of the military presence on the frontier relate to prostitutes of all races, including Navajo women at Fort Fauntleroy in New Mexico and Sioux women at Fort Randall in the Dakota Territory.[47]

One anecdote reflects extremely good relations between Fort Fauntleroy and the local Navajo population, such that on one occasion, Navajo men, women, and children were at the garrison for horse racing. The Navajo accused the soldiers of cheating, whereupon the soldiers massacred many of the Navajo, ending the previously good relations. Military commanders attempted to send a Navajo prostitute with clients among the officers as an emissary, but she was whipped by her tribesmen rather than welcomed.[48]

CONCLUSION

Frontier life was a hard existence for all, but prostitutes in frontier towns experienced varying levels of discrimination based upon class and race in addition to gender and the stigma of prostitution. Prostitutes were nonetheless simultaneously service providers and members of communities, and shunned by established society in the old west. These multiple roles illustrate far more intriguing lives than the one-dimensional stereotypes of the old west's "hooker with a heart of gold."

NOTES

1. Marion S. Goldman, *Gold Diggers and Silver Miners* (Ann Arbor, MI: University of Michigan Press, 1981), 59.

2. Goldman, 1981, 1–3.

3. Anne M. Butler, *Daughters of Joy, Sisters of Misery: Prostitutes in the American West 1865–90* (Urbana and Chicago: University of Illinois Press, 1985), 12.

4. Butler, 1985, 11.

5. Butler, 1985, 4.

6. Howard B. Woolston, *Prostitution in the United States* (New York: Century, 1921), 15.

7. Woolston, 1921, 16; Butler, 1985, 13.

8. Goldman, 1981, 69.

9. Tomoko Yamazaki, *The Story of Yamada Waka* (New York: Kodansha, 1985).

10. Benson Tong, *Unsubmissive Women: Chinese Prostitutes in Nineteenth-Century San Francisco* (Norman, OK: University of Oklahoma Press, 1994).

11. Tong, 1994, 42.

12. Tong, 1994, 54.

13. Tong, 1994, 75.

14. Tong, 1994, 104.

15. Jacqueline Baker Barnhart, *The Fair but Frail* (Reno, NV: University of Nevada Press, 1986).

16. Tong, 1994.

17. Barnhart, 1986; Goldman, 1981, 67–69.

18. Butler, 1985.

19. Barnhart, 1986, 35.

20. Butler, 1985, 50.

21. Goldman, 1981, 111.

22. Goldman, 1981, 109–11.

23. Goldman, 1981, 74.

24. Goldman, 1981, 71.

25. Butler, 1985, 38.

26. Butler, 1985, 37.

27. Butler, 1985, 39, 41.

28. John D'Emilio and Estelle M. Freedman, *Intimate Matters: A History of Sexuality in America* (Chicago: University of Chicago Press, 1988).

29. Butler, 1985, 144.

30. Goldman, 1981, 120.

31. Goldman, 1981, 120.

32. Butler, 1985, 99.

33. Goldman, 1981, 145–47.

34. Woolston, 1921, 25.

35. Woolston, 1921, 24; Butler, 1985, 100.

36. Butler, 1985, 58.

37. Tong, 1994, 104.

38. Butler, 1985, 100.

39. Butler, 1985, 102.

40. Tong, 1994, 114–17.

41. Tong, 1994, 136–37.
42. Butler, 1985, 110.
43. Butler, 1985, 111.
44. Goldman, 1981, 34.
45. Butler, 1985, 65–67.
46. Butler, 1985, 138.
47. Butler, 1985, 137.
48. Butler, 1985, 134.

7

Immigration Law and State Legislation of Morality to "Protect" Women

Throughout history, many efforts to protect women have actually limited women's actions and opportunities. The regulation of women's sexuality has often ostensibly been motivated by health concerns or a desire to protect women and children. These possibly well-intentioned aims frequently masked an underlying agenda to regulate morality, and even a certain prurience on the part of those who proposed them. Moreover, while the intention of such acts may have been protective, they were seldom empowering—they typically disregarded women's rights and acted to restrict rather than extend the options available to them. In addition to reflecting that men made these laws to govern women, re-enforcing gender roles and the male privilege of autonomy, these laws also reflected racial and religious beliefs of white male legislators. The selective enforcement of these laws fell along racial and political lines, thereby reinforcing the existing power dynamics in which white men made the rules for everyone in the United States.

This chapter will analyze a number of different laws, including the 1882 Chinese Exclusion Act, immigration acts from the early 20th century, and the Mann Act of 1910.[1] The laws under consideration include laws on trafficking, immigration, and prostitution. There are good reasons to consider these in tandem. One is that activists addressing prostitution also concerned themselves with traffic in women and girls. These acts, especially the Mann Act, give the historical background of the changing interpretation of prostitution, as commercial sex was made illegal in the United States during the early 20th century.

Another reason to address these categories of laws together is how they affect other issues. Some immigration policy is overtly concerned with prostitution, and the perception of specific immigrants, particularly the Chinese and southern Europeans, as morally lax or even as prostitutes and "white slavers." Trafficking policy additionally affects migration with its stipulations about who can enter and stay in the United States. The Chinese Exclusion Act may have promoted trafficking in Chinese women, because Chinese women were unable to legally enter the United States. The Mann Act is most known for its interstate aspect, but it also addressed recent immigrants. Additionally, the Immigration Acts of 1903, 1907, and 1910[2] stipulated the deportation of aliens who were prostitutes. Therefore, the Chinese Exclusion Act and Immigration Acts from 1903, 1907, and 1910 will be discussed, as well as the Mann Act of 1910 and state laws passed against prostitution in the wake of the Mann Act, as well as prominent cases in their enforcement. Each of the acts named above provide the legal and political context in which to examine current efforts. These specific legal and political instruments are analyzed because they illustrate the continuing effectiveness of efforts to regulate morality in the guise of women's issues.

"WHITE SLAVERY" SCARES AND PROTECTIONIST LEGISLATIVE EFFORTS

The power of laws designed to combat "white slavery," such as the Mann Act, as instruments of social control came in part from the absence of clear definitions of the phenomena that they address—white slavery, immoral acts, or prostitution. White slavery at that time referred to seduction (synonymous at the time with rape)[3] and prostitution but also was used against moral laxity. White slavery and "immoral acts" were conflated and undefined, resulting in overly broad use based not on law but on the interpretation of these terms by law enforcement officials. Commercial sex and prostitution were ill defined at best, sometimes encompassing sex in ways that today we would consider "dating" rather than an overt commercial exchange. The definition or lack thereof in legislation of prostitution, focusing on "immoral acts" and circumstantial evidence as opposed to crimes committed, reflects general anxiety about sexuality rather than about prostitution specifically.

The Mann Act, also known as the White Slave Traffic Act, was motivated by the fear that large numbers of young, white girls were being stolen and forced into sexual servitude. There is no evidence to suggest that this was in fact the case, but the act had enormous social impact. Women's travel was effectively limited, especially between 1915 and 1932, when women who traveled across state lines with or to meet a man were prosecuted for conspiring to violate the Mann Act.[4] The Mann Act remains a sacred cow to imagined propriety in the United States, but it was amended in 1986 and its application strongly reduced. The following sections explore the history of these acts and their enforcement, with a view to the ways that they attempted to exert social control and restraint of women. The selective enforcement of the Mann Act in both its original and revised forms is also analyzed, as an illustration of the way laws may be selectively enforced to yield results different from their original, ostensible intention.

The Mann Act and the Criminalization of Prostitution

The Mann Act was passed in 1910. Within 10 years, nearly all states passed legislation making prostitution a crime.[5] Female promiscuity and prostitution were widely conflated well into the 20th century. For example, the Mann Act refers to "immoral acts" without specificity and was used to address promiscuity and miscegenation as well as sexual exchange. After 1917, laws criminalizing prostitution were passed across the United States.[6] These statutes varied in their levels of ambiguity but in some ways were fairly consistent.

Prior to World War I, prostitution was widely addressed using vagrancy laws. Historian H. B. Woolston writes that prior to 1917, only Indiana defined prostitution in criminal law, but that in 1918 alone, 10 states passed laws including definitions of prostitution.[7] Prohibition of prostitution is currently the dominant legislative approach across the United States. For example, Woolston writes,

In 1918 ten states (Conn., Dela., N.H., N.C., N.D., Ohio, R.I., Vt. and Md.) passed laws which included as a definition of prostitution, "The giving or receiving of the body for sexual intercourse for hire, or the giving or receiving of the body for indiscriminate sexual intercourse without hire."[8]

Note that "prostitution" in these laws is not dependent on the exchange of money. No distinction is made between promiscuity ("without hire") and prostitution ("for hire").

AMERICAN IMMIGRATION ACTS

While Victorian British concerns with white slavery focused on the removal of innocent British girls to other nations, American concerns in the early 20th century focused on the immigration of white slavers and immoral women to the United States. The context for the Immigration Acts was a growing wave of immigration to the United States, as well as a change in the ethnic background of the immigrants. Earlier waves had brought predominantly northern Europeans, especially Norwegians, Germans, and Irish. Now established, these groups clamored loudly against the newer turn-of-the-century immigrants, largely Italians and Eastern European Jews.

The concern with white slavery during the late 19th and early 20th centuries included fears about changing morality and changes in immigration. It is not accidental that white slavery hysteria escalated during a period of increased immigration. To this day, the ethnic cast assigned to supposed white slavers in urban myths closely reflects changing patterns of immigration.[9] Legal historian Frederick K. Grittner cites the stereotypes of Chinese white slavers in the 1890s.[10] In the following decades, racist fears portrayed white slavers as Jewish;[11] the current focus is on organized criminals from eastern Europe and Asia. Ironically, historical evidence shows that the new immigrants actually were less likely to be involved in prostitution than native-born women.[12] "Loose morals" may have been more of an American than an immigrant characteristic.

Immigrants from Europe, unlike those entering from the Pacific, arrived through Castle Clinton, and later, Ellis Island. Before 1875, the date of the first of many restrictive immigration laws, immigration personnel administered open immigration,[13] rather different from the current border enforcement function of the Immigration and Customs Enforcement. The first act to limit immigration, passed in 1875, and prohibited the entry of criminals and prostitutes.[14] As prostitution was not a crime, it had to be mentioned separately. Stereotypes of the Chinese as criminals and prostitutes justified not allowing Chinese people into the country even before the Chinese Exclusion Act of 1882, the second act to limit immigration to the United States.[15] Race was a greater issue for those entering from the Pacific than from Europe, specifically for the Chinese but also for other Asians.

Chinese Immigration

Sociologist Peter Kwong describes the kidnapping of a quarter of a million "coolies" or indentured servants and slaves, mostly men, from China into the United States between the 1840s and the 1870s, as black slavery declined and another source of cheap labor was sought.[16] Ironically, this real traffic in persons garnered less interest than the exaggerated "white slave trade" and the reaction to it was not motivated by humanitarian concerns. A racist and nativist platform promoted by whites, some of whom were themselves immigrants, encouraged the restriction and ultimate end of Asian immigration. Restricting Asian immigration began with the Chinese Labor Exclusion Act of 1882 and culminated in the 1924 Oriental Exclusion Act. These acts reflect a larger racism seen also in the labor movement and popular preconceptions of the time including stereotypes of Chinese white slavers.

The Chinese Labor Exclusion Act of 1882 eliminated the option for Chinese in the United States to become naturalized citizens[17] and forced Chinese would-be migrants to enter the United States illegally, often by land from Mexico.[18] This policy was intended to prevent permanent settling by Chinese men in the United States. Stereotypes of the Chinese at the time were those of criminals and prostitutes[19] rather than today's "model minority." Seagraves writes that of the several thousand Chinese women in San Francisco in 1870, "[l]ess than one hundred were respected members of the community."[20] Low numbers of Chinese women in the United States limited the possibilities of marrying and having children. However, a man who claimed citizenship (made possible for many by the destruction of birth records in San Francisco's 1906 earthquake) could return to China and bring his children to the United States from China, who were then citizens. The "slots" for these "paper children," as they were called, were frequently sold until new immigration policies eliminated this system in 1965.[21]

These restrictions on women were lessened in the 1940s, when veterans were allowed to bring brides from China, but only 100 women were allowed to enter as wives each year.[22] It was not until the civil rights movement of the 1960s that all immigration laws specific to colored minorities, including Asians, were repealed.[23] Like newer policies that restrict women's movement (which will be discussed later), this policy did not entirely eliminate the entry of Chinese women into the United States. A *San Francisco Chronicle* article from 1932 describes outright slavery.[24] The piece profiles Donaldina Cameron, who made her name rescuing enslaved Chinese prostitutes in San Francisco until 1939. It seems the Chinese Exclusion Act offered no improvement for Chinese women in the American West, and may have encouraged traffic in Chinese women because they could not enter the country legally. Chinese women were not necessarily well off in the United States before the Exclusion Act.

Luc Sante's colorful history of New York City's underworld notes that there were unconfirmable claims of Chinese women and children being sold as slaves in Mexico for between $38 and $45 before being brought to New York.[25] Sante describes Chinatown tours to see criminal figures and "slave wives."[26] Some of these women were possibly "mail order brides," while others may have been prostitutes. There were more Chinese in California than in the eastern United States, but the numbers of Chinese women were very low throughout the United States. Sante cites an 1890s poll recording three Chinese prostitutes or slaves and 800 Chinese men in New York.[27]

Historian Timothy Gilfoyle's thorough history of prostitution in New York City supports such a low number with the information that most Chinatown prostitutes were not Chinese but white women.[28] Legal historian Grittner quotes Jacob Riis's renowned *How the Other Half Lives* (1890), which depicts Chinese ability to handle opium as greater than that of whites, especially white women. Langum further cites a variant on white slavery rumors of the time that women should not enter Chinese laundries for fear of "kidnapping, druggings, and sexual abuse."[29] Racist depictions of the Chinese precede the anti-Semitic racism of later "white slavery" tracts.[30]

Immigration Acts Referring to Prostitution

The United States 1903 and 1907 Immigration Acts referred directly to prostitution, not in the vague terms later used by the Mann Act. The 1903 Act specified a one-to-five year prison term and a fine not exceeding $5,000 for this felony.[31] The 1907 Act further specified deportation for the prostitute involved.[32]

The Immigration Act of 1910 went further and applied to "[a]ny alien who shall be found an inmate of or connected with the management of a house of prostitution or practicing prostitution."[33] The connection could be tenuous: an alien might be liable to deportation if found in a music or dance hall, public sites of working class entertainment and places where prostitutes often met their clients at that time.[34] The exact wording of the relevant statute is:

Any alien who shall be found an inmate of or connected with the management of a house of prostitution or practicing prostitution after such alien shall have entered the United States, or who shall receive, share in, or derive benefit from any part of the earnings of any prostitute; or who is employed by, in, or in connection with any house of prostitution or music or dance hall or other place of amusement of resort habitually frequented by prostitutes, or where prostitutes gather, or who in any way assists, protects, or promises to protect from arrest any prostitute, shall be deemed to be unlawfully in the United States and shall be deported.[35]

This provision could have been used against anyone who happened to be in the wrong place at the wrong time.

The 1903 Immigration Act saw an increase in the numbers of people barred from entry, but the numbers remained low. For example, in 1904, nine alien women were barred from entry, and in 1905, 24 alien women were barred from entry. This number jumped to 30 in 1906, and dropped to 18 in 1907. The numbers of alien women barred as procurers ranged from one to four between 1904 and 1907, with only one woman barred in 1907.

Table 7.1
Numbers Barred from Entry under 1903 and 1907 Immigration Acts

	1904	1905	1906	1907	1908
Alien women barred from entry	9	24	30	18	124
Alien women barred from entry as procurers	3	4	2	1	43

Figures are from U.S. Senate, *Importation and Harboring* (1910): 60–61, quoted in Connolly, 1980, 175.

The 1907 Immigration Act, however, led to a marked jump to 124 alien women barred and 43 alien women barred as procurers in 1908. Even as the numbers of women deported or denied entry increased substantially in 1908, following the passage of the 1907 Act, the numbers were still small in the grand scheme of things: less than 300 (see Table 7.1). Numbers of aliens deported as prostitutes and procurers also jumped significantly after the passage of the 1907 Immigration Act. From June 1907 to June 1908, 65 aliens were deported as prostitutes, and two were deported as procurers, and that the following year, and from June 1908 to June 1909, these numbers increased dramatically to 261 and 30, respectively (see Table 7.2).[36] However, such small numbers from an era of enormous immigration suggest that—even with the rise in deportations and the numbers barred from entry of prostitutes and procurers following the 1903 and 1907 Immigration Acts—the scale of the problem was hardly large enough to warrant the legislative efforts deployed against it. Such numbers suggest that the association between immigrants and prostitution had little basis in fact. Prostitution-related offenses involving native-born women at this time in any large American city were greater in

Table 7.2
Numbers Deported under 1907 Immigration Act

	June 1907–June 1908	June 1908–June 1909
Aliens deported as prostitutes	65	261
Aliens deported as procurers	2	30

Figures are from U.S. Senate, *Importation and Harboring* (1910): 60–61, quoted in Connolly, 1980, 175.

number.[37] Prostitution was a local issue; the sections of the Immigration Acts relating to prostitution and "white slavery" were a response to an imagined problem that had been inflated out of proportion by irrational fears. Yet these fears did not end here: they were to find further expression in the Mann Act.

The Mann Act (1910) and Immigration

The Mann Act had two areas of enforcement: first, immigration, where it was used both to deport people and to reject potential immigrants (much as in the Immigration Acts of 1903, 1907, and 1910), and second, the more well known area of federal trade, where it extrapolated from interstate commerce to the movement of women. The association demonstrates a perception of women as chattel rather than as residents and full citizens. This perception was perhaps not inappropriate: at the time of the Act, women were not yet able to vote.

In both its immigration and interstate aspects, the Mann Act specifically targeted "white slavery":

Every person who shall keep, maintain, control, support, or harbor in any house or place for the purpose of prostitution, or for any other immoral purpose, any alien woman or girl within three years after she shall have entered the United States from any country, party to the said arrangement for the suppression of the white slave traffic [Agreement between the United States and other powers for the repression of the trade in white women, 1908], shall file with the Commissioner-General of Immigration a statement in writing setting forth the name of such alien woman or girl, the place at which she is kept, and all facts as to the date of her entry into the United States, the port through which she entered, her age, nationality, and parentage, and concerning her procuration to come to this country within the knowledge of such person.[38]

Such reports are not included in the thorough studies of the Mann Act by Connolly, Grittner, and Langum, perhaps indicating a lack of informants. The focus on white women—with the implication that sexual servitude of other, non-white women was apparently permissible—is, however, clearly evident from the title of the international agreement cited, the Agreement between the United States and Other Powers for the Repression of the Trade in White Women, 1908.

INTERSTATE ENFORCEMENT OF THE MANN ACT

The Mann Act is far better known for its interstate aspect than its immigration aspect. This interstate aspect was so much a part of the collective imagination that the Mann Act figured in literature. F. Scott Fitzgerald used it in *Tender is the Night* (1934), in which the main character has an affair with a teenager, and *This Side of Paradise* (1920),[39] in which the act is referred to by name when the main character is found in a hotel room with a young woman in a state different from the state in which his car in the parking lot is registered. It was also a constant reference in legal cases. Prostitution is normally dealt with at the state level; by introducing the issue of travel across state lines, the Mann Act brought prostitution into the federal jurisdiction. The Act relies on the federal authority to legislate interstate commerce and on international agreement to enable enforcement by federal agents without infringing on local police jurisdiction.

Initial enforcement of the Act focused on prostitution, in accordance with the intent of this law, but the language of the Mann Act left it open for wider application. The Act prohibited interstate travel (physical movement from one state to another) for "immoral acts," with a specific focus on women. Women constituted the largest group prosecuted under the Mann Act.[40] In some cases (between 1915 and 1932), women were charged with conspiracy, along with their boyfriends, for their participation in their own travel plans, for "agreeing to go along on the trip."[41]

The Mann Act was open to extension, both with regard to the question of what constituted an "immoral act," and to the nature of the travel. For many women who lived close to state lines—such as the Hudson River valley, near New York City—even local travel might be "interstate." Similarly, the act was soon extended from prostitution to other sex acts. In 1911, it was clearly stated in a court that the Mann Act addressed commercial sex;[42] by 1917, it had been established that the Mann Act did not apply solely to persons engaging in commercial sex or to actions involving minors but also to consensual, adult acts. This principle was definitively established by the highly publicized Caminetti case, in which two married men and their extramarital partners traveled across state lines, from California to Nevada in 1913. The two men, Caminetti and Diggs, were convicted and then appealed, but the guilty verdict was upheld by the U.S. Supreme Court in 1917. Subsequently, the two men involved in the case divorced their wives, and one married his female partner in this crime before he entered prison to serve time for traveling to Reno with her.[43]

What spurred the change in interpretation to include a wider range of social and sexual activity under the Mann Act? Was it the difference in social ideals of the respective judges? Or a sea change in U.S. society? One thing to consider is the shifting social mores and situation of the age.[44] The Mann Act was originally enacted during a flurry of concern about changing immigration patterns, and an (unfounded) fear that white women were being bought and sold by swarthy foreign immigrants. As this moral panic slowly died away, a new one took its place.

At the time that the interpretation of the Act began to shift, increasing numbers of young women were beginning to move from rural areas to the cities. But urbanization had been happening for decades, and worries about prostitution had ebbed and flowed with this migration to the cities.[45] Simultaneously, the end of the Victorian Era saw growing public and particularly legislative concern with social issues. The Progressive Era was an age of concern about social hygiene. This was when John D. Rockefeller began funding social hygiene outfits, such as the Bureau of Social Hygiene (founded 1913) for "the study, amelioration, and prevention of those social conditions, crimes, and diseases which adversely affect the well-being of society, with special reference to prostitution and the evils associated therewith."[46] It was also the time of the publication of *The Social Evil in Chicago*, a municipal study of prostitution soon replicated in many other cities around the United States. Fears about unsupervised single women included fears that they might succumb to the temptations of city life, such as dancing, drinking, and theater, three activities linked to prostitution.[47] Such ideas were supported by the fact that women's wages were so low that many women turned to prostitution or "going on the town" for extra money, so many that some professions "in the public mind were linked with prostitution."[48] In 1922 the U.S. government published information stating that the white slave gangs had been eradicated, amid discussion of whether they ever actually existed.[49] Most cases prosecuted individuals and not rings.[50] But instead of simply declaring victory over white slavery, the authorities transferred the focus of enforcement: white slaves and white slavers were simply replaced by prostitutes and pimps, and enforcement was stepped up.[51] From there, selective enforcement of the law provided the mechanism for the imposition of a specific morality. This enforcement did not correspond to factual incidents but rather reflected shifting socially constructed fears.

Contested Concepts

Laws that use terms without offering a clear definition are subject to problems because the meanings of the terms may change over time. A common characteristic of legislation and policy addressing trafficking or prostitution is the vagueness and incompleteness of the definitions given of these phenomena. Some do not attempt a definition at all. There may be various reasons for this: legislators and policy-makers might assume that these are well-understood phenomena that require no definition, they might realize that reaching consensus on a definition will be extremely difficult if not impossible, or they might wish to cater to what may be termed "delicate sensibilities." Regardless of the reasons, however, imprecise language in policy presents a number of dangers. Legislation such as the Mann Act, which cites "immoral activity," is open to wide interpretation. Thus, the Mann Act has been used in cases of interracial sex and other consensual adult sex as well as prostitution, "white slavery," and cases involving minors. Given an existing tendency to conflate distinct issues—such as prostitution, "white slavery," and trafficking—and imprecise language referring to open ended concepts such as "immorality," it is easy for laws to be selectively applied and enforced. While selective enforcement can never be eradicated, a clear definition of terms is necessary to allow the enforcement of laws, as opposed to the enforcement of one regulator's sensibilities and personal preferences.

As with other poorly defined concepts, the interpretation of the term "prostitution" has changed over time. Prostitution as we now define it, involving a clear monetary exchange, was not the sole meaning when the Mann Act was enacted. Prostitution included the activities of so-called "charity girls"[52] who would date men without parental supervision and perhaps indulge sexual desires after a night on the town. But similar behavior, which would have been identified as prostitution at the time of the Mann Act, is a normal activity for many adults today. Our notions of romance have changed—from courtship under parental supervision to dating without supervision.[53] But this is not the case everywhere. Women like "charity girls," who would accept gifts or travel or other entertainment in exchange for sex, have a present day counterpart in the Cuban *jineterias* who perform the same social functions and interactions with men wealthier than themselves, often foreign (American) businessmen.[54]

In the early part of the 20th century, the term "prostitute" did not necessarily imply a financial exchange. Earlier reformers in Boston and elsewhere included a variety of sexual behaviors under the rubric of prostitution in their desire to distinguish the virtuous working family from its incorrigible and sinful neighbors.[55] Before 1919, there was no clear determination of whether a prostitute was a "loose" woman or a woman for hire. A 1920 Alabama ruling determined a prostitute to be "a loose woman or strumpet,"[56] after which the legal tendency was a non-commercial definition of prostitution. The Mann Act may have been passed as an effort to combat "white slavery" and forced prostitution, but it easily became an instrument of moral and social control of sexual behavior. The concerns expanded from forced prostitution and in some cases prostitution per se to fears about changing morality, including female independence and therefore female sexual activity and autonomy. The enforcement of the Mann Act after the Caminetti case made clear that

female sexuality was not to be treated lightly but was to be protected by limiting women's autonomy, most obviously regarding travel.

The Mann Act refers to "immoral acts" without specification. The 1910
Immigration Act assumed that all women in places where prostitutes congregated at that time (theaters, dance halls) were necessarily prostitutes. The
assumption that any woman out in the evening could be taken to be a prostitute offered women very little alternative save to stay home and avoid the
majority of recreational activities, as the consequences could have been
severe. A female immigrant who had been in the United States for less than
three years might be subject to deportation, and the laws could be applied
to women for nothing more than being in the wrong place at the wrong time.
The ostensible purpose of these laws was to address the issue of prostitution
(forced or otherwise): imprecise definitions and arbitrary assumptions turned
them into powerful instruments for legislating and regulating female sexual
expression and morality.

The Mann Act refers to prostitution, debauchery, and immoral acts without defining any of these terms. Initially the Act addressed solely those cases
that clearly involved commercial sex, but the terms used were conveniently
ambiguous. The U.S. Supreme Court ruled in 1917 that immoral acts certainly included adultery and sex outside marriage, regardless of the age or
consent of partners and irrespective of whether any payment or exchange
occurred.[57]

Commissions were created to examine prostitution and working class life.
Reports on prostitution included *The Social Evil in Chicago*[58] and *The Social
Evil in Syracuse*[59] as well as hygiene reports. Reports on working class women
included "Commercialized Prostitution in New York City,"[60] "Social Life in
the Streets,"[61] and *Making Both Ends Meet: The Income and Outlay of New
York Working Girls*[62] among many others, all addressing New York City.
These reports cited women's low wages as leading toward "treating"—which
we might compare with modern-day dating, where a man pays for the costs
of an outing with a woman, stereotypically dinner and a movie—and thus
down a slippery slope to prostitution.[63] At the time, promiscuity or pre-
marital sex could be and was construed as prostitution.

OTHER ENFORCEMENT OF THE MANN ACT

The Mann Act's strictures against "immoral acts" were also used to prosecute cases involving interracial sexual activity, most notably in cases involving Jack Johnson, an early 20th-century black boxer who married and dated
white women, and the rock and roll star Chuck Berry (1960).

Jack Johnson was convicted under the Mann Act in 1913. Johnson was first tried for traveling between Minneapolis and Chicago in 1912 with Lucille Cameron, a white woman. She stated that she had been a prostitute before meeting Johnson and did not implicate Johnson in her leaving Minneapolis.[64] He was acquitted, and they later married. Johnson, however, traveled with a number of white women, and this led to another Mann Act case. Belle Schreiber was another prostitute involved with Johnson. In 1910, he gave her money to move to Chicago and to set up her own business.[65] Johnson was convicted for transporting Schreiber in 1913. Racism was demonstrated in the verdict, although the trial may have been fair.[66] Upon Johnson's conviction, the prosecutor stated,

[T]his negro, in the eyes of many, has been persecuted. Perhaps as an individual he was. But it was his misfortune to be the foremost example of the evil in permitting the intermarriage of whites and blacks.[67]

This statement seems still more incredible when you consider that the case in question did not involve either of Johnson's white wives, so the question of intermarriage did not even technically arise.

Chuck Berry was arrested with Joan Mathis, a white woman, while traveling across state lines from Kansas to Missouri in 1958. She stated that she "had not been molested."[68] No Mann Act charges were filed until later, in tandem with another Mann Act case. In 1959 Berry brought a prostitute, Janice Escalante, from Mexico to Missouri to be a hatcheck girl in his nightclub. They traveled together and purportedly engaged in sex during the two-week trip to Missouri. She worked in his club for a few days, but the relationship did not last, and they parted. She may have been underage, but this was never confirmed. Age would be a clear reason to bring charges. However, the police brought charges against Berry for the earlier Mathis incident at this time, apparently in order to prejudice the jury that would hear the Escalante case. Berry gratefully wrote that Mathis "chose to open herself to what was then considered indignity by declaring that she was in love with a Negro."[69] Berry was convicted in the Escalante case, but this conviction was thrown out because of the overt racism of the court—demonstrated with quotes from the judge—and re-tried. He was convicted in the second trial of the Escalante case and served 20 months.[70] The Escalante case may have been brought legitimately, but the racist motive of the Mathis case is clear. Considering the dismissal of the first conviction, it is impossible to ignore the racism of the prosecution of the Escalante case.

In addition to racist enforcement, a striking feature of the Mann Act was the gender inequality inherent in the act. In some notable Mann Act cases, prosecution was brought because a woman traveled alone to visit a man elsewhere. Had he traveled to visit her, there would have been no case.[71] Other cases that followed the Caminetti case effectively proscribed travel for women, either with a man or with intent to meet a man in another state. Such a gender differential and lack of parity could not be upheld today, yet no legislator has proposed repeal of this act. The Final Report of the Attorney General's Panel on Pornography (also known as the Meese Commission Report, 1986)[72] recommended that the Mann Act be amended to use gender-neutral language. This change was made in the Child Sexual Abuse and Pornography Act of 1986.[73] This was bundled with another amendment limiting the Mann Act only to acts that were criminal in the jurisdiction where they were committed.[74] This change effectively remanded morality enforcement to the state level (as specified in Article I of the U.S. Constitution) and probably more closely reflects current sexual mores.

The vagueness of the Mann Act gave it enormous scope. As already remarked, it was used to enforce a code of sexual behavior on women and to punish interracial relationships. While J. Edgar Hoover was director of the Federal Bureau of Investigation, it was also used for political purposes and personal vendettas, taking advantage of the flexibility and range of the Act to implement selective enforcement. Hoover led many "white slavery" raids and encouraged publicity around them. Numerous headlines about the FBI Director's involvement in such raids ran during the 1930s and 1940s.[75] Hoover used the information gleaned in raids for political ends. He instructed agents to include data such as address books, especially those containing prominent persons, in "administrative" files to which he had complete access and which he sometimes leaked to the press.[76]

Hoover sought a Mann Act case against Charlie Chaplin for Chaplin's overt Communist sympathies and perceived immorality.[77] Grittner cites Chaplin's biographer's use of the Freedom of Information Act to learn about Hoover's specific involvement. Hoover himself assigned the agent involved and encouraged Chaplin's prosecution.[78] Chaplin paid for train tickets for his mistress and her mother to travel from Los Angeles to New York in 1942. At the end of their affair the following year, the woman in question went to gossip columnists with her story. This brought public and prosecutory attention.[79] Even though Chaplin was acquitted, his public image and career were unsalvageable, and he relocated to Europe.[80]

The Mann Act was cited in divorce cases in order to demonstrate adultery or alienation of affection, which is cited in cases involving love triangles in which one person leaves a spouse. The third person can be sued for alienation of affection, which amounts to stealing a person's spouse or partner. Frank Lloyd Wright was charged in this way under the Mann Act in 1926, but this case was dismissed in 1927 when it became apparent that his wife was pressing the charge in order to obtain a better divorce settlement—demonstrated by the fact that Miriam Wright also sued her husband's new companion for alienation of affection.[81] Miriam Wright's use of the Mann Act in her divorce is ironic, in light of the fact that a housekeeper had earlier suggested Mr. Wright be brought up on Mann Act charges for crossing state lines with Miriam in 1915, before they were married.[82]

The Mann Act also provided a weapon against organized crime figures who could not be convicted due to a lack of evidence for more serious crimes. Other "undesirables" (such as prostitutes, strip club dancers, and club owners), were also prosecuted under the Mann Act. Caminetti and Diggs (convicted in 1917 and mentioned above) fall into this category. It may be impossible to discover how widespread such abuse of law actually was, but Langum makes a clear case that the Mann Act was selectively applied and points out that as the number of Mann Act cases declined, the seemingly selective use of the Mann Act increased.[83]

CONCLUSION

Definitions of prostitution, white slavery, and trafficking are still confounded to this day, although the terminology has changed, from "white slavery" to "traffic in women and children" to "traffic in persons." The interpretation of "white slavery" changed over time from wage labor in the mid-19th century[84] to rape and prostitution. This shift may in part have been because prostitution was not a crime in and of itself, and so other methods outside law enforcement were implemented to constrain prostitution and social mores until laws were passed against prostitution in the 20th century. Ambiguous definitions promote selective enforcement and interpretation of legislation, as demonstrated in racist and sexist enforcement of the Mann Act and immigration laws and use of the Mann Act against political dissidents. The laws discussed in this chapter are vain efforts to regulate morality, as social mores continue to change and prostitution remains as common as ever. This historical grounding is intended to help understand the ways legislation passed at the end of 2000 addressing "human trafficking"[85]—to be discussed in Chapter 8—is not new at all but in fact very similar to earlier attempts to address trafficking in persons. Protectionist legislation continues to limit women's self-determination, including freedom of movement, rather than empowering women. This is especially true of legislation addressing women's travel, particularly in morality clauses and in legislation passed to promote public health but only addressing women, as will be demonstrated in the chapter on sexually transmitted infections and associated panics.

NOTES

1. United States Mann Act of 1910.

2. United States Immigration Act of 1903, United States Immigration Act of 1904, United States Immigration Act of 1907.

3. Mark Thomas Connolly, *The Response to Prostitution in the Progressive Era* (Chapel Hill: University of North Carolina, 1980).

4. David J. Langum, *Crossing Over the Line: Legislating Morality and the Mann Act* (Chicago: University of Chicago, 1994), 10.

5. Howard Brown Woolston, *Prostitution in the United States [V. 1] Prior to the Entrance of the United States into the World War* (New York: Century, 1921).

6. Woolston, 1921, 25.

7. Woolston, 1921, 35.

8. Woolston, 1921, 35–36.

9. Connolly, 1980; Pamela Donovan, "Crime Legends in Old and New Media" (PhD diss., Graduate Center of the City University of New York, 2001).

10. Frederick K. Grittner, *White Slavery: Myth, Ideology, and American Law* (New York: Garland, 1990), 47.

11. Donovan, 2001.

12. Connolly, 1980.

13. Jan C. Ting, "*301 'Other Than a Chinaman' [Fnd]: How U.S. Immigration Law Resulted from and Still Reflects a Policy of Excluding and Restricting Asian Immigration," *Temple Political and Civil Rights Law Review* (Spring 1995).

14. Ting, 1995.

15. Ting, 1995.

16. Peter Kwong, *Forbidden Workers* (New York: New Press, 1997), 42–43.

17. Kwong, 1997, 142.

18. Kwong, 1997, 76.

19. Ting, 1995.

20. Anne Seagraves, *Soiled Doves: Prostitution in the Early West* (Hayden, Idaho: Wesanne Publications, 1994), 139.

21. Kwong, 1997, 93–95.

22. Ting, 1995.

23. Kwong, 1997, 13.

24. Seagraves, 1994, 147.

25. Luc Sante, *Low Life: Lures and Snares of Old New York* (New York: Vintage, 1991), 144.

26. Sante, 1991, 128.

27. Sante, 1991, 144.

28. Timothy Gilfoyle, *City of Eros* (New York and London: Norton, 1994), 218.

29. Langum, 1994, 47.

30. Donovan, 2001.

31. Connolly, 1980, 49–50.

32. Connolly, 1980, 50.

33. Connolly, 1980, 56.

34. Gilfoyle, 1994.

35. U.S. Statutes at Large, 1910, v. 36, 265, quoted in Connolly.

36. Figures are from U.S. Senate, *Importation and Harboring*, 1910, 60–61, quoted in Connolly, 1980, 175.

37. Gilfoyle, 1994, 61; Connolly, 1980, 175 [footnotes].

38. U.S. Statutes at Large, 1910, v. 36, 827, quoted in Connolly, 1980, 57–58.

39. Francis Scott Fitzgerald, *Tender Is the Night* (New York: Scribner, 1934); Francis Scott Fitzgerald, *This Side of Paradise* (New York: Scribner, 1920).

40. Grittner, 1990; Langum, 1994, 172.

41. Langum, 1994, 10.

42. Langum, 1994.

43. Langum, 1994, 97–138.

44. Connolly, 1980, 124.

45. Gilfoyle, 1994.

46. The Rockefeller Archive Center, Bureau of Social Hygiene Archives, http:// www.rockarch.org/collections/rockorgs/bsh.php (accessed September 11, 2010).

47. Gilfoyle, 1994; Langum, 1994.

48. Gilfoyle, 1994, 60.

49. Langum, 1994.

50. Langum, 1994, 156–57.

51. Langum, 1994, 168.

52. Barbara Meil Hobson, *Uneasy Virtue* (New York: Basic Books, 1987); Kathy Peiss, " 'Charity Girls' and City Pleasures: Historical Notes on Working-Class Sexuality, 1880–1920," in *Powers of Desire*, edited by Ann Snitow, Christine Stansell, and Sharon Thompson (New York: Monthly Review Press, 1983), 74–87.

53. Gilfoyle, 1994, 311; Langum, 1994, 121; Michael Pearson, *The £5 Virgins* (New York: Saturday Review Press, 1972).

54. Coco Fusco, "Hustling for Dollars: Jineterismo in Cuba," in *Global Sex Workers*, edited by Kempadoo and Doezema (New York: Routledge, 1998), 151–66.

55. Hobson, 1987, 21.

56. Langum, 1994, 123.

57. Grittner, 1990, 141; Langum, 1994, 113.

58. Chicago Vice Commission, *The Social Evil in Chicago* (Chicago: Gunthorp-Warren, 1911), http://www.archive.org/details/socialevilinchic00chic (accessed November 5, 2009).

59. Syracuse Moral Survey Committee, "The Social Evil in Syracuse" (Syracuse, 1913), http://www.archive.org/stream/cu31924021846047/cu31924021846047 _djvu.txt (accessed November 5, 2009).

60. George Kneeland, "Commercialized Prostitution in New York City" (New York: The Century Company, 1913), cited in Peiss, 1983.

61. Sue Ainslie Clark and Edith Wyatt, *Making Both Ends Meet: The Income and Outlay of New York Working Girls* (New York: Macmillan, 1911), cited in Peiss, 1983.

62. Clark and Wyatt, 1911, cited in Peiss, 1983.

63. Hobson, 1987; Peiss, 1983.

64. Langum, 1994, 181.

65. Langum, 1994, 183.

66. Langum, 1994, 185.

67. "U.S. Jury Finds Johnson Guilty; May Go to Prison," *Chicago Tribune*, May 14, 1913, 1, quoted in Langum, 1994, 185.

68. Langum, 1994, 186.

69. *Chuck Berry: The Autobiography*, quoted in Langum, 1994, 187.

70. Langum, 1994, 186–88; Grittner, 1990, 181.

71. Langum, 1994.

72. Final Report of the Attorney General's Panel on Pornography 1986, http://www.communitydefense.org/lawlibrary/agreport.html (accessed November 5, 2009).

73. United States Child Sexual Abuse and Pornography Act of 1986, Details of amendments are available from http://www.law.cornell.edu/uscode/html/uscode18/usc_sec_18_00002251- - - -000-notes.html (accessed November 5, 2009).

74. Langum, 1994, 249–50.

75. Langum, 1994, 170.

76. Langum, 1994, 171.

77. Grittner, 1990, 149.

78. Grittner, 1990, 149.

79. Langum, 1994, 192.

80. Grittner, 1990, 150.

81. Grittner, 1990, 93, 145.

82. Langum, 1994, 95.

83. Langum, 1994.

84. Grittner, 1990, 119.

85. United States Trafficking Victims Protection Act of 2000: Trafficking in Persons Report, http://www.state.gov/g/tip/rls/tiprpt/2004/ (accessed November 5, 2009).

8

21st-Century Campaigns and Laws against Trafficking in Persons

Anti-trafficking initiatives at the turn of the millennium echoed earlier attempts to address "white slavery": the same tactics, the same motivations, and the same policies, not to mention the same conflation and similar problems with definitions, make their appearance, with an agenda aimed at the regulation of morality and sexuality hidden beneath a veneer of social concern. Anti-trafficking movements are marked by some of the same features as the social reformers of the Victorian and Progressive eras a century before—a tendency to hyperbole and over-dramatization, and a need to distinguish between "good women and children"—deserving of protection—and "bad women"—deserving anything they get. In order to better understand latter-day efforts to legislate sexual morality in the name of human interests, this chapter presents a history of some of the white slavery panics as well as the legislation that addressed white slavery, traffic in women, and prostitution.

The United Nations and the United States both passed anti-trafficking laws in 2000. These laws addressed forced labor and human trafficking in a wide variety of economic sectors in addition to sex work. The negotiations leading to these laws began in 1998. Subsequently, state laws were passed in Washington, New York, and elsewhere. The process and the use of these laws once they took effect are discussed in this chapter because their successes and failures illuminate the effects of the conflation of modern-day slavery and sex work.

Sex work has historically been a moral battleground for feminists and reformers.[1] This is an industry where workers can control their bodies and make a living wage,[2] two basic feminist goals. Unfortunately, this is not always the

case, as in any industry. Sex workers would have more autonomy and better
conditions if policies protected women from violence and if feminists themselves honored their pledge to protect women's choices regarding their bodies.
Perhaps even more frequently, sex work may supplement the wages of another
job. This chapter attempts to explore the necessary feminist transformation
from didacticism about sex work to respect for the autonomy of sex workers.
In it, I examine the effects on sex workers of systems regulating prostitution—
the most morally condemned and frequently best paid sex work. I further offer
suggestions about how exchanges between feminists and sex workers with
diverging political opinions about sex work and prostitution can positively
affect policy on this subject, ensuring that people who engage in sex work are
guaranteed the same kinds of protections that we expect for other workers.

SEX WORK IS REAL WORK

The International Labour Organization (ILO) defines sex work as "the provision of sexual services for reimbursement or material gain."[3] Sex work
includes not only prostitution but also stripping and pornography and all
other varieties of sexual services in commercial exchange. The term "sex work"
was coined by sex workers[4] to emphasize the labor aspect of the sex industry,
and to create a term without moral judgment or emotional connotations.

Those who advocate the elimination of the sex industry cite sexual commerce as the sale of a person.[5] Sex work, however is not the sale and purchase
of a person, but rather of a person's services or time,[6] much like the "emotion
work" of nurses and flight attendants. Rather than declaring sex work in itself
an abuse, feminist organizers ought to work to see that sex work is afforded the
same standards they seek for workers in other industries. Addressing sex work
as labor, as recommended by the ILO, enables application of minimum standards for employment and attendant requirements for occupational safety and
health. It is fitting that the ILO recommends recognition of the sex industry as
labor, as ILO statutes governing minimum standards of working conditions
could be applied to the sex industry. The violations of labor standards within
the sex industry are not specific to the sex industry but problems for persons
providing informal labor, particularly in the service industries.

Sex work is an occupation that provides income to workers in the sex
industry and their families. While repugnant to some people, sex work, like
house cleaning, child care, or other work traditionally done by women, is
not inherently degrading or a violation of a woman's human rights. In fact,
many people opt for sex work because it is less degrading, better paying,
and provides more freedom than other available options (such as work in

export processing zone factories or food service jobs).[7] There is no doubt that some people turn to sex work out of desperation and that abuses, including trafficking, take place, but these realities are too often used to divert attention from the fact that there are many others who prefer sex work to other work.

SEX WORK IS A FEMINIST ISSUE–DIVERGENCE WITHIN A MOVEMENT

Feminism and sex work have a volatile history in America. There exist volumes of essays pitting sex workers against didactic feminists.[8] Such debates reinforce the misleading idea of a monolithic and dogmatic feminism. This vision is very much at odds with the open-minded and inclusive approach necessary to move beyond this schism to a more nuanced understanding of the sex industry. Many sex workers call themselves feminists, and feminism, contrary to public perception, is prone to factionalism and lacks a uniform line on sex work. In fact, many feminists have done work with sex workers, and their work is immensely valuable.[9]

One might expect feminism to address sex work differently. American feminists should inquire how this population of women, largely outsiders because of their work, is affected by both by legislation addressing sex work and by the divisions within feminism. However, the stereotyped feminist response to the sex industry is that it objectifies women and therefore should be eradicated; that all sex work is coerced and abusive; and that women who do sex work do not understand and are not concerned with sexism. Some press coverage has been given to the sex workers' rights advocates and first amendment hard-liners, but not nearly as much as to anti-pornography activists. This has led to the impression that feminism offers only two directly opposing views on the topic of pornography, without addressing other aspects of the sex industry. Unfortunately, respectful inclusion of sex workers within feminist dialogue and policy-making has never been easy.[10] Sex workers have had to insist on inclusion on bodies governing policy and advisement on issues affecting them.[11] It is already difficult for people whose work may be illegal to be outspoken about their activities. Such divisions among feminists make organizing around other issues related to sex work even more difficult.

Lynn Chancer describes four positions addressing sex work:[12]

1. Conservative, right-wing moralism stands against sex work in all its forms.
2. Feminist puritans stand similarly against sex work and what they deem sexual exploitation, seemingly without qualms at their political alliance with conservatives, who have rarely been supporters of women's rights.

3. First-Amendment hard-liners see the erosion of civil rights in legislation addressing morality.

4. Legitimately pro-sex factions, such as activists for gay and prostitutes' rights, suffer the de-legitimatization of their opinions by virtue of the fact that they address sexuality without a morally prescriptive stance.

While certain anti-pornography and anti-sex work spokespersons have had great influence on the issue of pornography,[13] too often they have neglected the voices of those who live with the regulation and prohibition of various aspects of sex work. In recent years the prescriptive tendencies described above have met with opposition from a number of feminists whose motivation comes from having witnessed the use of regulations "protecting" women from themselves. They have grown suspicious of the negative effects of such policies. Their suspicions are congruous with those stemming from the protective legislation enacted to prevent women's overwork earlier this century. In protecting women by limiting their working hours, policy-makers rendered it impossible for these women to support their families.[14] Policy ostensibly aimed at improving women's conditions may often, whether through its conception or implementation, have precisely the opposite effect.

Well-intentioned efforts have actually worsened situations for sex workers in ways that would not have occurred had sex workers of varied backgrounds and experiences been consulted. Feminists have not always recognized sex workers' autonomy. Instead, some feminists have accused sex workers who defend their work of false consciousness regarding their own oppression and exploitation. This perspective is patronizing to all women in that it suggests that some women do not know what is good for them. This attitude is also patronizing to sex workers in that it suggests that women involved in sex work cannot see the social and economic structure that has made their services valuable yet their situations, in providing these services, untenable, as they are outlawed and shunned. Finally, the perspectives of many feminists on sex work is naive, in that it suggests that some women (but of course not sex workers) can get outside the oppressive and exploitative nature of much work. This disregard of sex workers' autonomy is changing, in part due to third wave feminism's insistence on inclusion of a plurality of experiences and voices. Feminism increasingly recognizes sex workers' rights to control their bodies, including the choice to work or not to work in the sex industry, as sex workers insist on participating in the discussions of sex work and related policies.

Consensus is hard to attain. The National Organization for Women's stance on prostitution recommends decriminalization, but this is not reflected in the practices of each chapter.[15] Just as within feminism, within organizations serving sex workers, there is also enormous division of opinion on sex work. Some organizations endeavor to offer services to sex workers with the ultimate aim of their quitting the sex industry,[16] others, like the Durbar Mahila Samanwaya Committee of Calcutta[17] and California's Exotic Dancers Alliance,[18] endeavor to serve sex workers while recognizing the reality of their economic needs and other needs met by the sex industry. Abolitionist organizations have influenced the implementation of legislation restricting pornography in the United States and Canada, while Feminists for Free Expression, a New York based anti-censorship organization, has female and feminist pornographers among their founding members and board of directors.

Feminism has lost out due to the exclusion of divergent views. After years of factionalism, it is time not only to address differing opinions, but to productively move forward toward making policy addressing sex work with the input of those most affected by it: sex workers themselves. This need not merely add more voices to the mix. By actively seeking plurality not merely by the inclusion of sex workers, but the inclusion of sex workers with diverse points of view, a more realistic view of sex work is encouraged. This wider view could enable well-informed policy and affect the lives of many women for the better.

LEGISLATION

Little work exists addressing the varied legalities surrounding prostitution.[19] At the same time, prostitution is the sole aspect of the sex industry that is almost universally addressed via legislation. An exploration of the conditions of prostitution under differing legal systems may enlighten us to the varied needs not addressed in prostitution legislation and ultimately affect policies that are in the best interests of those most affected by them—sex workers themselves.

Laws concerning sex work are sometimes written with the ostensible intent of helping women, but are usually written for moralistic reasons or for the purposes of protecting clients.[20] Furthermore, these laws are often enforced in ways that further victimize sex workers.[21] In most states and countries, sex workers are actually hunted by authorities (during crackdowns, morals sweeps, and stings) for their work or for necessary business practices including advertising and managerial relationships.[22] This vigilance about the enforcement of prostitution laws affects the mental and physical health of sex workers and their families. It pushes sex work underground and thereby makes it more difficult to ensure health and safety. Legal penalties are similar for those who engage in sex work and those who commit abuses within sex work.[23] Medical regulations seem typically to seek to protect the (male) client from the prostitute rather than addressing the medical needs of the (usually female) prostitute.

PROSTITUTION POLICIES

The definition of prostitution itself varies by location and interpretation, so that what may be prostitution in one place at one time is not in another. For example, exotic dancers may be charged under ambiguous statutes.[24]

There are three ways to legislate prostitution: prohibition, legalization, and decriminalization. The most common, prohibition, makes it a crime to prostitute, to procure prostitutes, or to solicit or patronize prostitutes. Additionally, it may criminalize the taking of money from a prostitute, or living off the earnings of prostitution. Legalized prostitution is usually heavily regulated. Regulation might include mandating health tests and permitting prostitution only in specific zones of operation. Prostitution venues may also be subject to regulations not imposed on other businesses.[25] Where prostitution is decriminalized, prostitution and attendant activities (such as advertising) are regulated merely as any other business would be regulated under normal labor and business stipulations.

Prohibition

An outright ban on prostitution has never successfully eliminated prostitution but instead caused sex workers and their associates to find or create new venues.[26] Thus legislating morality is unproductive and contrary to what people want. Instead bans have marginalized the prostitute, making him or her more likely prey for violence since legal recourse is not available without the admission of illegal activity. In places where prostitution is a criminal act, prostitutes rarely turn to the police for help.

The police have entrapped prostitutes and their clients to make arrests, assaulted or even raped prostitutes,[27] and encouraged and accepted bribes to allow prostitutes to work in spite of local laws.[28] Prostitutes may also be subject to arrest while not working, even though there is no legal basis for this.[29] For these reasons, some prostitutes take greater risks with clients in order to avoid the police and arrest.[30] Crackdowns tend to fall disproportionately hard on street workers, the most visible prostitutes. Legislation that includes an "intent to commit prostitution" clause leaves arrest entirely at the discretion of the arresting officer. No actual activity of prostitution is required to commit the crime of intent. This method of enforcement effectively renders prostitution a status crime, where the crime at hand is existence rather than a particular activity. This law places almost unlimited power in the hands of the police, isolates the prostitute from others, and prevents prostitutes from seeking legal recourse.

Laws against living off the earnings of prostitution, which are intended to prevent exploitative pimping or third party management, further isolate sex workers by making it a criminal act to do business with a prostitute. Maintaining personal or familial relationships is also made difficult, as cohabitation or even supporting children can be considered living off the earnings of a prostitute.[31] For example, in one such case from Santa Barbara, California, the prostitute ran a business and her husband was charged with living off her earnings. Their house was forfeited and he served time in prison.[32] Such laws also prevent prostitutes from working with each other as agents or as security for each other.[33]

Repression of prostitution forces some prostitutes to work in unsafe and unhealthy conditions. Repression of prostitution also means that prostitutes do not have legal recourse in cases of violence and abuse and cannot turn to police for protection. Ergo, repression of prostitution effectively denies prostitutes some of their fundamental human rights. When violence is committed against sex workers, the problem is violence, not the victim's occupation. In no other occupation does society so incessantly blame the victim of the violence. We do not blame a victim of gay bashing for being beaten, even in areas where homosexual acts remain in local criminal statutes. Nor do we blame people for acts committed against them in jobs generally considered prone to violence (such as convenience store clerks and livery drivers). Yet we blame workers in the sex industry for the violence committed by others against them. In countries where sex workers have access to legal recourse, including parts of Australia and the Netherlands, sex workers are able to avail themselves of the same help accorded other victims of violence, including rape and battery.

Feminist response to violent crime includes redressing the pattern of blaming women for violence done to them. Some feminists have striven to end this practice. This includes eliminating a rape victim's sexual history as evidence in the courtroom. This should be the goal of feminists regarding violence against sex workers. Violence against sex workers parallels the more widespread violence against women, particularly rape, as a crime where the victim is blamed for her misfortune.

Legalization

Legalization usually incorporates regulation of prostitution, as seen in the Philippines and Nevada.[34] While legalized prostitution may benefit those who choose to practice it in some places, regulation is for the most part implemented with the intent of protecting the client from the prostitute. This has important ramifications for prostitutes, who would prefer that regulatory behavior focused on enforcing occupational safety and health regulations.

In some places, prostitutes pay higher taxes than others and receive fewer benefits of health care and social security.[35] Registration of prostitutes is a thorny matter, as removing oneself from the register of prostitutes can be difficult. For example, in Geneva, Switzerland, a prostitute must be out of sex work for two years before her name can be removed from the register, even though being registered can preclude obtaining other work, creating a catch-22 situation with officially endorsed stigma.[36] Prostitutes can be subject to forcible "rehabilitation" and removed from their homes under systems of legalization, as seen in the case of the Tanbazar, the oldest brothel in Bangladesh. In July 1999, 235 women were forcibly removed from their homes in the Tanbazar red light district and relocated to be rehabilitated against their will.[37]

Legislation may involve proscription of the sex workers' physical movements. In Nevada, for example, most licensed prostitutes work for three-week stints at a brothel, during which time they may or may not be allowed to leave the brothel. Workers may or may not be allowed to negotiate prices and acts with clients, or to refuse a client, based on brothel policy and management. Each month, prostitutes must undergo mandated gynecological examinations with the aim of preventing the spread of sexually transmitted infections. (No equivalent examination is required of clients.)

A serious concern is that many licensed and regulated workers' health records are not confidential.[38] The World Health Organization states that sex workers should not be tested by the state for disease.[39] Such health checks may make negotiations of safe sex more difficult, because if clients feel reassured that they are seeing a "clean" prostitute, they may resist condom use. Testing is not an effective way to prevent the spread of sexually transmitted infections, as many ailments have a latency period during which they may remain undetected. (HIV is only one example of this.) Furthermore, prevention efforts often focus on HIV to the exclusion of other less publicized but more widespread sexually transmitted infections.

Decriminalization

Decriminalization of prostitution means removing all laws pertaining to prostitution from the criminal code. Within this context, the sex industry and its participants are governed under business and labor law, like any other business. Decriminalization of prostitution is the system most often recommended by prostitutes' rights groups and in the World Charter for Prostitute Rights.[40] Decriminalization is in place in specific states of Australia and South Africa. Recognizing sex work as a labor issue rather than a moral issue enables its regulation with attendant requirements for occupational safety and health, including standards of cleanliness, provisions for safe sex, and the right to decline a client. Taxation of the sex industry provides large amounts of government revenue in the state of Nevada (where prostitution is heavily regulated).[41]

Under decriminalization, consenting adults are enabled to work as they choose with the protection provided under codes and statutes against forced labor. Decriminalization offers prostitutes the opportunity to work on the street, in a brothel, or independently, without fear of police harassment or corruption.

INTERNATIONAL LEGISLATION AND TRAFFICKING IN PERSONS

The same problems already observed with respect to laws applying to prostitution can be seen in laws concerning trafficking in persons.[42] These laws, particularly the United Nations 1949 Convention Against Trafficking in Women and Children, are written with the intent of helping trafficked persons, but by their implementation and application, they too often harm the very people they set out to help, especially women.[43] Some people are trafficked into sex work, but sex work itself is not the problem. The existence of slavery-like conditions in the sex industry does not equate all sex work with slavery, much as the existence of sweatshops does not equate all garment manufacture with poor working conditions, but highlights the need for the application of occupational standards to the sex industry. The problem is organized deceit and coercion, not sex work.[44]

Trafficked persons in the sex industry remain unlikely to seek legal recourse as long as they have reason to fear law enforcement.[45] Despite this, the same laws used to prosecute sex workers are often applied to trafficked women.[46] Trafficked women in the sex industry are not always identified as trafficked women, they may be prosecuted as prostitutes and their status as trafficked women may remain unaddressed. Laws prohibiting sex work are actually at odds with laws against trafficking in women, because they encourage prosecution of trafficked women under legislation targeting prostitutes. Furthermore, it is impossible to accurately address the issue of trafficking as long as there is a clear benefit for the worker to claim to have been coerced, such as in places where trafficked persons are accorded rights once they are ascertained to have been trafficked.[47]

Not enough research has been devoted to the concerns of those who can admit to wishing to remain in the industry. This is why those who take a stance on prostitution based solely on trafficking often appear to have the facts on their side. In cases where trafficked persons are able to seek monetary redress, women trafficked into prostitution are excluded.[48] This is because as prostitution is not recognized as work, these people have not worked according to the law, and so cannot be paid for their work as prostitutes. As with anti-prostitution law, misinterpretation and irresponsible enforcement of anti-trafficking law worsens rather than improves the situation of trafficked persons.

The best-known example of such abuses and misinterpretation of the law comes from Thailand.[49] Women who have been victims of trafficking, working in brothels in debt bondage under slavery-like conditions are subject to arrest and imprisonment. This is ostensibly the exact opposite of what was intended and expected upon the introduction of laws addressing trafficking in women. Nor is this unique to Thailand: William J. Knisley, an immigration lawyer who has represented women arrested in brothels in New York City, described similar happenings in New York where trafficked women were arrested and prosecuted as prostitutes.[50]

Recent enaction of laws applying to clients[51] may often also be unenforceable or of little practical utility. "Sex tourists" have been the object of some legislation attempting to prosecute nationals of one country for illegal acts (under the national's flag) committed in another country.[52] Such efforts focus on preventing abuse of children, certainly a worthwhile endeavor, but neglect the fact that the overwhelming majority of most prostitutes' clientele remains local.[53] Considering this, it may be worthwhile to reconsider such efforts in order to have greater impact. Punitive efforts in home countries geared at what goes on elsewhere require the as yet unsecured cooperation of local authorities and are rendered unenforceable by differing laws regarding labor, prostitution, and age of consent. As there is no transnationally agreed upon and enforced age of majority, laws affecting acts with children are not transnationally enforceable.[54]

Finally, it should be noted that clients may actually have a positive role in preventing abuse. Clients are frequently the most sympathetic ears for sex workers as well as trafficked women in abusive or coercive situations. Clients who are educated to the problems of trafficking are often the people who bring the situation of women held against their will to the attention of the police or non-governmental organizations.[55] Rather than criminalizing the participants of any sexual act between consenting adults, it would be more efficacious to prosecute acts of violence committed against prostitutes, including rape, abduction, and child abuse.

The Anti-Prostitution Pledge

A specific example of policy that inhibits work with sex workers is a funding restriction requiring recipient organizations of U.S. federal funding to adoption of a written statement that they oppose prostitution and sex trafficking.[56] No service organization promotes prostitution or trafficking, and so the pledge is moot, but guidance is unclear and some organizations opted to exclude sex workers rather than risk their funding. Excluding sex workers from programming is counter to an unenforced non-discrimination clause that rules out the denial of services to anyone in the funding contracts.[57]

The pledge has adversely affected sex workers and threatened gains made in the fight against HIV by organized sex workers. Lawsuits were filed to contest the implementation of the pledge, and appeals by the U.S. government against rulings that the pledge unlawfully restricted speech in HIV-prevention programming by U.S.-based organizations were dropped when U.S. President Barack Obama took office in 2009.[58] However, revised guidance in effect since May 2010 about the use of anti-trafficking and HIV-prevention and other foreign aid does not offer relief from the pledge.[59] At the time of going to press, U.S.-based organizations were preparing to file suit against the pledge in anti-trafficking funding.

RECOMMENDATIONS FOR POLICY ADDRESSING THE SEX INDUSTRY

Regulations addressing the sex industry must be very specific about what is to be regulated in order not to affect a sex worker's everyday life outside of work. Practices such as registering with the state must not be encouraged if they can prevent the mobility of the worker, or his or her ability to legitimately acquire credit, housing, and other employment. Follow-up on policy implementation by advocates and sex workers to ensure that sex workers are not adversely affected by legislation intending to benefit them is of great importance. This should include scrapping ineffective or detrimental policy like legislation that is subject to misuse.

There are some aspects of the sex industry that cannot be condoned. In particular, the involvement of children in the sex industry is indefensible. Rather than condemning all aspects of the sex industry, more effective efforts may include education countering mistaken notions about sex with virgins[60] and punishing acts involving minors.[61] In many countries sexual abuse of children cannot be more illegal than it already is, so measures other than further legislation must be taken. Punishment of minors in the sex industry serves no purpose.[62] Better efforts could include non-legislative programs encouraging and offering incentives to minors to identify and speak for themselves, and offering services to them, especially in cases where runaways are unable or unwilling to return to their families.

Sex workers should receive the same social benefits as others in their societies, without special levies or taxes applied only to them. Where these services do not include health insurance, sex workers should be able to purchase health insurance as would a person in any industry. The elimination of registration requirements for sex workers, and "good moral character" clauses[63] pertaining to business, property ownership, and other circumstances would benefit sex workers as well as others. Additional recommendations include decriminalization of all parties participating in consensual adult commercial sex and activities ancillary to the sex industry. This includes third party management and agents, and the practice of making referrals to sex workers. Sex workers should have freedom of assembly, to be effected by eliminating bawdy house laws and allowing sex workers' organizations to meet without fear of arrest.[64] As Georgia's Supreme Court decision regarding sex toys[65] and the landmark *Lawrence v. Texas* case attest, it is inappropriate for the state to curtail private behavior among consenting adults.

Sex workers in brothels must be able to decline a client and to negotiate services offered on an individual basis. Safe sex precautions have led to the absence of transmission of HIV in the legal sex industry in Nevada and Australia.[66] Other safe sex related policies could include requiring businesses to keep condoms and lubricant on the premises and eliminating police confiscation of condoms in order to use them as evidence in prostitution cases.

Police should address violence against sex workers promptly and seriously using already existing legislation against battery and other violence, like the use of force and abduction. Slow police reaction may have enabled violence including murder to continue in many places.[67] This is one area where feminist activism could have immediate and beneficial effect were feminists to mobilize to educate law enforcement to take complaints from sex workers seriously and to effect the policies necessary to encourage sex workers to report incidents of violence. This could include programs to educate police on how to deal with prostitutes, in a similar manner to police education programs on how to deal with rape victims in practice since the 1960s.[68] This could include developing protocol for dealing with sex workers in police stations.

CONCLUSIONS AND COMMON GROUND

Follow-up on policy implementation is paramount. Policy should be geared toward bettering conditions rather than enforcing a vision of morality. Already existing laws that criminalize violence such as rape, battery, and corruption (e.g., regulations against police extortion) could be better utilized in efforts to stop abuse of sex workers. Feminists can help address this situation and have already affected legislation and enforcement (particularly in legislation and enforcement addressing domestic violence and rape) in some parts of the world, including the United States. Unfortunately, this has not always been done by working with sex workers or in ways that address the everyday lives of sex workers. This has led to the lack of police attention to crimes against sex workers, including murder, which would not be tolerated for any other victim.

Those with divergent views of sex work have common interests. Abolitionist groups seeking to eliminate the sex industry and sex workers' rights groups can find common ground in initiatives aimed at increasing the safety, rights and workplace conditions of sex workers, particularly as regards the ability to seek redress in cases of abuse. For example, in June 1999 Anti-Slavery International and the International Movement Against Discrimination and Racism (IMADR), in cooperation with the United Nations Working Group on Contemporary Forms of Slavery, organized discussion and negotiation of international trafficking policy recommendations by abolitionists and sex workers' rights organizations. Despite divergent philosophies, both groups strongly recommended the elimination of state prosecution of sex workers. More broadly, both favored ending punitive legislation aimed at women in the sex industry. This discussion would not have occurred without the inclusion of sex workers as policy advocates. As feminism continues to embrace people formerly excluded, it becomes paramount to further include sex workers in public policy discourse.

NOTES

1. Barbara Meil Hobson, *Uneasy Virtue* (New York: Basic Books, 1987).
2. Presentations by Jo Doezema, Mala Singh et al., United Nations Working Groups on Contemporary Forms of Slavery (presented June 21, 1999). See also Frédérique Delacoste and Priscilla Alexander, eds., *Sex Work* (Seattle: Cleis, 1987) and Lin Lean Lim, ed., *The Sex Sector* (Geneva: ILO publications, 1998).
3. Lim, 1998, 1.
4. Carol Leigh (a.k.a. Scarlot Harlot), "Inventing Sex Work," in *Whores and Other Feminists*, edited by Jill Nagle (New York: Routledge, 1997), 223–31.

5. Presentations by the Coalition against Trafficking in Women at the United Nations International Working Group on Contemporary Forms of Slavery meeting, Geneva, Switzerland, (presented June 21, 1999).

6. Presentations by the International Human Rights Law Group at the United Nations International Working Group on Contemporary Forms of Slavery meeting (presented June 21, 1999). See also Wendy Chapkis, *Live Sex Acts* (New York: Routledge, 1997) in which she uses the idea of "emotion work" from caretaking and service industries, to address the sex industry.

7. Nury Pernia, presentation at the United Nations International Working Group on Contemporary Forms of Slavery meeting (presented June 21, 1999); Barbara Meil Hobson, *Uneasy Virtue* (New York: Basic Books, 1987); Timothy Gilfoyle, *City of Eros* (New York: Norton, 1994); and Annie Sprinkle, *Post Porn Modernist: My 25 Years as a Multi-Media Whore* (San Francisco: Cleis, 1998).

8. For example, Laurie Bell, ed., *Good Girls/Bad Girls* (Seattle: Seal Press, 1987).

9. I refer to Carole Vance, Anne Snitow, Ellen Willis (see Vance, ed., *Pleasure and Danger* [Boston: Routledge & K. Paul, 1984]), among others.

10. Lynn Chancer, *Reconcilable Differences* (Berkeley: University of California Press, 1998).

11. Such as the Atlanta Task Force on Prostitution (Gail Pheterson, ed., *A Vindication of the Rights of Whores* [Seattle: Seal Press, 1989]), 78; Dolores French, *Working: My Life as a Prostitute* (New York: E. P. Dutton, 1988); and at the Fourth International Conference on Women in Beijing in 1995, conversation and correspondence with Norma Jean Almodovar, 1995–1999.

12. Chancer, 1998, 61–80.

13. I refer to laws influenced by Catharine MacKinnon against pornography. See Chancer, 1998, particularly chapter three, and to the work of Andrea Dworkin, particularly *Pornography* (New York: Perigee, 1981). This is part of a larger trend of sexual repression in the United States, as exemplified by new zoning laws addressing adult entertainment, usually places with strippers or adult materials, implemented in New York and other cities around the United States.

14. Protective labor legislation was a generic label for a host of state laws applicable only to women that restricted, among other things, the number of hours women could work. See Elizabeth Baker, *Technology and Women's Work* (New York: Columbia University Press, 1964), 91–96; and Jo Freeman, "From Protection to Equal Opportunity: The Revolution in Women's Legal Status," in *Women, Politics and Change*, edited by Louise Tilly and Patricia Gurin (New York: Russell Sage, 1990), 457–81.

15. Teri Goodson, "A Prostitute Joins NOW," in *Whores and Other Feminists*, edited by Jill Nagle (New York: Routledge, 1997).

16. One example of such an organization was New York's From Our Streets with Dignity (FROSTD) at its founding.

17. Presentation by Dr. Smarajit Jana, Washington, DC (presented April 1998).

18. Conversation with Carol Leigh, a.k.a. Scarlot Harlot, San Francisco, January, 1996.

19. Perhaps the best exploration of the legal and political context of sex work is Jo Bindman with Jo Doezema, "Redefining Prostitution as Sex Work on the International Agenda," http://www.walnet.org/csis/papers/redefining.html (accessed November 9, 2009).

20. Lim, 1998; and Pheterson, 1989.

21. Juhu Thukral and Melissa Ditmore, *Revolving Door* (New York: Sex Workers Project at the Urban Justice Center, 2003); Lim, 1998.

22. Jo Doezema, described efforts criminalizing every aspect of sex work aside from the work itself in Canada and the United Kingdom in her presentation to the United Nations Working Group on Contemporary Forms of Slavery, June 21, 1999.

23. Asia Watch Women's Rights Project, *A Modern Form of Slavery Trafficking of Burmese Women and Girls into Brothels in Thailand* (New York, Washington, Los Angeles and London: Human Rights Watch, 1993).

24. See the website of the Prostitutes' Education Network, maintained by Carol Leigh, a.k.a. Scarlot Harlot, http://www.bayswan.org/notes.html, "As prostitution is defined in the (California) State Penal Code as 'Any lewd act between persons for money or other consideration,' some of the activities have been viewed by police as prostitution. In fact, periodically, in cities across the United States, dancers are charged with prostitution. In January and February of 1985, the Market Street Cinema and the Mitchell Brothers were raided and performers were arrested, some on PC 647(a) and others on PC 647 (b). Numerous raids have taken place at clubs around the country including a raid of The Kit Kat Club in Sunnyvale in July 1994, in which dancers were charged with prostitution. Also, Spectator August–September 1994."

25. For example, health testing of workers. Additionally, New York City's zoning of adult oriented businesses includes a stipulation to prevent clustering of similar businesses, which is not done with any other sort of business. As prostitution would certainly be considered adult business, it could conceivably be subject to such regulations elsewhere. The newly enacted regulations were initially proposed in the Mayor's Task Force Report on Adult Oriented Businesses (New York: 1994).

26. Helen Fisher, *Anatomy of Love*, see chapter four (London: Simon and Schuster, 1992); and also Barbara Meil Hobson, *Uneasy Virtue*, chapter five (New York: Basic Books, 1987).

27. Bill Gang, "Metro Officer to Be Tried in Sexual Extortion—Court Views Video Showing Activity with Prostitute," *Las Vegas Sun*, February 28, 1997; and Peter O'Connell, "A Former Policeman Who Used His Job to Get Sex Will Serve 45 Days in Jail and Be Put on a Sex Offenders' List," *Las Vegas Review-Journal*, August 11, 1999.

28. Pheterson, 1989, 78.

29. Thukral and Ditmore, 2003.

30. Pheterson, 1989, 87.

31. In France, where prostitution is not illegal, it is illegal for a prostitute to live with anyone, including her adult children. Pheterson, 1989, 68–70.

32. Chris Meagher, "Santa Barbara Fugitive Arrested after 10 Years on the Run," *The Santa Barbara Independent*, November 13, 2008, http://www.independent.com/

news/2008/nov/13/santa-barbara-fugitive-arrested-after-10-years-run/ (accessed September 13, 2010).

33. Jo Doezema's presentation at the Non-governmental Organizations Consultation for the United Nations Working Group on Contemporary Forms of Slavery in Geneva (presented June 21, 1999); and Jo Weldon in her talk at the 1999 Socialist Scholar's Conference.

34. Information about specifics of legalization in the Netherlands were enabled by conversations at the Prostitutes Center in Amsterdam (presented July 1998). On the situation of brothels in the Philippines (see Lim, 1998). Information on legal situations in Nevada were informed by conversations with former Nevada brothel workers during 1996 and 1997.

35. Specifically Germany, "German Prostitutes May Get Benefits," Associated Press; "Rights for hookers" via News Services, *Province*, August 6, 1999, A38.

36. Pheterson, 1989, 83–84. See also Bindman with Doezema, 1997.

37. Reuters, July 24, 1999, "Police Swoop on Century-Old Bangladeshi Brothel."

38. Pheterson, 1989, 71–72.

39. World Health Assembly (WHA45.35).

40. International Committee for Prostitutes' Rights, "World Charter for Prostitutes' Rights" in Pheterson, 1989, 40–42.

41. Scott Sonner, "Mustang Ranch Closure Nevada County Officials Say They Will Miss Legal Brothel—for Its License Revenue," *National Post*, August 5, 1999, A14. Associated Press; and "the Storey County Commission, which stands to lose $233,000 a year or more—one-sixteenth of the tiny county's entire budget—in taxes and licensing fees it receives from the Mustang." Mike Henderson, *Reno Gazette-Journal*, August 8, 1999.

42. Asia Watch Women's Rights Project, *A Modern Form of Slavery Trafficking of Burmese Women and Girls into Brothels in Thailand* (New York, Washington, Los Angeles and London: Human Rights Watch, 1993); Marjan Wijers and Lin Lap-Chew, *Trafficking in Women Forced Labour and Slavery-like Practices in Marriage Domestic Labour and Prostitution* (Utrecht: Foundation Against Trafficking in Women [STV], 1997) defines trafficking as the use of force, deceit, or coercion into labor practices including slavery-like conditions and debt-bondage.

43. Asia Watch Women's Rights Project; Wijers and Lap-Chew, 1997.

44. See Wijers and Lap-Chew, 1997, for a more in-depth discussion of trafficking in persons.

45. For a more in-depth account of this, see Bindman with Doezema, 1997.

46. Asia Watch Women's Rights Project.

47. Wijers and Lap-Chew, 1997.

48. For example, in the Mariana Islands, women trafficked into prostitution were not able to seek damages from their traffickers, while people enslaved in sweatshops by the same traffickers were awarded large settlements. The justification for this was that the prostitutes were not working as prostitution is not labor in U.S. Territory. Conversations with the International Human Rights Law Group and Human Rights Watch, July 1999.

49. Asia Watch Women's Rights Project.

50. Talk given at the Global Fund for Women's conference in Reno, Nevada, October 1996.

51. Most notably, in Sweden (Lillian Andersson and Petra Östergren, letter to *Aftonpolicies*) addressed to clients include seizures, usually cars, of assets in various U.S. jurisdictions.

52. Recent legislation from Sweden and the United Kingdom intend to prosecute nationals who commit crimes in other nations, specifically geared at clients of prostitution.

53. Lim, 1998, 136, 169.

54. Lim, 1998, 214–18.

55. Melissa Ditmore, *The Use of Raids to Fight Trafficking in Persons* (New York: Sex Workers Project at the Urban Justice Center, 2009), http://www.sexworkers project.org/publications/reports/raids-and-trafficking/ (accessed November 2, 2009).

56. See *Taking the Pledge*, http://sexworkerspresent.blip.tv/file/181155/ (accessed February 2, 2010); and Melissa Ditmore, "New U.S. Funding Policies on Trafficking Affect Sex Work and HIV-prevention Efforts World Wide," *SIECUS Report* 33, no. 2, 26–30.

57. *Taking the Pledge*, http://sexworkerspresent.blip.tv/file/181155/ (accessed February 2, 2010).

58. Jodi Jacobson, "DOJ Drops Appeal of 'Prostitution Pledge' Injunction," *RHRealityCheck*, July 21, 2009, http://www.rhrealitycheck.org/blog/2009/07/21/ department-justice-withdraws-appeal-injunction-against-prostitution-pledge (accessed February 2, 2010.)

59. Zoe Hudson, "Bad Health, Bad Law," April 19, 2010. Open Society Foundations blog, http://blog.soros.org/2010/04/bad-health-bad-law/ (accessed September 13, 2010); Brennan Center for Justice, "Memorandum to Advocates Interested in the Anti-Prostitution Policy Requirement," April 13, 2010, http://www.scribd.com/doc/ 30047571/Memo-to-Advocates-Final-04-13-10 (accessed September 13, 2010).

60. Myths about sex with virgins healing disease encourage others to seek out sex with children. Educational efforts must counter this. Lim, 1998, 177; Dean Murphy, *Los Angeles Times*, July 15, 1999; UN Wire, July 15.

61. Jayson Blair, "3 Officers at Jail Accused of Sex Acts with Prisoner," *New York Times*, September 16, 1999.

62. In the United States federal law, all commercial sex with a minor is considered trafficking in persons and the minors in question are considered victims of human trafficking under the Trafficking Victims Protection Act of 2000. However, state laws vary and minors who are arrested may be charged with other offenses that are not prostitution-related and may not be recognized as crime victims.

63. Regulations requiring "good moral character" in India effectively deny prostitutes of the right to own property in India. Conversations and presentations by members of the Durbar Mahila Samanwaya Committee of Calcutta, at the 1998 XII International Conference on AIDS.

64. The United Kingdom's Disorderly Houses Act of 1751 [25 Geo. 2. C. 36] defines a disorderly house as a house "not regulated by the restraints of morality, and which is so conducted as to violate law and good order." It refers to brothels and other sex work venues. See also, John Lowman, "Prostitution Law Reform in Canada," http://mypage.uniserve.ca/~lowman/ (accessed September 13, 2010). "In addition to the communicating law, 'bawdy houses' are prohibited (Criminal Code sections 210 and 211). . . . A common bawdy house is a place kept, occupied or used by at least one person for the purposes of prostitution or indecent acts. 'Keeping' a bawdy house (section 210(1)) is an indictable offence liable to up to two years in prison. Being 'found in' or an 'inmate' of a bawdy house (Criminal Code sections 210(2) and 211) are summary offences carrying a maximum term of six months in prison and/or a $2,000 fine."

65. Amy Frazier, Associated Press, "Federal Judge Throws out Alabama's Sex Toy Ban," March 30, 1999.

66. James A. Geffert, "Anti-Prostitution Activity and Public Health" (Answers to Action, Grant MacEwan Community College, Edmonton, AB, Canada, presented May 4–6, 2000).

67. David Crary, Associated Press, *Missing Prostitutes Worry Vancouver*, July 24, 1999; Allan Dowd, Associated Press, July 27, 1999: Missing 31 women in Canada fan serial killer fears. These articles are two of many detailing such sentiments.

68. N. Connell and C. Wilson, ed., *Rape: The First Sourcebook for Women* (New York: Plume, 1974); and M. Bard, "The Rape Victim: Challenge to the Helping System," *Research Utilization Briefs* 1, no. 2 (1976).

9

From Prostitutes to Sex Workers: A Movement for Rights

The contemporary sex workers' rights movement is vibrant and well documented as sex workers make use of old media and new technology to promote their voices.[1] Associations of prostitutes have existed before, for example, assisting prostitutes who had medical expenses, but not usually with the documentation and attention garnered by current media efforts. Prostitutes have often given generously to local organizations. One known example is Julia Bulette's generosity to the fire department in her Nevada mining town.[2] It is likely that many such efforts remain undocumented and lost to history. However, technological advances have enabled greater information sharing than ever before, and this has facilitated networking around the country and internationally, both at the local level and within umbrella networks.

The prostitutes' rights movement overlaps and intersects with many other social movements, including war efforts, reproductive rights, gay liberation, and feminism. However, in each instance, prostitutes and sex workers were working to undo or stave off discrimination and damage rather than starting from a position of social strength. One episode in the history of the prostitutes' rights movement that deserves to be more widely known is the strike by brothel workers in Hawaii during World War II.

FORGOTTEN HISTORY: HONOLULU HOOKERS' STRIKE[3]

In 1942, prostitutes in Honolulu went on strike for three weeks. The events leading up to this were specific to wartime and the war effort. During World War II, brothels in Honolulu were concentrated on Hotel Street and were controlled by the police, notwithstanding that prostitution was illegal. The movement of the women who worked in them was severely restricted. Upon arrival, a woman would be met by the vice squad, fingerprinted, given a license, and informed of the rules of her stay, rules that would not be applied to anyone else in Hawaii: "She may not visit Waikiki Beach or any other beach except Kailua Beach," "She may not patronize any bars or better class cafes," and "She may not own property or an automobile." Regulations that limit the mobility of sex workers are a common attempt to segregate prostitutes from the larger population in regulated prostitution and are a feature of licensed prostitution in Nevada today. Other aspects of life were also severely restricted. Regulations additionally specified, "She may not marry service personnel" and "She may not telephone the mainland without permission of the madam."[4] Many women accepted these strictures because of the money they could earn. These regulated brothels featured white women from the mainland. Unregulated brothels also existed, featuring local women.

After the Japanese attacked Pearl Harbor in 1941, brothels were turned into makeshift hospitals and the women living and working in them moved out in order to make room for wounded soldiers. The women moved and lived in places where they had not previously been allowed. They socialized in places where they had not been allowed to go, patronizing restaurants and cafes that had been off-limits to them prior to the bombing. The military had essentially stripped local police of their power over prostitutes. When local police attempted to reassert control and evict prostitutes from areas where they formerly had not been allowed, military police asserted that they were handling prostitution-related matters. Police Chief William Gabrielson acknowledged military control of prostitution in Administrative Order No. 83 issued in 1942.[5] This order was issued not to recognize or cede control to the military, but to embarrass military commanders and force them to return control of prostitution to the police. The year before, the U.S. Congress had passed the May Act, which made prostitution in military areas a federal offense, enabling federal agents to take action to close prostitution districts and venues near military and defense installations.[6] The May Act was rigorously enforced, and so, in order to avoid problems with federal law enforcement, the military governor of Hawaii, General Delos Emmons, wrote to Chief Gabrielson that the military sought no control over prostitution and instructed him to "Cancel Administrative Order No. 83."[7] Despite this, local police and military police continued to spar over actual implementation and enforcement. Beth Bailey and David Farmer write that prostitutes from the Hotel Street venues "did not want to go back to the pre-war order. It was one thing to choose to service 100 men a day, but it was another to abide by rules that denied them their basic freedoms. They framed the issues that way and they went on strike" and picketed police headquarters.[8]

The strike lasted for nearly three weeks and was resolved by compromise between the military and the local police. The military undertook responsibility for the physical exams of the women, as well as brothel inspections, the most onerous jobs for the local police. Local police were expected to enforce other regulations, but other regulations were relaxed because prostitution was seen as critical to soldiers' morale and therefore critical to the war effort. Prostitutes enjoyed their freedom of movement and could choose to live where they pleased. These freedoms were won not due to any arguments about rights but because the military wanted prostitutes to be available to soldiers and this compromise was seen as the most convenient way to ensure this aim.

As the end of the war drew near, martial law was lifted. Civilian government was restored, and the prostitutes were ordered to return to the Hotel Street red light area. Newly appointed Governor Ingram Stainback eventually closed the brothels as part of the return to civilian rule.[9] The triumph of the prostitutes' strike may have been short-lived, but it would not be prostitutes' last effort to combat restrictive laws and policies.

UPRISINGS AND LOOSE ORGANIZATIONS

Groups of prostitutes around the United States formed loose organizations during the 1970s, when the sexual revolution was well under way. This was the genesis of the contemporary movement for the rights of sex workers. The most known organizations remain Prostitutes of New York (PONY) and Call Off Your Old Tired Ethics (COYOTE), both of which carry on to this day. Neither PONY nor COYOTE has formalized its structure or funding, and both have experienced dormant periods and resurrections. Similar organizations emerged and today, a contemporary national movement includes numerous organizations across the country.

There were and are significant similarities and overlap between the sex workers' rights movement and the gay rights movement, particularly during the time when same-sex sexual activity and dressing counter to one's sex were used as justifications to arrest people in gay bars and other venues. For example, an important but often overlooked fact is that some of the gay men, lesbians, transgender, and cross-dressing people involved in the riots at Compton's Cafeteria in San Francisco in 1966[10] and the Stonewall Inn in New York City in 1969[11] were actively selling sex. Sex workers were very active in these responses to routine police harassment, both of which were landmarks in the struggle for gay rights.

One focus and motivation of the struggle for the rights of sex workers continues to be laws used against sex workers and their enforcement. The reasons for this are three-fold. First, many people who sell sex report unlawful arrest, when they are arrested for being known to police rather than for being arrested for actions breaking the law.[12] Second, anecdotal observation by outreach organizations and analysis of policing by watchdog groups[13] demonstrate that racial and ethnic minorities are disproportionately affected by law enforcement efforts to address sex work. Finally, laws against prostitution deter sex workers who experience violence from reporting these crimes. Perpetrators of violent crimes recognize that sex workers are not likely to turn to the police for assistance, and so many target sex workers and sex work venues for robbery and violence.[14] In this way, laws against prostitution render sex workers the prey of law enforcement agents and violent criminals. For these reasons, the prostitutes' rights movement has frequently attempted law reform and sought to combat violence against sex workers.

Efforts to prevent violence began at a very grassroots level and typically focus upon sharing information about known attackers. This information may be compiled in a "bad date list." Bad date lists and information about specific perpetrators circulate in samizdat fashion or by telephone, sometimes published specifically for sex workers. For example, *danzine*, discussed below, occasionally included information about people to avoid. Technological advances have enabled faster and wider sharing of information, including photographs.

Efforts at legal reform, to challenge laws used against sex workers, have necessarily taken more formal channels, including attempts to generate strategic support. California's state legal system has contributed to the number of attempts to change statutes; COYOTE was in the vanguard of these attempts.

COYOTE

Margo St. James first started a group she called Whores, Housewives, and Others, which later became COYOTE. COYOTE's initial finances came in the form of grants from Glide Memorial Church and the Playboy Foundation. Glide specifically wanted to support the formation of a prostitutes' union.[15] Later on, income was generated in part from gala events, including five Hooker's Balls. These extravaganzas were media events attended by celebrities. Revelers came in costume; collectible posters from the balls depict scantily clad women and a carnivalesque theme. The 1977 ball grossed over $93,000.[16]

St. James worked closely with ally Priscilla Alexander. St. James was a public spokesperson, while Alexander and others worked toward political and policy goals. Throughout the 1970s, St. James traveled the country making many media appearances and trying to bring lawsuits that would lead to the decriminalization of prostitution.[17] Most of these had little effect, but in Rhode Island, St. James brought a suit that was dismissed when prostitution law was changed in 1980. Prostitution was made a misdemeanor so that it would move more quickly through the courts, but legislators, perhaps unwittingly, later deleted a section addressing prostitution, rendering indoor prostitution legal. (Rhode Island re-criminalized indoor prostitution in 2009.[18])

St. James and anthropologist Jennifer James spearheaded a successful campaign to encourage the National Organization for Women (NOW) to pass a resolution supporting the decriminalization of prostitution. This was accomplished in 1971 with significant support and networking, especially among feminists. COYOTE members and representatives continued to attend meetings and work to promote resolutions supporting the decriminalization of prostitution. The San Francisco Bar Association passed such a resolution supporting the decriminalization of prostitution. In 1974, COYOTE successfully contested California practice of detaining women arrested for prostitution until they had been examined for sexually transmitted diseases. Surprising alliances grew out of the networking necessary for these significant accomplishments. For example, Alexander represented COYOTE at meetings of Women Against Pornography.

COYOTE's political networking flourished when Alexander worked in the office of California State Senator Milton Marks in the 1980s and 1990s. Political successes included abolishing the use of condoms as evidence. It had been police policy to use three or more condoms as evidence of intent to commit prostitution. One of COYOTE's triumphs was to encourage sex workers to join a major democratic club working with gay people in San Francisco.[19] At the time, there was a risk of being arrested for felony conspiracy if there were more than two prostitutes discussing prostitution. However, in this situation, it was explained that to arrest people present in the meetings of the democratic club would require the arrest of the legislators and elected officials present. The realization of the risks faced created an environment in which sex workers could speak out and legislators would listen to them. This context contributed to the creation of the St. James Infirmary.

In 1984, COYOTE hosted a gathering of sex workers and activists including international activists. One product of this meeting was a Bill of Rights that was the forerunner to the International Charter for Prostitutes' Rights drawn up at the first World Whores Congress held in Amsterdam the following year. St. James attended, and she and Alexander attended the follow-up meeting in Brussels in 1986. Capitalizing on ties to the European Green Party, sex workers from around the world delivered a resolution at the European Parliament.

St. James left the United States in the mid-1980s and returned in 1993 to run for San Francisco Supervisor in 1996, and received 76,000 votes but was not elected. While less active now, she continues to support efforts by many organizations to promote the rights of sex workers.[20]

Prostitutes of New York

PONY was started in the mid-1970s by street prostitutes. PONY's creation is linked to the reproductive rights movement and the legalization of abortion across the country in 1973. Abortion was permitted in New York State after 1973, and women traveled to New York City from around the country for abortions, which were offered at low cost by the Center for Reproductive and Sexual Health (CRASH). Once abortion was available elsewhere, demand dropped by three-quarters.[21] Judson Church opened the Professional Women's Clinic in 1975, publicized among "professional women" with outreach to massage parlors, prostitutes working the street, and word of mouth among members of PONY. In more formalized venues, women were expected to have weekly medical examinations, and many people who worked in these venues used the services of the Professional Women's Clinic. Judson Church also conducted outreach using a van starting in 1978. Medical services were not offered in the van.

Jean Powell and, later, Iris de la Cruz were influential PONY members. De la Cruz died of HIV in the mid-1980s and is the namesake of Iris House, a women's shelter in New York City. PONY had close ties to Judson Memorial Church on Washington Square. Reverend Howard Moody and Arlene Carmen conducted mobile outreach to street prostitutes.[22] Judson Church continues to host sex work-related groups and events to this day. PONY includes people from all aspects of the sex industry but like many sex worker groups has gone through dormant periods. Porn stars Veronica Vera and Annie Sprinkle revitalized PONY and were instrumental in the production of *PONY X-Press*. The Sprinkle Salon, hosted by Sprinkle, offered a venue for cultural events and discussions about sex work and sex politics in New York City. Other notable members of PONY include writer Tracy Quan, "Mayflower Madam" Sydney Biddle Barrows, and burlesque dancer and teacher Jo Weldon.

THE EMERGENCE OF ORGANIZATIONS ACROSS THE UNITED STATES

Numerous other groups of prostitutes and other people in the sex industry arose throughout the 1970s and 1980s, many with animal-themed names, such as Miami's DOLPHIN and Kansas City Kitties. Dolores French founded Hooking Is Real Employment (HIRE) in Atlanta. These organizations formed a loose national network. The U.S. Prostitutes Collective (US-PROS), formed in 1980, is an offshoot of the English Collective of Prostitutes (ECP). The Collectives grew out of the Wages for Housework campaign. In line with their Marxist ideology, they opposed the regulation of prostitution, as in Nevada's licensed brothels, for removing control of the conditions of production from the worker.[23] The emphasis on work and income-generation is also reflected in the term "sex work."

Inventing "Sex Work"

The term sex work was coined by Carol Leigh in 1978 at a meeting organized by Women against Violence in Pornography and Media. Leigh hit upon the term in reaction to the term "sex use industry" as used at this meeting. Leigh wrote that she had initially intended to disclose herself as a prostitute but realized that this would not be fruitful because of the stigma surrounding the word prostitute. She therefore sought to acknowledge her work and emphasize that prostitution is work, as well as to emphasize the activities of women as sellers of sex rather than men as buyers of sex.[24] Hence the term "sex work," which is now standard in public health, social sciences, and other academic disciplines.

HIV/AIDS, SEX WORK, AND INNOVATIVE PROGRAMS

The emergence of HIV changed the climate and practice of sex work across the country and around the world. The HIV/AIDS epidemic created obstacles and opportunities for sex worker rights activism in the United States. Promiscuity was associated with HIV/AIDS, and so prostitutes were doubly stigmatized, first for contravening social mores and second with blame for the spread of the new infection. Efforts to combat the stigmatization and scapegoating of sex workers forced sex worker organizations to change their focus,[25] and the funding allocated to preventing HIV both enabled the creation of some good programs for sex workers and determined the direction that sex worker organizations would go. While funding streams supported specific efforts to prevent the transmission of HIV, it could be argued that this was in some ways a step back for the rights of sex workers. Fear and panic about disease contributed to stigmatization and discrimination against prostitutes, most notably with the Chamberlain-Kahn Act described earlier, which subjected women found near military bases to imprisonment during United States involvement in the first World War. Fears of HIV did not lead to detention, but energies devoted to promoting the rights of sex workers were transferred to the prevention of HIV.

Funding for HIV prevention programs supported the creation of organizations like the California Prostitutes Education Project (CAL-PEP) to offer HIV-prevention services to sex workers even as the epidemic contributed to increased stigmatization and scapegoating of sex workers, similar to the ways prostitutes had been stigmatized for sexually transmitted infections prior to the development of effective antibiotics.

Efforts to combat the HIV/AIDS epidemic included mobile outreach to sex workers, very like Judson Church's bus but typically undertaken with medical aims rather than the holistic concern that grounded the efforts of Judson Church's Prostitution Project. In New York, Dr. Joyce Wallace started the Foundation for Research on Sexually Transmitted Diseases (FROSTD), first distributing condoms to sex workers on the streets from her car, and later with a van. Wallace's research documented oral transmission of HIV in people with oral sores from the hot glass pipes used to smoke crack.[26] Wallace had strong feelings for sex workers but strong feelings against sex work.[27] Wallace and CAL-PEP pioneered mobile outreach to sex workers on the street for HIV-prevention, which is now standard practice. Organizations dedicated to sex workers in which participants have a strong hand in determining activities avoid judgment. For example, Helping Individual Prostitutes Survive (HIPS) is a Washington, D.C.-based organization that conducts mobile outreach overnight for three nights every weekend. HIPS was founded in 1993 and utilizes a rights-based approach and is not judgmental toward sex workers.[28] The rights-based approach has been advocated by the Joint United Nations Programme on HIV/AIDS (UNAIDS) because it facilitates interactions with vulnerable people, in contrast to a judgmental approach.

An unforeseen consequence of the emergence of the AIDS pandemic was the involvement of affected people. People perceived to be at greater risk than others, including sex workers, have become part of the infrastructure established to address HIV/AIDS. Researchers, health educators, health departments, even some government agencies, have had to work with people like sex workers, people whom they may never have encountered otherwise. These encounters have ranged from hostile, as in protests against mandatory HIV testing, to embracing, as with some public health outreach programs that are led by sex workers. Sociologist Valerie Jenness points out that, "In an effort to attend to the threats posed by AIDS, the prostitutes' rights movement has at best circumvented and at worst abandoned its original goal" of the decriminalization of prostitution.[29] Since Jenness wrote her book, the sex workers' rights movement has moved forward in both well-organized funded organizations implementing innovative programs and with less formal associations.

St. James Infirmary

Priscilla Alexander had the idea of opening a clinic for sex workers. St. James Infirmary, named for St. James, began offering health services to sex workers in 1999. The name is not only a tribute to St. James but also a reference to the blues song of the same name, which tells the story of a "sweet man" (pimp) finding his prostitute girlfriend in the hospital, dead. Initial capital included a substantial donation from a transgender sex worker's settlement after a wrongful strip search by the San Francisco Police Department. The infirmary operates in partnership with the University of California-San Francisco and opened with the support of the police and the city for HIV prevention.

St. James Infirmary offers health services including primary health care services, gynecological services, services related to sexually transmitted infections, acupuncture, massage therapy, anti-retroviral therapy for people with HIV/AIDS, syringe distribution and disposal, hormone therapy for transgender people, and counseling and support groups to sex workers and their families. The infirmary conducts outreach to sex workers and offers nutrition and clothing and works to develop skills and capacity in order to build leadership among sex workers. The infirmary collaborates with the University of California-San Francisco on research projects.[30]

The Sex Workers Project at the Urban Justice Center

St. James Infirmary is one of a handful of innovative projects that promote sex worker rights that have been realized in the United States. Juhu Thukral, an attorney, contacted PONY in 2001 because she wanted to start a legal project to assist sex workers. The Sex Workers Project at the Urban Justice Center (SWP)[31] was founded at the end of 2001 and continues to offer social and legal services and to advocate for the rights of sex workers. It is the first and only organization offering legal services to sex workers in the United States. Prior to this, the extent of formal legal services offered by not-for-profit organizations had been limited to legal referrals and "know your rights" programs and cards, such as the pamphlet "How Not to Get Hooked by the New Prostitution Law," developed by the New York Civil Liberties Union in 1976 when a state law against loitering for the purpose of prostitution was passed, and distributed by Judson Church.[32] In 2009, SWP secured funding to expand programming to offer social services, including counseling to sex workers. SWP has produced three reports about sex work, with emphasis on law enforcement practices and economic justice.[33]

SWP advocates to promote legislation that supports the rights of sex workers. These efforts have included working with a coalition of anti-trafficking organizations that distinguish between sex work and trafficking in persons to enhance human rights protections in national laws addressing human trafficking. SWP has also advocated for similar inclusions in anti-trafficking laws at the state level. SWP continues to assist sex workers and trafficked persons with diverse matters including but not limited to housing disputes, name changes, immigration status, and family reunification.

Organizations Dedicated to Youth

Two organizations have emerged that specifically address youth in the underground sexual economy. The Young Women's Empowerment Project was started in 2001 in Chicago,[34] and the Girls of Banteay Srei has served the Southeast Asian community of the San Francisco Bay Area since 2004.[35] Both organizations use a harm-reduction and rights-based approach to address systemic issues and immediate needs. Because these organizations work with minors, they do not use the term sex work, in recognition of the lack of economic options available to adolescents. More services are available for girls than for boys and transgender youth.

THE RE-EMERGENCE OF A NATIONAL MOVEMENT

After Gary Ridgway, called the Green River Killer, was convicted of killing a number of sex workers in 2003, sex workers in California recognized December 17 as a day of remembrance for slain sex workers. Events were held around the United States and the world in the memory of men, women, and transgender sex workers slain for being sex workers. This annual event continues, typically including the reading of names of sex workers killed in the past year.

California state law permits ballot initiatives, in which items can be petitioned for and with enough signatures put to popular vote. Sex workers and their advocates in California have used this twice to bring local legislation to a vote. In 2004, Measure Q, a proposal to decriminalize prostitution in Berkeley was defeated. In 2008, Proposition K, a similar bill to decriminalize prostitution in San Francisco was defeated. Despite the failure of Measure Q, it was significant for its role galvanizing support and sparking momentum for the sex workers' rights movement in the United States. Measure Q was spearheaded by Robyn Few, after being arrested and charged with a felony related to prostitution. Few and colleagues started the Sex Worker Outreach Project (SWOP-USA), modeled on the Sex Workers Outreach Project in Australia. SWOP-USA is the largest and most geographically diverse organization promoting the rights of sex workers in the United States. Like the previous emergence of sex worker organizations across the nation, 13 SWOP chapters have formed across the United States.[36] Chapters are typically small and led by one or two dedicated individuals but the chapters are well-networked together and in the wider movement, capitalizing on the availability of social networking on the Internet to limit the isolation experienced by many sex workers[37] while promoting activism by offering social support and encouragement.

SWOP chapters and other organizations are members of the Desiree Alliance, a national umbrella organization of people and organizations dedicated to the rights of sex workers.[38] Desiree Alliance held its first national meeting in 2006 in Las Vegas. SWOP-USA also holds national events and SWOP members organize the meetings of Desiree Alliance. In 2008, SWOP-USA convened a national march on Washington, D.C., on December 17, to promote the rights of sex workers.[39]

PUBLICATIONS

The most colorful artifacts of the movement for sex workers' rights are the publications produced by various groups and individuals. Jean O'Hara, a Hotel Street prostitute and madam, distributed her manuscript, *My Life as a Honolulu Prostitute*.[40] Other examples include the single-issue COYOTE *Growls* and four issues of COYOTE *Howls* (1974–1979). Judson Church produced *The Hooker's Hookup: A Professional Journal*,[41] including contributions from women who worked in the places where Judson reached out to women working. PONY produced two issues of the well-written *PONY X-Press* in the early 1990s. One of the most memorable was *Whorezine*, made like a collage and photocopied. Low production values belied the humor of Vic St. Blaise, the bi-coastal sex worker who produced *Whorezine*. *danzine* was produced by Teresa Dulce out of Portland, Oregon, from 1995 into the beginning of the new millennium. *danzine* and *Whorezine* were low-cost, low-production value 'zines circulated by post. HOOKonline was a website dedicated to information for men who sell sex, featuring interviews with escorts and stunning graphics. HOOKonline's visual beauty was the work of designer Hawk Kincaid.

The most successful sex worker-produced publication is *$pread magazine*, with national distribution. The first issue appeared in 2005, and production values steadily increased through 2009. *$pread magazine* was written, edited, and produced by sex workers, featuring stories about clients, professional advice, product reviews including condoms and personal lubricants, interviews, and regular columns.

Digital media has opened up possibilities for many writers, artists, and organizations to share their ideas and work. Weblogs and social networking sites have been used to share information, to generate support for issues, and to publicize events and programs.

NOTES

1. The author is grateful to Priscilla Alexander, Teresa Dulce, Hawk Kincaid, Tracy Quan, Audacia Ray, Annie Sprinkle, Margo St. James, Juhu Thukral, Veronica Vera, and many others who spoke about these events and organizations.

2. Marion S. Goldman, *Gold Diggers and Silver Miners* (Ann Arbor, MI: University of Michigan Press, 1981), 88.

3. Information for this section comes from Beth Bailey and David Farmer, "Prostitutes on Strike: The Women of Hotel Street during World War II," in *Women's America: Refocusing the Past*, edited by Linda K. Kerber and Jane Sherron De Hart (New York and Oxford: Oxford University Press, 1995), 431–39; and Emily Yellin, *Our Mother's War: American Women at Home and at the Front during World War II* (New York: Simon and Schuster, 2004), 313–17.

4. Bailey and Farmer, 1995, 433.

5. Bailey and Farmer, 1995, 436.

6. Marilyn E. Hegarty, *Victory Girls, Khaki-wackies, and Patriotutes: The Regulation of Female Sexuality during World War II* (New York and London: New York University Press, 2008, 32); Yellin, 2004, 315.

7. Bailey and Farmer, 1995, 437.

8. Bailey and Farmer, 1995, 437.

9. Bailey and Farmer, 1995, 438; Yellin, 2004, 314.

10. *Screaming Queens* (film, 2005).

11. David Carter, *Stonewall* (New York: St. Martin's Press, 2004).

12. Arlene Carmen and Howard Moody, *Working Women: The Subterranean World of Street Prostitution* (New York: Harper and Row, 1985); Juhu Thukral and Melissa Ditmore, *Revolving Door: An Analysis of Street Prostitution in New York City* (New York: Sex Workers Project, 2003), http://sexworkersproject.org/publications/

reports/revolvingdoor (accessed November 2, 2009); Amnesty International, *Stonewalled: Police Abuse and Misconduct against Lesbian, Gay and Transgender People in the U.S.* (New York: Amnesty International, 2005), http://www.amnestyusa.org/lgbt-human-rights/stonewalled-a-report/page.do?id=1106610 (accessed November 2, 2009).

13. Valerie Jenness, *Making It Work: The Prostitutes' Rights Movement in Perspective* (Hawthorne, NY: Aldine, 1993), 53–54; Carmen and Moody, 1985; Thukral and Ditmore, 2003; Amnesty International, 2005; Ditmore, 2009.

14. Thukral and Ditmore, 2003; Juhu Thukral, Melissa Ditmore, and Alexandra Murphy, *Behind Closed Doors: An Analysis of Indoor Prostitution in New York City* (New York: Sex Workers Project, 2005), http://sexworkersproject.org/publications/BehindClosedDoors.html (accessed November 2, 2009).

15. Jenness, 1993, 42.

16. Jenness, 1993, 59.

17. Jenness, 1993, 48–49.

18. CNN AMFix, "RI Closes Loopholes on Minors Stripping, Indoor Prostitution," http://amfix.blogs.cnn.com/2009/11/02/ri-closes-loopholes-on-minors-stripping-indoor-prostitution/ (accessed November 2, 2009).

19. Personal correspondence with Margo St. James, 2010.

20. Personal correspondence with Margo St. James, 2010.

21. Carmen and Moody, 1985, 20.

22. Carmen and Moody, 1985.

23. Heather Miller, "Prostitution," in *Encyclopedia of U.S. and Working Class History*, edited by Eric Arneson (New York, NY and Oxon, UK: Routledge, 2006), 3: 1140.

24. Carol Leigh, *Unrepentant Whore: Collected Works of Scarlot Harlot* (San Francisco: Last Gasp, 2004), 68.

25. Jenness, 1993, 90–93.

26. Joyce Wallace, Judith Porter, Adele Weiner, and Allen Steinberg, "Oral Sex, Crack Smoking, and HIV Infection among Female Sex Workers Who Do Not Inject Drugs," *American Journal of Public Health* 87, no. 3 (March 1997), 470.

27. *Live Nude Girls Unite!* (video, 2000).

28. Helping Individual Prostitutes Survive, http://www.hips.org (accessed November 4, 2009).

29. Jenness, 1993, 103.

30. St. James Infirmary, http://stjamesinfirmary.org/ (accessed November 1, 2009).

31. Sex Workers Project, http://www.sexworkersproject.org (accessed November 1, 2009).

32. Carmen and Moody, 1985, 35.

33. Thukral and Ditmore, 2003; Thukral, Ditmore, and Murphy, 2005; Melissa Ditmore, *The Use of Raids to Fight Trafficking in Persons* (New York: Sex Workers Project, 2009), http://www.sexworkersproject.org/publications/reports/raids-and-trafficking/ (accessed November 2, 2009).

34. Young Women's Empowerment Project, http://www.youarepriceless.org (accessed November 4, 2009).

35. Banteay Srei, http://www.girlsempoweringthemselves.com (accessed November 4, 2009).

36. SWOP-USA, http://www.swop-usa.org (accessed November 1, 2009).

37. Thukral, Ditmore, and Murphy, 2005.

38. Desiree Alliance, http://www.desireealliance.org (accessed November 1, 2009).

39. *National March for Sex Workers Rights in DC* (video), http://redlightchicago.blip.tv/file/1619080/ (accessed November 15, 2009).

40. Yellin, 2004, 310.

41. Carmen and Moody, 1985, 47.

Timeline

1722	*The Fortunes and Misfortunes of the Famous Moll Flanders*, by Daniel Defoe, published.
1834	Helen Jewett murdered in a New York City brothel.
1848	California gold rush begins.
1851	Committee of Vigilance formed in San Francisco.
1857	After original Mormon settlers leave San Bernardino, California, a period of lawlessness begins that coincides with a thriving red light district around D Street.
1859	High-grade silver discovered on the Comstock Lode.
1870	St. Louis passes legislation to regulate prostitution, rescinded by Missouri state law in 1874.
1871 and 1874	Chicago instituted regulations of prostitution.
1873	Act of the Suppression of the Trade in, and Circulation of, Obscene Literature and Articles of Immoral use, called the Comstock Act, passed.
1875	The Page Act prohibits importing women to the United States for prostitution.
1882	Chinese Exclusion Act passed.
1893	Chicago institutes licensing for massage parlors.
1894	William Stead publishes *If Christ Came to Chicago*.
1897	New Orleans red light district Storyville opened.

1902	The Committee of Fifteen issued *The Social Evil* about prostitution in New York.
1903	Prostitutes explicitly prohibited from entering the United States.
1904	United States agreed to abide by but does not sign the International Agreement for the Suppression of the White Slave Traffic.
1908	Creation of the Federal Bureau of Investigation
1910	Mann Act (White Slave Traffic Act) passed
	Emma Goldman's "The Traffic in Women" published.
1911	Chicago Vice Commission issues *The Social Evil in Chicago*.
1913	John D. Rockefeller incorporates the Bureau of Social Hygiene.
1916	Release of D. W. Griffith's *Intolerance*.
1917	New Orleans's Storyville shut down.
1918	Chamberlain-Kahn Bill codifies internment for women suspected of prostitution near military bases.
1919	Alcohol prohibited by the 18th Amendment.
	Mamie Smith's "Crazy Blues," considered the first blues record, released.
1921	International Convention for the Suppression of the Traffic in Women and Children signed.
1931	Hull House co-founder Jane Addams receives the Nobel Peace Prize.
1941	May Act makes prostitution near military and defense installations a federal crime.
	Pearl Harbor, Hawaii, attacked by the Japanese. Brothels in Honolulu's Hotel Street are turned into makeshift hospitals for the wounded.
1942	Prostitutes in Honolulu's Hotel Street strike and picket the police department.
1944	Martial law is lifted in Hawaii and regulated brothels are closed.
1949	United Nations Convention for the Suppression of the Traffic in Persons and the Exploitation of the Prostitution of Others signed.
1952	Radio debut of "Gunsmoke."
1967	U.S. Secretary of Defense Robert McNamara arranges military R&R in Bangkok.
1971	Brothels permitted in rural Nevada.
1973	National Organization for Women passes a resolution supporting the decriminalization of prostitution.

1973	Creation of Call off Your Old Tired Ethics (COYOTE).
1975	Creation of Prostitutes of New York (PONY).
1978	Carol Leigh coins the term "sex work."
1979	Convention on the Elimination of All Forms of Discrimination Against Women is signed.
1985	First World Whores Conference held in Amsterdam.
	First International AIDS Conference held.
1986	Second World Whores Congress held in Brussels.
1987	*Sex Work* published.
1995	First "John School" started in San Francisco.
1999	St. James Infirmary founded in San Francisco.
2000	Trafficking Victims Protection Act passed.
	United Nations Optional Protocol on Trafficking in Persons, Especially Women and Children, signed.
2001	Sex Workers Project at the Urban Justice Center founded.
2002	Anti-prostitution pledge attached to federal funding.
2003	December 17 named Day of Remembrance for slain sex workers
	U.S. Leadership against HIV/AIDS, Tuberculosis and Malaria Act passed.
2004	Measure Q, to decriminalize sex work in Berkeley, defeated.
2008	Proposition K, to decriminalize sex work in San Francisco, defeated.
2009	Rhode Island criminalizes indoor prostitution.
	U.S. President Barack Obama drops appeal of the injunction against the anti-prostitution pledge applied to federal funding.

Appendix 1

Historical Accounts

"THE TRAFFIC IN WOMEN" BY EMMA GOLDMAN

From *Anarchism and Other Essays*, 1911

Our reformers have suddenly made a great discovery—the white slave traffic. The papers are full of these "unheard-of conditions," and lawmakers are already planning a new set of laws to check the horror.

It is significant that whenever the public mind is to be diverted from a great social wrong, a crusade is inaugurated against indecency, gambling, saloons, etc. And what is the result of such crusades? Gambling is increasing, saloons are doing a lively business through back entrances, prostitution is at its height, and the system of pimps and cadets is but aggravated.

How is it that an institution, known almost to every child, should have been discovered so suddenly? How is it that this evil, known to all sociologists, should now be made such an important issue?

To assume that the recent investigation of the white slave traffic (and, by the way, a very superficial investigation) has discovered anything new, is, to say the least, very foolish. Prostitution has been, and is, a widespread evil, yet mankind goes on its business, perfectly indifferent to the sufferings and distress of the victims of prostitution. As indifferent, indeed, as mankind has remained to our industrial system, or to economic prostitution.

Only when human sorrows are turned into a toy with glaring colors will baby people become interested—for a while at least. The people are a very fickle baby that must have new toys every day. The "righteous" cry against the white slave traffic is such a toy. It serves to amuse the people for a little while, and it will help to create a few more fat political jobs—parasites who stalk about the world as inspectors, investigators, detectives, and so forth.

What is really the cause of the trade in women? Not merely white women, but yellow and black women as well. Exploitation, of course; the merciless Moloch of capitalism that fattens on underpaid labor, thus driving thousands of women and girls into prostitution. With Mrs. Warren these girls feel, "Why waste your life working for a few shillings a week in a scullery, eighteen hours a day?"

Naturally our reformers say nothing about this cause. They know it well enough, but it doesn't pay to say anything about it. It is much more profitable to play the Pharisee, to pretend an outraged morality, than to go to the bottom of things.

However, there is one commendable exception among the young writers: Reginald Wright Kauffman, whose work *The House of Bondage* is the first earnest attempt to treat the social evil—not from a sentimental Philistine viewpoint. A journalist of wide experience, Mr. Kauffman proves that our industrial system leaves most women no alternative except prostitution. The women portrayed in *The House of Bondage* belong to the working class. Had the author portrayed the life of women in other spheres, he would have been confronted with the same state of affairs.

Nowhere is woman treated according to the merit of her work, but rather as a sex. It is therefore almost inevitable that she should pay for her right to exist, to keep a position in whatever line, with sex favors. Thus it is merely a question of degree whether she sells herself to one man, in or out of marriage, or to many men. Whether our reformers admit it or not, the economic and social inferiority of woman is responsible for prostitution.

Just at present our good people are shocked by the disclosures that in New York City alone one out of every ten women works in a factory, that the average wage received by women is six dollars per week for forty-eight to sixty hours of work, and that the majority of female wage workers face many months of idleness which leaves the average wage about $280 a year. In view of these economic horrors, is it to be wondered at that prostitution and the white slave trade have become such dominant factors?

Lest the preceding figures be considered an exaggeration, it is well to examine what some authorities on prostitution have to say:

A prolific cause of female depravity can be found in the several tables, showing the description of the employment pursued, and the wages received, by the women previous to their fall, and it will be a question for the political economist to decide how far mere business consideration should be an apology—on the part of employers for a reduction in their rates of remuneration, and whether the savings of a small percentage on wages is not more than counterbalanced by the enormous amount of taxation enforced on the public at large to defray the expenses incurred on account of a system of vice, which is the direct result, in many cases, of insufficient compensation of honest labor.[1]

Our present-day reformers would do well to look into Dr. (William) Sanger's book. There they will find that out of 2,000 cases under his observation, but few came from the middle classes, from well-ordered conditions, or pleasant homes. By far the largest majority were working girls and working women; some driven into prostitution through sheer want, others because of a cruel, wretched life at home, others again because of thwarted and crippled physical natures (of which I shall speak later on). Also it will do the maintainers of purity and morality good to learn that out of two thousand cases, 490 were married women, women who lived with their husbands. Evidently there was not much of a guaranty for their "safety and purity" in the sanctity of marriage.[2]

Dr. Alfred Blaschko, in *Prostitution in the Nineteenth Century*, is even more emphatic in characterizing economic conditions as one of the most vital factors of prostitution.

Although prostitution has existed in all ages, it was left to the nineteenth century to develop it into a gigantic social institution. The development of industry with vast masses of people in the competitive market, the growth and congestion of large cities, the insecurity and uncertainty of employment, has given prostitution an impetus never dreamed of at any period in human history.

And again Havelock Ellis, while not so absolute in dealing with the economic cause, is nevertheless compelled to admit that it is indirectly and directly the main cause. Thus he finds that a large percentage of prostitutes is recruited from the servant class, although the latter have less care and greater security. On the other hand, Mr. Ellis does not deny that the daily routine, the drudgery, the monotony of the servant girl's lot, and especially the fact that she may never partake of the companionship and joy of a home, is no mean factor in forcing her to seek recreation and forgetfulness in the gaiety and glimmer of prostitution. In other words, the servant girl, being treated as a drudge, never having the right to herself, and worn out by the caprices of her mistress, can find an outlet, like the factory or shopgirl, only in prostitution.

The most amusing side of the question now before the public is the indignation of our "good, respectable people," especially the various Christian gentlemen, who are always to be found in the front ranks of every crusade. Is it that they are absolutely ignorant of the history of religion, and especially of the Christian religion? Or is it that they hope to blind the present generation to the part played in the past by the Church in relation to prostitution? Whatever their reason, they should be the last to cry out against the unfortunate victims of today, since it is known to every intelligent student that prostitution is of religious origin, maintained and fostered for many centuries, not as a shame, but as a virtue, hailed as such by the Gods themselves.

It would seem that the origin of prostitution is to be found primarily in a religious custom, religion, the great conserver of social tradition, preserving in a transformed shape a primitive freedom that was passing out of the general social life. The typical example is that recorded by Herodotus, in the fifth century before Christ, at the Temple of Mylitta, the Babylonian Venus, where every woman, once in her life, had to come and give herself to the first stranger, who threw a coin in her lap, to worship the goddess. Very similar customs existed in other parts of western Asia, in North Africa, in Cyprus, and other islands of the eastern Mediterranean, and also in Greece, where the temple of Aphrodite on the fort at Corinth possessed over a thousand hierodules, dedicated to the service of the goddess.

The theory that religious prostitution developed, as a general rule, out of the belief that the generative activity of human beings possessed a mysterious and sacred influence in promoting the fertility of Nature, is maintained by all authoritative writers on the subject. Gradually, however, and when prostitution became an organized institution under priestly influence, religious prostitution developed utilitarian sides, thus helping to increase public revenue.

The rise of Christianity to political power produced little change in policy. The leading fathers of the Church tolerated prostitution. Brothels under municipal protection are found in the thirteenth century. They constituted a sort of public service, the directors of them being considered almost as public servants.[3]

To this must be added the following from Dr. Sanger's work:

Pope Clement II issued a bull that prostitutes would be tolerated if they pay a certain amount of their earnings to the Church.

Pope Sixtus IV was more practical; from one single brothel, which he himself had built, he received an income of 20,000 ducats.

In modern times the Church is a little more careful in that direction. At least she does not openly demand tribute from prostitutes. She finds it much more profitable to go in for real estate, like Trinity Church, for instance, to rent out death traps at an exorbitant price to those who live off and by prostitution.

Much as I should like to, my space will not admit speaking of prostitution in Egypt, Greece, Rome, and during the Middle Ages. The conditions in the latter period are particularly interesting, inasmuch as prostitution was organized into guilds, presided over by a brothel queen. These guilds employed strikes as a medium of improving their condition and keeping a standard price. Certainly that is more practical a method than the one used by the modern wage-slave in society.

It would be one-sided and extremely superficial to maintain that the economic factor is the only cause of prostitution. There are others no less important and vital. That, too, our reformers know, but dare discuss even less than the institution that saps the very life out of both men and women. I refer to the sex question, the very mention of which causes most people moral spasms.

It is a conceded fact that woman is being reared as a sex commodity, and yet she is kept in absolute ignorance of the meaning and importance of sex. Everything dealing with that subject is suppressed, and persons who attempt to bring light into this terrible darkness are persecuted and thrown into prison. Yet it is nevertheless true that so long as a girl is not to know how to take care of herself, not to know the function of the most important part of her life, we need not be surprised if she becomes an easy prey to prostitution, or to any other form of a relationship which degrades her to the position of an object for mere sex gratification.

It is due to this ignorance that the entire life and nature of the girl is thwarted and crippled. We have long ago taken it as a self-evident fact that the boy may follow the call of the wild; that is to say, that the boy may, as soon as his sex nature asserts itself, satisfy that nature; but our moralists are scandalized at the very thought that the nature of a girl should assert itself. To the moralist prostitution does not consist so much in the fact that the woman sells her body, but rather that she sells it out of wedlock. That this is no mere statement is proved by the fact that marriage for monetary considerations is perfectly legitimate, sanctified by law and public opinion, while any other union is condemned and repudiated. Yet a prostitute, if properly defined, means nothing else than "any person for whom sexual relationships are subordinated to gain."[4]

"Those women are prostitutes who sell their bodies for the exercise of the sexual act and make of this a profession."[5]

In fact, Bangert [Bonger] goes further; he maintains that the act of prostitution is "intrinsically equal to that of a man or woman who contracts a marriage for economic reasons."

Of course, marriage is the goal of every girl, but as thousands of girls cannot marry, our stupid social customs condemn them either to a life of celibacy or prostitution. Human nature asserts itself regardless of all laws, nor is there any plausible reason why nature should adapt itself to a perverted conception of morality.

Society considers the sex experiences of a man as attributes of his general development, while similar experiences in the life of a woman are looked upon as a terrible calamity, a loss of honor and of all that is good and noble in a human being. This double standard of morality has played no little part in the creation and perpetuation of prostitution. It involves the keeping of the young in absolute ignorance on sex matters, which alleged "innocence," together with an overwrought and stifled sex nature, helps to bring about a state of affairs that our Puritans are so anxious to avoid or prevent.

Not that the gratification of sex must needs lead to prostitution; it is the cruel, heartless, criminal persecution of those who dare divert from the beaten track, which is responsible for it.

Girls, mere children, work in crowded, over-heated rooms ten to twelve hours daily at a machine, which tends to keep them in a constant over-excited sex state. Many of these girls have no home or comforts of any kind; therefore the street or some place of cheap amusement is the only means of forgetting their daily routine. This naturally brings them into close proximity with the other sex. It is hard to say which of the two factors brings the girl's over-sexed condition to a climax, but it is certainly the most natural thing that a climax should result. That is the first step toward prostitution. Nor is the girl to be held responsible for it. On the contrary, it is altogether the fault of society, the fault of our lack of understanding, of our lack of appreciation of life in the making; especially is it the criminal fault of our moralists, who condemn a girl for all eternity, because she has gone from the "path of virtue"; that is, because her first sex experience has taken place without the sanction of the Church.

The girl feels herself a complete outcast, with the doors of home and society closed in her face. Her entire training and tradition is such that the girl herself feels depraved and fallen, and therefore has no ground to stand upon, or any hold that will lift her up, instead of dragging her down. Thus society creates the victims that it afterwards vainly attempts to get rid of. The meanest, most depraved and decrepit man still considers himself too good to take as his wife the woman whose grace he was quite willing to buy, even though he might thereby save her from a life of horror. Nor can she turn to her own sister for help. In her stupidity the latter deems herself too pure and chaste, not realizing that her own position is in many respects even more deplorable than her sister's of the street.

"The wife who married for money, compared with the prostitute," says Havelock Ellis, "is the true scab. She is paid less, gives much more in return in labor and care, and is absolutely bound to her master. The prostitute never signs away the right over her own person, she retains her freedom and personal rights, nor is she always compelled to submit to man's embrace."

Nor does the better-than-thou woman realize the apologist claim of Lecky that "though she may be the supreme type of vice, she is also the most efficient guardian of virtue. But for her, happy homes would be polluted, unnatural and harmful practice would abound."

Moralists are ever ready to sacrifice one-half of the human race for the sake of some miserable institution which they cannot outgrow. As a matter of fact, prostitution is no more a safeguard for the purity of the home than rigid laws are a safeguard against prostitution. Fully fifty percent of married men are patrons of brothels. It is through this virtuous element that the married women—nay, even the children—are infected with venereal diseases. Yet society has not a word of condemnation for the man, while no law is too monstrous to be set in motion against the helpless victim. She is not only preyed upon by those who use her, but she is also absolutely at the mercy of every policeman and miserable detective on the beat, the officials at the station house, the authorities in every prison.

In a recent book by a woman who was for twelve years the mistress of a "house," are to be found the following figures: "The authorities compelled me to pay every month fines between $14.70 to $29.70, the girls would pay from $5.70 to $9.70 to the police." Considering that the writer did her business in a small city, that the amounts she gives do not include extra bribes and fines, one can readily see the tremendous revenue the police department derives from the blood money of its victims, whom it will not even protect. Woe to those who refuse to pay their toll; they would be rounded up like cattle,

if only to make a favorable impression upon the good citizens of the city, or if the powers needed extra money on the side. For the warped mind who believes that a fallen woman is incapable of human emotion it would be impossible to realize the grief, the disgrace, the tears, the wounded pride that was ours every time we were pulled in.

Strange, isn't it, that a woman who has kept a "house" should be able to feel that way? But stranger still that a good Christian world should bleed and fleece such women, and give them nothing in return except obloquy and persecution. Oh, for the charity of a Christian world!

Much stress is laid on white slaves being imported into America. How would America ever retain her virtue if Europe did not help her out? I will not deny that this may be the case in some instances, any more than I will deny that there are emissaries of Germany and other countries luring economic slaves into America; but I absolutely deny that prostitution is recruited to any appreciable extent from Europe. It may be true that the majority of prostitutes of New York City are foreigners, but that is because the majority of the population is foreign. The moment we go to any other American city, to Chicago or the Middle West, we shall find that the number of foreign prostitutes is by far a minority.

Equally exaggerated is the belief that the majority of street girls in this city were engaged in this business before they came to America. Most of the girls speak excellent English, are Americanized in habits and appearance—a thing absolutely impossible unless they had lived in this country many years. That is, they were driven into prostitution by American conditions, by the thoroughly American custom for excessive display of finery and clothes, which, of course, necessitates money—money that cannot be earned in shops or factories.

In other words, there is no reason to believe that any set of men would go to the risk and expense of getting foreign products, when American conditions are over flooding the market with thousands of girls. On the other hand, there is sufficient evidence to prove that the export of American girls for the purpose of prostitution is by no means a small factor.

Thus Clifford G. Roe, ex-Assistant State Attorney of Cook County, Ill., makes the open charge that New England girls are shipped to Panama for the express use of men in the employ of Uncle Sam. Mr. Roe adds that "there seems to be an underground railroad between Boston and Washington which many girls travel." Is it not significant that the railroad should lead to the very seat of Federal authority? That Mr. Roe said more than was desired in certain quarters is proved by the fact that he lost his position. It is not practical for men in office to tell tales from school.

The excuse given for the conditions in Panama is that there are no brothels in the Canal Zone. That is the usual avenue of escape for a hypocritical world that dares not face the truth. Not in the Canal Zone, not in the city limits—therefore prostitution does not exist.

Next to Mr. Roe, there is James Bronson Reynolds, who has made a thorough study of the white slave traffic in Asia. As a staunch American citizen and friend of the future Napoleon of America, Theodore Roosevelt, he is surely the last to discredit the virtue of his country. Yet we are informed by him that in Hong Kong, Shanghai, and Yokohama, the Augean stables of American vice are located. There American prostitutes have made themselves so conspicuous that in the Orient "American girl" is synonymous with prostitute. Mr. Reynolds reminds his countrymen that while Americans in China are under the protection of our consular representatives, the Chinese in America have no protection at all. Everyone who knows the brutal and barbarous persecution Chinese and Japanese endure on the Pacific Coast, will agree with Mr. Reynolds.

In view of the above facts it is rather absurd to point to Europe as the swamp whence come all the social diseases of America. Just as absurd is it to proclaim the myth that the Jews furnish the largest contingent of willing prey. I am sure that no one will accuse me of nationalistic tendencies. I am glad to say that I have developed out of them, as out of many other prejudices. If, therefore, I resent the statement that Jewish prostitutes are imported, it is not because of any Judaistic sympathies, but because of the facts inherent in the lives of these people. No one but the most superficial will claim that Jewish girls migrate to strange lands, unless they have some tie or relation that brings them there. The Jewish girl is not adventurous. Until recent years she had never left home, not even so far as the next village or town, except it were to visit some relative. Is it then credible that Jewish girls would leave their parents or families, travel thousands of miles to strange lands, through the influence and promises of strange forces? Go to any of the large incoming steamers and see for yourself if these girls do not come either with their parents, brothers, aunts, or other kinsfolk. There may be exceptions, of course, but to state that large numbers of Jewish girls are imported for prostitution, or any other purpose, is simply not to know Jewish psychology.

Those who sit in a glass house do wrong to throw stones about them; besides, the American glass house is rather thin, it will break easily, and the interior is anything but a gainly sight.

To ascribe the increase of prostitution to alleged importation, to the growth of the cadet system, or similar causes, is highly superficial. I have already referred to the former. As to the cadet system, abhorrent as it is, we must not ignore the fact that it is essentially a phase of modern prostitution—a phase accentuated by suppression and graft, resulting from sporadic crusades against the social evil.

The procurer is no doubt a poor specimen of the human family, but in what manner is he more despicable than the policeman who takes the last cent from the street walker, and then locks her up in the station house? Why is the cadet more criminal, or a greater menace to society, than the owners of department stores and factories, who grow fat on the sweat of their victims, only to drive them to the streets? I make no plea for the cadet, but I fail to see why he should be mercilessly hounded, while the real perpetrators of all social iniquity enjoy immunity and respect. Then, too, it is well to remember that it is not the cadet who makes the prostitute. It is our sham and hypocrisy that create both the prostitute and the cadet.

Until 1894 very little was known in America of the procurer. Then we were attacked by an epidemic of virtue. Vice was to be abolished, the country purified at all cost. The social cancer was therefore driven out of sight, but deeper into the body. Keepers of brothels, as well as their unfortunate victims, were turned over to the tender mercies of the police. The inevitable consequence of exorbitant bribes, and the penitentiary, followed.

While comparatively protected in the brothels, where they represented a certain monetary value, the girls now found themselves on the street, absolutely at the mercy of the graft-greedy police. Desperate, needing protection and longing for affection, these girls naturally proved an easy prey for cadets, themselves the result of the spirit of our commercial age. Thus the cadet system was the direct outgrowth of police persecution, graft, and attempted suppression of prostitution. It were sheer folly to confound this modern phase of the social evil with the causes of the latter.

Mere suppression and barbaric enactments can serve but to embitter, and further degrade, the unfortunate victims of ignorance and stupidity. The latter has reached its highest expression in the proposed law to make humane treatment of prostitutes a crime, punishing any one sheltering a prostitute with five years' imprisonment and $10,000 fine. Such an attitude merely exposes the terrible lack of understanding of the true causes of prostitution, as a social factor, as well as manifesting the Puritanic spirit of the Scarlet Letter days.

There is not a single modern writer on the subject who does not refer to the utter futility of legislative methods in coping with the issue. Thus Dr. Blaschko finds that governmental suppression and moral crusades accomplish nothing save driving the evil into secret channels, multiplying its dangers to society. Havelock Ellis, the most thorough and humane student of prostitution, proves by a wealth of data that the more stringent the methods of persecution the worse the condition becomes. Among other data we learn that in France,

in 1560, Charles IX abolished brothels through an edict, but the numbers of prostitutes were only increased, while many new brothels appeared in unsuspected shapes, and were more dangerous. In spite of all such legislation, or because of it, there has been no country in which prostitution has played a more conspicuous part.[6]

An educated public opinion, freed from the legal and moral hounding of the prostitute, can alone help to ameliorate present conditions. Willful shutting of eyes and ignoring of the evil as a social factor of modern life, can but aggravate matters. We must rise above our foolish notions of "better than thou," and learn to recognize in the prostitute a product of social conditions. Such a realization will sweep away the attitude of hypocrisy, and insure a greater understanding and more humane treatment. As to a thorough eradication of prostitution, nothing can accomplish that save a complete transvaluation of all accepted values especially the moral ones—coupled with the abolition of industrial slavery.

Evidently the authorities are not anxious that the public be informed as to the true cause of prostitution.

NOTES

1. Dr. Sanger, *The History of Prostitution.*
2. It is a significant fact that Dr. Sanger's book has been excluded from the U.S. mails. Evidently the authorities are not anxious that the public be informed as to the true cause of prostitution.
3. Havelock Ellis, *Sex and Society.*
4. Guyot, *La Prostitution.*

5. Bangert [Bonger], *Criminalité et Condition Economique.*
6. *Sex and Society.*

Source: Emma Goldman, *Anarchism and Other Essays.* Second revised edition. (New York & London: Mother Earth Publishing Association, 1911), 183–200.

REPORT OF COMMITTEE ON THE SOCIAL EVIL

The Report of Committee on the Social Evil was released by the Honolulu Social Survey in 1914. These excerpts were chosen because they illustrate where prostitution occurred at the time.

1. Present status

Iwilei, Honolulu's Red Light District

Prostitution in our city is to a slight degree centered in the protected district of Iwilei, which is allowed to exist contrary to law by the police. The number of inmates in this district varies from 52 to 188.[1] Comparatively few prostitutes live in Iwilei, the majority renting rooms for the night and plying their trade there when conditions of weather and presence of transports or strangers favor good business. Honolulu's prostitute quarter is dirty, muddy, ill-kept and dingy. Most of the houses are mere shacks, devoid of sanitary appliances, poorly lighted and most unattractive. Vice has no gilded dens in our city. Most of the women who are segregated in Iwilei are Japanese; only one Hawaiian was there at the time of investigation. Of the 107 found at one visitation, 82 were Japanese, fourteen Porto Rican, six French, five American, and none Hawaiian. Owing to police protection there is rarely any disorder or open unseemliness in Iwilei. Occasionally, however, a bold crime startles the lethargic authorities. Women living in or frequenting the district are supposed to have a certificate from a practicing physician attesting freedom from venereal disease. These papers are presumably inspected once a week by the police. But this is a form often disregarded. Prostitutes who are not disorderly are unmolested. This system of regulation is so lax that the military authorities track from 75 to 90 percent of the cases of venereal disease among their men to Iwilei. No effort is made to restrict prostitution to this quarter except that no house outside the district is allowed to keep open doors for business.

Unregulated Prostitution

By far the larger part of commercialized vice and the extensive clandestine prostitution known to exist in Honolulu is carried on outside of Iwilei. The trade is prosecuted in recognized houses of assignation, tenements, cottages, parks, and open spaces, and by means of hacks and automobiles.

Houses of Assignation

There are sixteen well-known houses of assignation clustered about the center of the city, besides three at Waikiki. These do a thriving business, some hotels harboring prostitutes for longer or shorter periods, others asking no questions of persons registering without baggage for the night, still others serving as headquarters for men who take girls from the street. In some of these places liquor can be had and the police occasionally raid them. Others are quiet and known as "safe houses," never being molested by the authorities. The list of nineteen houses of assignation on our files does not include all such places but only the more prominent. A large percentage of prostitution in Honolulu centers in these places.

Tenements

Numbers of women ply their trade in tenements, safe from police interference. Little or no attempt is made by the owners to prevent the abuse, which is quite open and may be easily detected by any casual visitor day or night. As a rule the pimp does not figure in tenement house prostitution.

Cottages

The number of detached cottages in Honolulu is steadily increasing. These rent as low as from $10 to $20 a month. Hence they offer to women plying this trade a safe and lucrative base of operations. The cottage trade has close connection with the hack and automobile business, which will be considered under another section.

Street Solicitation

Solicitation by word of mouth such as characterizes mainland cities is largely absent here. Many women ready for business do appear on the streets, waiting about to go to houses of assignation or to be transported by vehicles, but they do not openly solicit to any great, extent. To any one of observant habit what they are out for is, however, quite apparent.

Number Engaged

It has been found impossible to ascertain the number of women engaged in prostitution in Honolulu. Our open-air conditions favor clandestine trade and render it so safe that it would require for many months the services of trained investigators well acquainted with the habits of the various races in our population to make anything like a reliable estimate. It is apparent, however, that the evil is very, wide spread, that social vice in Honolulu is most insidious and that its virus affects family life more extensively than one who has not given the subject careful study would suspect.

. . . .

5. The Saloon as a Factor

There is no organized system of solicitation of men by women or pimps in the saloons of Honolulu. Lewd pictures or cards are not distributed therein. Nor do the saloons connect with sleeping rooms or places for assignation. Pimps occasionally enter saloons of the lower order and solicit for prostitutes but no evidence of direct connection of any kind between the saloons and the social evil has been discovered. This is largely due to the excellent work of the License Commission.

6. Restaurants and Coffee Shops

Among the most dangerous centers in Honolulu are the cheap restaurants and coffee houses. These are frequented at night by men, women and children. They are made the meeting place for boys and girls too young to be away from parental authority. Young girls buying food at these restaurants to take home are frequently seduced by employees or unscrupulous frequenters. The general seclusion and inaccessibility of many of these coffee shops render them little better than dives. While saloons are admirably supervised, these eating places are not the especial care of any licensing commission. Neither the police nor juvenile officers afford their patrons any protection. Many of these shops are nightly the resort of women of loose habits and their companions. Young girls who visit the shops without suitable escorts are exposed to contact with this class and are easily led astray. These shops are particularly dangerous as they are kept by men who often make a practice of seducing the girls who enter them. Many of these restaurants are open and thronged with patrons, among whom are children, as late as eleven o'clock at night.

7. The Relation of the Police to the Evil

Our police force reflects the general spirit of toleration of vice characteristic of the public sentiment of our community. No sustained attempt is made to keep women known to be prostitutes off the streets. Now and again a spasmodic effort is instituted but it quickly subsides. The main reliance of the police is upon the policy of segregation. Iwilei is, however, a melancholy commentary upon the utter futility of this measure. It is both disease-cursed and a travesty. All reports thereupon covering many months revealed the presence in Iwilei of only one Hawaiian woman, while prostitution among Hawaiian women is rife outside the district and is confined to no one locality in the city. Though such a condition is a constant temptation to the police, this investigation has failed to disclose evidence of graft in connection with commercialized vice. In this, as in many other respects, Honolulu presents a marked contrast to mainland cities.

8. The Army and Navy and the Social Evil

There are now some eight thousand men connected with the army and navy of the United States stationed at Honolulu and Leilehua. So large an addition to the number of unmarried men in our community has greatly increased the gravity of the problem of social vice. The attitude of the military authorities toward the question is one mainly of solicitude for physical efficiency in the army. The sole object of the regulations seems to be to guard their men from disease. Soldiers are encouraged to use prophylactics, which are freely dispensed. When venereal disease makes its appearance the patient is punished by segregation and loss of pay. Prostitution is not allowed on the reservations. In the community it is a matter of common observation that prostitution has greatly increased since the coming of the army. Very few cases of rape by men of the service are on record. From time to time there has been complaint of soldiers accosting women in public places and even of assault on the streets. Those in position to know avouch that Hawaiian girls have had to contend with far more temptation since the establishment of the large army posts.

It should be stated, however, and emphasized as the finding of this Committee after careful investigation, that as a whole, the men of the service in Honolulu have given a notable example of good conduct and self-control. The addition of eight thousand men to the community, the large majority of them voting, vigorous and unmarried, could not have been expected to result otherwise than in some increase of sexual vice.

As a rule, the enlisted men are markedly courteous in their demeanor and well-behaved when outside the rigorous discipline of barracks. In proportion to their numbers, the increase of disorder and sexual vice has been less than might be expected. The soldier in Honolulu, as a rule, believes in maintaining the reputation of the uniform and the Flag and in condemning his comrade who casts discredit upon either.

There are a number of officers also who are endeavoring earnestly to increase the morals of the service and aid the men in living decent and self-respecting lives.

9. Hacks and Automobiles

One of the unique features of the social evil as it exists in Honolulu is its connection with the public hack and automobile business. Hack drivers constitute practically the only class of pimps we have. There are of course not a few drivers and chauffeurs of all nationalities who will have nothing to do with the business. Those who engage in the illicit trade procure girls for their customers by arranging to meet the former at some specified place and by driving the couples either to an assignation house or to some secluded spot out of doors. They do not carry men to the homes of the girls as that would deprive them of valuable business secrets. The hacks convey many also to Iwilei. For this latter business the automobiles are too expensive. The chauffeurs who cater to prostitution practice seduction for their own personal pleasure. Their habit is to give free rides to young girls from whom they finally exact as payment their ruin. Sometimes this is accomplished by means amounting to compulsion. Girls thus seduced are led into the trade by the associations cultivated by the chauffeurs. Of late the latter have cut into the procuring business of the hack drivers by getting from them the better class of girls. Automobiles are also engaged by joy riders for immoral purposes. There is no evidence of any organization of hack drivers and chauffeurs in the business of prostitution but the practices just outlined are very wide spread and offer peculiar difficulties in dealing with social vice in our community. Not a few hack drivers have definite business connections with the women to whom they bring trade, while the chauffeurs form with the girls of their pernicious clientele social groups that exert a very evil influence.

10. Agencies for Rescue and Reform

No definite rescue or reform work for prostitutes is carried on in Honolulu, though in a quiet way the Christian forces of the city have for generations done not a little in this direction through unorganized personal channels. The Salvation Army Home and the Industrial Schools for Boys and Girls are willing to receive the children of prostitutes and care for them intelligently. Public sentiment upon the question of social vice is so advanced that a program of scientific reformation would receive the enthusiastic cooperation and support of the best women in town. The motto of Jesus, "Neither do I condemn thee. Go and sin no more," finds more sympathetic understanding here than in most enlightened communities.

11. Public Health

Venereal disease is as prevalent in Honolulu as in any other city. It causes here as elsewhere one-third of all the blindness, more than one-half the sterility and 60 to 75 percent of the gynecological operations performed upon chaste married women. Gonorrhea is more prevalent here among children under ten than in any place known to the cooperating physicians on our Committee. Army prophylactics are not used generally by the soldiers, who when diseased often consult city practitioners to escape the punishment prescribed by the regulations. The hospitals of the city are open to all suffering from venereal diseases. Very few prostitutes have children because they have been sterilized by gonorrheal infection. They rarely abort. No abortionist is known to the Honolulu profession. There is practically no medical examination of women, that in connection with Iwilei being a farce.

NOTE

1. Conditions in Iwilei have entirely changed since the investigation of the committee. The U.S. Immigration authorities have deported all aliens and there are now no Japanese in the district. A visit there recently showed ten "French" women and two Porto Ricans. The French women are of both French and American extraction, at least two of them being apparently Americans. There were no Hawaiian women there. There was one woman of Hawaiian birth, but of Portuguese parentage. The women are living entirely in the detached cottages, each of which has fair sanitary arrangements.

Source: Report of Committee on the Social Evil (Board of Trustees of the Kaiulani Home for Girls, Report of Committee on the Social Evil: Honolulu Social Survey), May 1914.

Appendix 2

Documents by Sex Workers

OBITUARY OF IRIS DE LA CRUZ

It is with resigned sadness that we write that Iris died of AIDS on May 11, 1991 in New York City, at the age of 37. She is survived by her mother, Beverly Rotter, her brother Randy, and her daughter Melissa.

Iris was loved and respected as an activist by people in the Life. After she became aware of her diagnosis, she became active in the People With AIDS (PWA) Coalition. Iris used every medium to educate her constituencies about AIDS. Iris began and ran support groups for heterosexual, bisexual and women PWAs. Her column in *PWA Newsline*, "Kool-Aids With Ice" was a humorous assault on bourgeois pieties which flirted with the bizarre. Her writings were filled with salty memories of street life and practical (if weird) advice on living with illness. She produced political and educational materials and became a widely sought-after public speaker.

Iris's memorial service was a moving occasion, with family and friends, including activists from the AIDS Movement and the Prostitutes' Movement recalling her courage and her character. Those who came to Judson Memorial Church to honor Iris, filled the room beyond capacity. Friends with AIDS recounted Iris's finer and funnier moments.

Her work in PONY and in the PWA Coalition will not be forgotten.

Source: The obituary of Iris de la Cruz was previously published in *PONY X-Press*, no. 2 (1991) and is used with the permission of PONY (Prostitutes of New York).

"TAXING: Q 'N A WITH A LICENSED TAX CONSULTANT"

danzine was published from 1995 to 2001. This is a reprint from number 17, Summer 2001. This information was checked for accuracy in 2009.

Taxing

Q 'n A with a Licensed Tax Consultant

By Your Mama

Three years ago Your Mama had a question and answer session with a professional who had been preparing people's taxes since 1977. The following is a reprint of those questions with a few changes after we had someone from the IRS double check the answers, year 2000. The licensed tax consultant offered good leads but a few of us went to go see him in person and he gave us the willies. If you want to know more about him as a resource, leave *danzine* a message and someone will get back to you.

[Lamer disclaimer: *danzine* does not give tax advice, a person should consult with their tax advisor about their particular situation.]

What is the Internal Revenue Service (IRS)?

The IRS is the agency that has the responsibility to collect all the different taxes that are in the laws of the United States Codes. It is an agency within the U.S. Treasury Department.

Do I have to file taxes?

If a person has more than $400 of net income from self-employment, they have an obligation to file an individual income tax return. (Net income is the money you clear, the profit.)

Where do my taxes go?

Tax revenues go into the General Fund of the United States Treasury. This is what pays for all the Federal government's and some of the State's public benefits such as roads, education, welfare, and other government activities.

I haven't done my taxes in 3 years (9 years, or never). Will I be audited, and for what reason?

An audit is an examination of a tax return that has been filed with the IRS or the State. Until a tax return is filed there cannot be an audit. However, if you have not filed a tax return, you may be required to do so if there is someone who reports to the IRS that you have been paid. This is usually a W-2 or a 1099-Misc.

Dancing/modeling/escorting is my only source of income. I don't get a pay check, and the money I make is from tips alone. How do I file?

If your only source of income is just tips, this is the same as being in business for yourself (self-employed sub-contractor.) You should file your income on Schedule C of the tax return (Form 1040).

What is a 1040? . . . 1099?

A 1040 is another name for "Form 1040 U.S. Individual Income Tax Return." This is the form used to report your income on. A 1099 is another form used by third parties such as businesses, banks, credit unions, mortgage companies, etc., to report to the IRS payments they have made to persons other than employees.

I get paid an hourly wage and I work for tips as well. How do I file?

You file a Form 1040 and Form 4137 "Social Security Tax on Tip Income Not Reported to Employer." If you report your tips to your employer, you do not have to file the Form 4137.

Do I have to tell the IRS I'm a "stripper" or an "adult entertainer?"

Call yourself an entertainer.

I haven't kept any receipts, nor have I recorded when I worked and how much I made from dancing. Where do I start?

The best place to start is reconstructing your income and expenses as best you can. Keep in mind that you should be reasonable in reporting your net income. By that I mean that you should show enough income to live.

I have never filed my taxes, will I be penalized if I file now? What are the penalties for filing late?

There are no penalties for a first-time filer. The penalty for filing late and interest can run to a maximum of 25 percent of the tax due on the return. However, tax evasion, willful failure to file a return or pay tax, and fraudulent returns are also subject to criminal penalties, including fines.

I've been reporting taxes from my other job that has nothing to do with the sex industry. Do I have to go back and report the money I made from dancing all this time?

This is a tough question. As I stated earlier, you need to report all income that you receive, especially if you receive a 1099-Misc. or a W-2. But, I would suggest that you start with the current year and try to accurately keep track of all your income and expenses.

What forms do I need if I'm married, single with children, single without children, get financial aid, receive government assistance?

Form 1040 is the form to file for an individual income tax return. On that form is a place to select your "filing status" such as single, married, head of household, etc.

I worked out of state last year, how do I file?

No matter what state you work in, you should file a U.S. Individual Income Tax Return Form 1040. Depending on the separate requirement for each state, you may also need to file a state return.

I work in town and live in a hotel. Can I write that off as a business expense?

Personal living expenses are not a deductible expense, however if you maintain a home base and go out of town to work, then those temporary living expenses are deductible.

Can I write off cab rides to and from work? . . . lingerie, shoes, outfits, makeup, tanning, hairstyles and manicures for work?

Commuting to and from work is not deductible, however if you go from one job to another before returning home, then that travel is deductible. As for the rest of the question, those items usually fall under the heading of personal expenses and are not deductible.

Is it true that I can write off the tampons I use at work because they are 'altered' (cut the string) for performance purposes?

Again, personal items are not a necessary business expense.

I trade for money, can I write off the condoms, lubrication, and latex I use for work?

All ordinary and necessary expenses for your business are deductible unless otherwise limited or not allowed, i.e., commuting.

When is my last chance to file?

The filing date for a tax return is usually the 15th day of the fourth month following the end of the tax year.

If I file and find out I owe, can I pay it off in payments?

The IRS has a payment plan. They charge [between $43 and $105] to set one up. If you do go on the payment plan, be sure and make all payments on time. Because if you default, all taxes are immediately due and payable.

I don't want to be in the system. Is there a way around all of this?

I don't know how to answer this question. I can think of all kinds of reasons to be included in the "system," however I do make it a practice to minimize the money I sent to Washington. I believe that it is my duty to arrange my affairs so as to pay no more in taxes than is absolutely required.

The IRS asks a lot of personal questions, who reads it and where does it go?

The IRS is required by law not to disclose any information about a taxpayer to another party without that person's written permission. Any information about a taxpayer's file is maintained at the Martinsburg, West Virginia master file system.

I don't have a Social Security number. Do I need one in order to file? Where do I get one?

You must have a Social Security number in order to file a tax return, but also in order to open a bank account, apply for credit, or any number of everyday activities. You get a Social Security number by applying for one at the nearest Social Security Office. Call 1 800 772 1213 for nearest location.

What is Social Security?

Social Security is the name for the benefits provided by the law passed in 1936 to give workers, who paid a part of their income in the form of a tax, a pension when they retired from work at age 62 or 65. It has been changed and modified many times to provide other benefits such as Medicare and Medicaid, and other welfare benefits.

I don't get a pay check, how do I establish good credit?

Find some lending company such as a bank, credit union, or finance company to lend you some money. Pay back the loan promptly, and when you have paid that one, go find another. This is how most of us who are self-employed do this.

What is tax evasion? . . . tax fraud?

Tax evasion and tax fraud are criminal offenses. A person who deliberately attempts to hide income, lies to an investigator, does not cooperate in an investigation by destroying records, or deliberately claims deductions and exemptions falsely, may be found guilty of defrauding the Government, or evading the proper collection of tax. These actions can result in criminal fines and/or imprisonment.

Source: "Taxing: Q 'n A with a Licensed Tax Consultant" was previously published in *danzine*, no. 17 (Summer 2001) and is used with permission of Teresa Dulce, publisher.

"MARKET PENETRATION: THE WAR ON PROSTITUTION ADVERTISING" BY CAROLINE ANDREWS

Back in 1973, the year Roe v. Wade decriminalized abortion and made women's lib front page news, the National Organization for Women passed a resolution supporting the decriminalization of prostitution. It emphasized the sentiment of the day—that women's bodies were their own domain and only they should decide how to use them.

Fast-forward to the present. In March, 2007, the National Organization for Women's New York City (NOW-NYC) chapter sent out a press release titled, "New York Press: The Marketing Arm of the Human Trafficking Industry." The press release highlighted the organization's "Ending the Business of Human Trafficking" campaign, in which print publications, particularly free weeklies, have been targeted in an effort to convince them to pledge not to accept "adult" ads for non-licensed massage parlors, escorts, and the like. In their press release, NOW-NYC took particular aim at the New York Press for initially refusing to accept their demands, charging that the Press, an alternative free weekly paper, "deliberately or not . . . has become the intermediary between trafficked people and the 'johns' who seek their services."

In bullet points, NOW-NYC laid out their evidence for the link between adult advertising and trafficking. First, the press release cited eight "spas" in East Midtown Manhattan that are actually brothels uncovered by NOW in its "Block by Block" campaign. Next, they described a john review website (www.spahunters.com) in which they claim men have reviewed their experiences with trafficked women in New York City brothels. (For the record, I couldn't find one example of a client posting on that website who described "trafficking . . . ") Then, NOW referenced a human trafficking bust by the FBI in Queens from January, 2007. Finally, they pointed to an August, 2006 bust on West 26th Street in Manhattan involving Korean women whose passports had been held by traffickers.

What do any of these examples have to do with the New York Press? No clue. Astoundingly, NOW-NYC didn't demonstrate any link between a single one of the hundreds of ads in the Press and any verifiable or even alleged instance of trafficking, including the examples cited in that press release. While it is almost certain that some truly exploited and trafficked women have been advertised in the Press at some point, what is disturbing is that it wasn't deemed necessary by NOW-NYC to actually prove that even one of the paper's adult ads were really a trafficking front. All they had to do was talk about the fact that trafficking is a problem in New York City (which I don't dispute) and then point out that those ads in the back of the Press are not actually for back rubs and companionship (duh!). The fact that prostitution is different from trafficking is irrelevant because to the general public, prostitution might as well be a synonym for trafficking.

In late 2007, the New York Press capitulated to the pressure and now no longer accepts adult advertising. To date *Time Out New York, The Brooklyn Paper, Hoy, Our Town, Westside Spirit, The Westsider, Our Town Downtown, City Hall, Chelsea-Clinton News, AVENUE, New York Family, The Queens Courier, L Magazine,* and *New York Magazine* have taken NOW-NYC's pledge. *The Village Voice* and Verizon's New York City Yellow Pages are future targets.

Earlier in NOW-NYC's campaign, a member of Prostitutes of New York (PONY) who wishes to be identified as "Eve," attended a NOW-NYC meeting to explain her concerns about the effort. Eve says,

I've been a NOW member for over a decade. I went to a meeting and told NOW that based on my personal experience the majority of these ads were for prostitution, not trafficking. They were very nice, but unfortunately the basic attitude was that anything ethnically advertised was *de facto* a trafficking operation. I'm not sure they wanted to believe that it was possible for escort agencies, parlors, or independent girls themselves to use ethnic advertising as a marketing strategy because of client fetishes for a particular nationality. "Hot Russian Girls 4 U" might not be politically correct or tasteful, but that doesn't mean the girls working there are trafficked, badly treated, or even necessarily Russian. But it fit NOW's campaign better to assume the worst. I also really believe that many of NOW's leaders are abolitionist about prostitution; they've spent time visiting the worst examples of trafficking in New York City brothels and know very little about the everyday life of more ordinary sex workers. My main goal in going to that meeting was to explain that limiting advertising options for prostitutes was bad policy. If it becomes impossible for prostitutes to advertise online or in cheap print publications then we're back to street soliciting, which is much more dangerous.

Cheap print ads in free papers have long been the mainstay of escort agencies, parlors, fetish houses, and independent sex workers because no special skills are necessary to get an ad printed and the costs are minimal. The wide availability of print advertising means that sex workers, particularly prostitutes, who lack access to the Internet or the skills to effectively advertise online, have an opportunity to avoid resorting to street work. Specific newspapers in every city are often well known for having sex industry ads in the back of their publications, so they represent a never-ending source of new clients for sex workers and sex industry businesses—as well as a major source of operating funds for independent and alternative news publishing. It's unclear how much traffickers rely on print ads to attract clients, and until some entity studies the subject, it's likely to remain that way.

One reason traffickers might actually choose to avoid print publications is all the unwanted attention. Last October, a U.K. newspaper, *South Wales Echo*, published an exposé about trafficked women in the Welsh capital of Cardiff. The paper was caught with its pants down when it was discovered that all the brothels that held the trafficking victims advertised in their paper (and in the exact same issue as the exposé). Local police were quoted as saying that one important factor in tracking down the traffickers was their print advertising.

While the Cardiff case is just one example, it's a general truism that what happens in plain sight is easier to monitor than what happens underground or behind closed doors. An effective ban on open advertising for the sex industry would mean the creation of an underground network of whispers to replace it—and anything that drives the sex industry further underground is not better for sex workers.

Last year, *The Economist* printed a story highlighting the debate around prostitution advertising in British newspaper classifieds and noted,

Allowing sex to be bought and sold in reasonably open circumstances can in fact make things safer for the workers involved [and] newspapers can do more by regulating their adverts than by dropping them altogether. In Suffolk, where five prostitutes were murdered last year, *Archant Regional*, a big local newspaper group, decided with the police that the small ads should continue in order to stop the trade going underground. The newspaper passes information to officers and has made simple changes—such as accepting payment only by che[ck] or credit card for adult listings—which mean that advertisers can be traced if illegalities are reported.

While print advertising keeps everything out in the open, the in-your-face aspect of the ads themselves means that there will always be plenty of people who are offended every time they pick up a paper and see the sex industry displayed. And if they can't stop the newspapers from printing the ads through public humiliation, some take the war on sex industry advertising to another level.

Orlando's Metropolitan Bureau of Investigation (MBI) got really creative last year. On October 19, vice agents arrested three employees of the *Orlando Weekly* whose job it was to sell classified advertising for the newspaper. The three workers were charged with 17 counts of "aiding in the commission of prostitution" and the newspaper itself was accused of racketeering. At the Orange County grand jury indictment, vice agents said that the paper earned $2.3 million in five years from prostitution-related ads. *The Weekly* charges $80 for a three line ad, so there is clearly a huge market share of Orlando represented in this paper. Vice agents went undercover to the newspaper's office and explicitly asked to place an ad for a prostitution business. The sting was part of MBI's pun-laden "Operation Weekly Shame."

Orlando Weekly publisher, Rick Schreiber, quickly denounced the arrests as "an outrageous abuse of process and an attempt to censor the First Amendment rights of a newspaper that has reported critically on the Metropolitan Bureau of Investigation."

The case is still pending and could have far-reaching and chilling effects on whether or not print publications continue to accept adult advertising. In a similar case two years ago, a grand jury in Tennessee indicted the *Nashville Scene* for promoting prostitution, but the state of Tennessee eventually dropped the case.

With print advertising under attack, the obvious refuge is Internet advertising, but this is a war zone too. Anyone who was selling or buying sex online in 2002 remembers Operation Flea Collar, when Florida police put together a major sting against Big Doggie website owner, Charles Kelly. As one of the net's largest escort review and advertising sites, when Big Doggie suddenly went dark, escorts and clients alike scurried for cover.

In retrospect, it's surprising that something like this didn't happen sooner. With sex being openly advertised all over the Internet, shutting down major advertising and review sites would seem like an obvious goal of law enforcement.

In the case of Big Doggie, however, the police weren't able to make any of the over 50 felony racketeering, obstruction, or procurement charges stick. All the chatter on the Big Doggie message boards are protected as free speech, so in order to prove their case the police needed witnesses (clients) to testify in open court, and no one was willing to talk. Moreover the operation was also extremely resource-heavy—vice officers were needed to create a fake escorting site, advertise it, entrap clients, and monitor the message boards; lawyers were needed to review the evidence and put together a case—and it's not good to tell the District Attorney or local Sheriff that you can't successfully prosecute the case that he or she has just sunk all the office's staff time and money into. At the end of the day, MSNBC reported that the Hillsborough County Sheriff's Office (who ran Operation Flea Collar) would not be renewing an investigation into Big Doggie.

Having realized how difficult it is to prosecute the owners of online advertising sites, police have turned their attention to the providers themselves. While it has always been the case that sex workers and clients occasionally find themselves on the receiving end of online police sting operations, recently the volume of arrests has begun to live up to the sex industry's paranoia on the subject. Nowhere is this truer than with Craigslist.

The Erotic Services section of Craigslist represents the online version of a stroll that accidentally found itself in a good neighborhood: Everyone's complaining. Ever since Craigslist broke into mainstream consciousness, there has been a spike in cultural chatter on the subject of prostitution being advertised online. When the sex marketplace was relegated to its own particular websites that no-one who wasn't looking for them would accidentally stumble across, the sex industry remained relatively under the radar, even though its market share of commerce on the Internet was significant and growing. With Craigslist, however, broader audiences of web users are suddenly being exposed to brazen prostitution on one of their favorite websites. If you ask most Americans about online prostitution advertising, they will probably answer, "Do you mean, Craigslist?"

Craigslist's huge audience as well as its basic structure has been great for sex workers: it's free, there are tons of people looking, and it's very simple to use. It's also a site that many former street workers have turned to as a way of leaving street solicitation. I spoke to "Frannie," a 47-year-old former street worker from the Bronx, about her postings on Craigslist after she responded to my Craigslist ad. Frannie told me about how Craigslist helped her to leave the street.

I never used no computer until last year when my kid—he's 21—showed me Craigslist and said to me, 'Yo, ma, here's where they look for some so you don't have to stand on no street corner. At my age, I don't get mad customers, not like when I was young. I have another job too, but I put up my ad every few days, check my hotmail, and every now and then I get some extra cash without freezing my butt off or messing with crack heads. I'm too old for that shit.

When I asked Frannie if she knew of others who were able to move their work off the streets because of Craigslist, she added, "Anyone who's not a crack head or just likes it out there for God-knows-what reason is coming inside if they have sense."

Last summer I attended a public meeting of Manhattan's 10th Precinct Community Council where a Hell's Kitchen neighborhood resident asked an officer making his report what the precinct was doing to arrest street prostitutes and clean up the area. The officer replied that NYPD sent out vice patrol every night to what were considered problem spots by the community but that there were very few arrests because they couldn't find any street prostitutes. A few residents commented on how the strolls tended to migrate to keep up with the police, but the officer interrupted and said, "You know, a lot of these people just do this online now."

The numbers tell the same story. The city of Chicago was reported by *The New York Times* to have had 43 street-based arrests in July of 2007—and

60 Craigslist arrests. The Times story that included that fact was published as a front-pager on September 5, 2007, "As Prostitutes Turn to Craigslist, Law Takes Notice." The article, which re-discovered Internet prostitution, describes how police departments from "Hawaii to New Hampshire" are spending more and more of their time trolling the Erotic Services section of Craigslist. In it, Nassau County Assistant Chief of Detectives Richard McGuire called Craigslist "the high-tech 42nd Street, where much of the solicitation takes place now."

As with print advertising, online advertising creates an openness and (digital) paper-trail that can make it easier for police to track down the bad guys. I don't just mean traffickers but also other men (clients or management) who may be abusing prostitutes.

Right now, the war on prostitution advertising is striking some serious blows against industry workers. The right to free speech guaranteed by the U.S. Constitution protects our ads where they appear in print (online or in print publishing), but if newspapers refuse to accept our business because they are afraid of being labeled as "facilitators of trafficking" and the major market share websites become unsafe because of police entrapment operations, there will soon be few choices left for prostitutes, many of them choices that make women less safe and less money.

Caroline Andrews is a former escort who lives and works in New York City.

Source: Andrews, Caroline. "Market Penetration: The War on Prostitution Advertising," *$pread* magazine, 3, no. 4 (2008). Used with permission.

"EPIDEMIC OF NEGLECT: TRANS WOMEN SEX WORKERS AND HIV" BY MACK FRIEDMAN

We call them *hijra* in India, *waria* in Indonesia, *katoey* in Thailand, *travestis* in Brazil. They've been plying their trade for thousands of years, since male slaves were sold wearing face paint at ancient Roman auctions. Here in America, we've come up with other vernacular through the centuries: man-monsters, faeries, transvestites. Academia has settled on the cumbersome term "male-to-female transgender individuals engaged in transactional sex" to define people who were born male but express a female gender identity when sex-working. That's a little rocky to read, so I'll use trans sex workers from now on.

The first American report of trans sex work that's been found was recorded in 1836 in a New York tabloid, when Peter Sewally (who used the aliases Eliza Smith and Mary Jones) was arrested for rolling a trick in a Manhattan alleyway. (She got five years in prison for running off with the man's bank book.) Trans sex work is not a new phenomenon, but I'm not here to oil you up with the glistening history of nancy boys (you can read my book, *Strapped for*

Cash, if that's what you're looking for). I want to talk about what's going on right now, because our trans street sisters are in serious danger, all over the world, and it's hard to find anyone who's doing anything about it.

We're talking, of course, about HIV. When we think about HIV infecting certain populations, trans sex workers may not be the first group that comes to mind. We might think about pregnant women in South Africa, over one-quarter of whom are infected. Or intravenous drug users in Moscow, almost half of whom are living with HIV. But trans sex workers have been shown to bear HIV rates from fifteen to 81 percent in the two dozen studies conducted since 1987. Eighty-one percent is one of the highest rates of HIV infection ever recorded anywhere, and it happened right here in America, in Georgia. Incredibly high HIV rates among trans sex workers have also been discovered in a number of other countries, as we will soon see.

In the 25-year history of HIV, only four HIV prevalence studies among trans sex workers have been conducted and published in the United States (in peer-reviewed journals). In Atlanta, San Francisco, and Los Angeles, hundreds of trans sex workers were tested for HIV; in each case, they had infection rates above 25 percent.

These studies are listed below (Appendix Table 2.1).

A sociologist named Jackie Boles analyzed the findings of a study in Atlanta. Comparing two main strolls, Foggy Bottom and Midtown, Boles found HIV prevalence rates of 81.1 percent and 37.5 percent, respectively. These differences were the first warning that HIV could be very dangerous for trans sex-working ethnic and racial minorities throughout the world. "Foggy Bottom," wrote Boles, "is characterized by extreme poverty, racial segregation (all participants from this locale were black), and a deteriorating physical environment." On the other hand, the trans women working in Midtown were more likely to be white (56 percent) and only 26 percent

Appendix Table 2.1
U.S. Studies of HIV Prevalence in Male-to-Female Transgender People Involved in Sex Work (TGSW), 1988–2001

City	Data Collected	HIV Prevalence	N (Enrolled TGSW)	Lead Author
Atlanta	1988–91	68%	53	Elifson
San Francisco	1997	40%	312	Clements-Nolle
Los Angeles	1998–99	26%	121	Simon
San Francisco	2000–01	26%	332	Nemoto

reported being paid for receptive anal intercourse. Because the Atlanta studies were conducted in 1987, we can view their results as a cross-section of the time when the first wave of HIV was peaking in the United States.

But why were trans sex workers getting the virus at such high rates? Boles points out that the high prevalence found in Atlanta might indicate that the trans sex-working community was "ghettoized ... an oppressed minority within an oppressed minority" and subject to a variety of negative social factors that quickly made it a reservoir for HIV. In most of the world, including the United States, transgender people face serious job discrimination. When you are being interviewed as a woman named Denise, and your state ID lists you as Harold, potential employers might get confused and angry and refuse to hire you. But that's just the edge of the blade. When you factor in the high school dropout rates among trans women (getting made fun of and beat up in class would make anyone not want to go to school anymore), and the inevitable gaps in the resume (can't exactly put sex work on your CV, can you?), employers don't always have to work too hard to find reasons not to hire transgender people while still abiding by the non-discrimination laws that some progressive cities have enacted. The difficulties transgender people encounter when looking for legal employment force many to engage in sex work in order to survive.

And when they do engage in sex work, transgender women generally find themselves at the low end of the totem pole in terms of prestige and power. They have been found to make less per trick than non-transgender male and female sex workers, and they are more likely to work the streets than in bars and clubs. In addition, researchers have found that the strolls that trans sex workers occupy are less desirable than the strolls available to non-transgender sex workers. Taking this one step further, the strolls that are available to trans sex workers of color tend to be less desirable than those available to whites. What does this mean? More competition; price gouging; less ability and economic incentive to negotiate safe sex with tricks. Less patrolled strolls can attract violent clients and lead to physical and sexual assaults; more patrolled strolls leave trans sex workers subject to high visibility and greater incarceration rates. All of these reasons and more contribute to the finding that trans sex workers of color in Atlanta were six times more likely to have HIV than their white colleagues.

In the late 1990s, after HIV had peaked in most American populations, Dr. Tooru Nemoto found that an alarming 47 percent of sex-working African American transgender sex workers in San Francisco were HIV positive. Among white trans sex workers, unprotected receptive anal intercourse was taking place primarily between primary and casual partners, not commercial partners. But this was *not* true for the African Americans Nemoto studied, who were five times more likely than whites to get paid for unsafe sex.

In Dr. Paul Simon's study, 44 percent of African American trans sex workers were HIV positive, compared with 16 percent of whites. Dr. Cathy Reback later analyzed Simon's data, and found that sex work "was not directly associated with HIV infection," although she found it was "associated with the other factors that related to HIV seroprevalence." These other risk factors included unsafe needle use, higher numbers of non-paying partners, and substance use during sex. Nemoto noted that "paying for drugs can increase financial strain and dependence on sex work for income." And, as many of us know from personal experience, tricking can increase the demand for drugs in order to cope with emotional and physical stresses that often ensue from engaging in unpleasant, forced, or unsafe sex.

Economic coercion seems also to heighten HIV risk among American trans sex workers. Many of us have been in a situation where a client offered us twice as much case (or more) to have unprotected sex. Dr. Boles reported that johns comparison-shopped, finding the individual who would "perform the desired sex act for the least money," and that African American trans sex workers generally were paid the least per act. Dr. Nemoto agreed with these pressures. His focus group findings suggest that "economic pressure compelled many to compromise their condom rules and engage in unsafe sex for increased money." Clements-Nolle writes that "many male-to-female transgender persons turn to sex work because they face severe employment discrimination," and that this might account for the "high numbers of sexual partners and prevalence of sex work" among study participants. Because American sex work is illegal and underground, there is not always room for sex workers to negotiate. In addition, trans sex workers frequently work on their own, independent of pimps and procurers who might find a john that wasn't playing by the rules and set him straight.

But even in countries where sex work was legal, HIV rates among trans sex workers soared in the 1990s. There are fifteen relevant international studies, and each of them corroborates our limited U.S. evidence of very high HIV rates among trans sex workers. HIV prevalence trends within the global trans sex work population are remarkably consistent, showing a sharp peak of infection in the late 1980s and early 1990s in Western countries (infecting 57 percent to 81 percent of street-based sex workers surveyed), and gradually decreasing since then to its current level of 11 percent to 26 percent (see Appendix Table 2.2). Smaller cities with less immigration, like Antwerp and Rotterdam, tended to have the lowest HIV rates, while larger ones with more immigration, like Rome and Sao Paulo, had higher rates. Both domestically

Appendix Table 2.2
International Studies of HIV Prevalence in Transgender Women Involved in Sex Work (TGSW), 1986–2004

City	Data Collected	HIV Prevalence	N (TGSW Enrolled)	Lead Author
Milan	1986–89	57%	49	Galli
Sao Paolo	1987	62%	37	Sulieman
Tel Aviv	1987–90	11%	36	Modan
Rome	1989–90	74%	57	Gattari
Sao Paolo	1992	61%	112	Grandi
Rome	1993–99	38% (declining)	353	Spizzichino
Rotterdam, NL	1994–95	8%	38	Wiessing
Amsterdam	1996	24%	25	Gras
Rio de Janeiro	1994–1996	63%	46	Inciardi
Rome	1997–98	20%	40	Verster
Montevideo	1999	22%	192	Russi
Spain (various)	2000–02	15%	76	Belza
Jakarta	2002	22%	241	Pisani
Madrid	1998-2003	23%	60	Gutierrez
Antwerp	1999–2004	11%	53	Leuridan

and internationally, one-third of all trans sex workers tested for HIV have come up positive.

These international studies also corroborate American findings of racial minorities bearing higher HIV rates in the trans sex work world. In Milan in the 1980s, 76 percent of South American foreign nationals were HIV positive compared to 38 percent of Italian natives. Typically, male sex worker HIV prevalence rates have been considerably lower, more in keeping with the gay male community: 18 percent in New Orleans, twelve percent in Long Beach, four percent in Jakarta. And compared to female sex workers, trans sex worker HIV rates have been exponentially higher: working girls had less than one percent HIV prevalence in Montevideo, Amsterdam, and Madrid, and a range in HIV prevalence from less than one percent to six percent in Rome, Barcelona, London, and other European cities. Meanwhile, trans sex worker HIV prevalence rates have been five to thirty times higher throughout North

Appendix Table 2.3
Aggregated Domestic and International HIV Prevalence among Transgender Women Involved in Sex Work (TGSW): 19 Research Studies, 1986–2004

City	Data Collected	HIV Prevalence	N (TGSW Enrolled)	N (HIV+ TGSW Enrolled)
Domestic United States	1988–1999	34%	818	279
International	1986–2004	33%	1415	471
All	1986–2003	34%	2233	750

America and Western Europe, and have approached rates seen previously only among female sex workers in sub-Saharan Africa.

Transgender sex workers have been significantly absent from the world's scientific literature (if not from the planet's sexual awareness). This is perhaps best described by the authors of a Thai study on drug-using men, who note that their participants often paid *katoey* for sex. "This cultural pattern has been remarkably little studied," they concluded.

A Medline search (on February 12, 2005) on the term "Katoey" yielded no scientific publications—a "Google" search on the same term (on February 12, 2005) yielded 25,600 results including bars, clubs, cabaret shows, dating services, and chat rooms dedicated to Thai Katoey. Although HIV and sexual health research may have overlooked Katoey, the sex and tourism industries have not.

The scarcity of HIV prevalence studies here in America indicates a more systemic bias in this country's research funding structure. If HIV prevalence rates in the four studies conducted here are any indication, corroborative studies should have been done in *every major city in America*. The literature is limited: there is no published data for HIV prevalence among trans sex workers in New York City, Miami, Philadelphia, Boston, or Seattle, and no HIV prevalence research available on Midwestern populations where substantial transgender sex work takes place, such as Chicago and Minneapolis.

In the United States, there is significant scientific stigma attached to lesbian, gay, bisexual, and transgender (LGBT) health research. Nemoto's group at the University of California-San Francisco Center for AIDS Prevention Studies was recently audited by the Department of Health and Human Services; Nemoto was one of several research scientists whose work on LGBT and sex work-related issues was targeted for audits. Dr. Emilia Lombardi, one of Dr. Simon's collaborators, made a recent Congressional "hit list" for her interest in transgender research. "Studies of gay men, prostitutes come under scrutiny," headlined a *Science* article of February 2005 in response to a Congressional inquiry on government-funded research in sexuality and health. The Association of Reproductive Health Professionals warned researchers against using "sex work" and "transgender," among several other terms, in government grant applications. The message: your research won't get funded if it has anything to do with transgender sex work.

This *de facto* censorship of American public health research has both direct and indirect elements and consequences, and clearly deters researchers from examining health conditions in trans sex work communities. It is difficult to get tenure if you cannot publish your research; it is difficult to publish when the journals are squeamish about your research focus; and it is difficult to get grants from a government agency that refuses to read grants involving the population you want to research. My own public health professors have suggested that I focus on something more "practical," for instance. (One in particular listened to me present on this health issue, and then asked, "Why should I care?") Other well-meaning advisers have suggested that I could still apply for grants by focusing on faith-based initiatives to help people escape prostitution. While I look quite fetching in my cape and boots, I have chosen to leave supernatural interventions to the Ghostbusters.

The crack and heroin research guru Dr. James Inciardi points out that barriers faced by our researchers aren't limited to America. Discussing Brazil, he writes, "Doctors who work with street people, prostitutes, and transvestites in Rio de Janeiro, for example, report hostile reactions on the part of their medical colleagues as they themselves, apparently through guilt by association, come to be seen as sources of contagion and risk." This has had the effect of squelching relevant research as well as diminishing necessary access to care.

There are no solid estimates for the number of transgender people who live in the United States, and no health data is collected routinely on transgender people in surveys administered by the U.S. Census or the National Center of Health Statistics. In none of these large government assays is "transgender" even a gender category to choose from. Local research centers, erstwhile academic studies, and community-based organizations are by default the only realistic mechanisms by which to collect trans sex work data.

In the studies we have cited, minority ethnicity consistently compounded already high HIV risks for trans sex workers. Ethnic and racial minorities were found to be marginalized even within trans sex-working communities. Their magnified HIV risk can be seen as a reflection of their extraordinarily limited social agency and grave economic coercion: when you're that low on the totem pole and you can't get a job, you have to make money somehow. Being transgender can often lead to severely reduced legal employment options via job discrimination. Racial and ethnic minority status (and/or foreign national status), while contributing to job discrimination, were also found to reduce individuals' market value within sex work. Being underpaid compared to male and female sex workers leads to reduced sexual safety within the sexual economy both by price constraint (having to turn more tricks to make as much money as non-minorities and non-transgender sex workers) and increased customer leverage (having unsafe sex to meet sex client demands or risk losing the client). Many of these studies cited violence (including frequent murder sprees) as another major occupational hazard faced by trans sex workers.

What can we do about this? First, we can insist on conducting our own research, getting degrees and grants, and doing it right. We can help established researchers gain interest in this community by alerting them to these criminally high infection rates and the massive health care costs associated with them, bills footed mostly by taxpayers—when was the last time you saw a trans sex worker with a health insurance plan besides Medicare? Second, we can keep reading, educating ourselves, and voting for politicians and ordinances that advocate targeted social services and expanding the employment rights of transgender people (as well as sex workers as a whole). Third, we can get out onto the streets and the Internet, and talk to the working girls and the johns, to remind them how risky unsafe sex work can be. And finally, we can keep doing our own research on the economic costs of managing health problems among sex workers instead of solving them. Ultimately, I bet it's cheaper to give a gal her own apartment, a day job, and health insurance than foot her ER bill when she gets stabbed or raped or has an overdose or a staph infection from the used needle she injected hormones with. When we can convince a narrow-minded public health professor that it makes economic sense to do the right thing, then we can convince the narrow-minded public, too.

Mack Friedman is the author of Setting the Lawn on Fire: A Novel, *winner of the Publishers Triangle/Edmund White Debut Fiction Award and* Strapped for Cash: A History of American Hustler Culture, *a Lambda Literary Award finalist in LGBT Studies. He is a researcher and doctoral student at the University of Pittsburgh.*

Source: An earlier version of Mack Friedman's "Epidemic of Neglect: Trans Women Sex Workers and HIV" was printed in *$pread* magazine, 2, no. 1 (2006). Used with permission.

"THE CRIMINALIZATION OF SURVIVAL: POVERTY, VIOLENCE AND PROSTITUTION"

The article below was written for a Community Dialogue on "Criminalization of Survival: Poverty, Violence and Prostitution" held in San Francisco on

June 9, 2005 and sponsored by the US PROStitutes Collective (US PROS). The organizing initiatives described below, from the groundbreaking Task Force on Prostitution in 1996 to the 2008 Proposition K voter ballot initiative to decriminalize prostitution in San Francisco were led by sex workers. Proposition K received 41 percent of the vote.

You need look no further than the case of serial rapist Jack Bokin to know why the San Francisco Board of Supervisors (BOS) resolution 810-00 Mitigating Violence Against Prostitutes should be immediately implemented. Bokin had attacked and violently raped at least three women when Judge Perker Meeks let him out on bail.

When the case came to court the prostitute women who testified against him faced a character assassination and were made to feel that they were on trial rather than their attacker. But a campaign spearheaded by US PROStitutes Collective and Legal Action for Women kept a constant presence of observers in and out of court, and ensured that the proceedings were publicized. This time the court was under public scrutiny. Bokin was finally convicted and sentenced to 231 years.

Rachel West from US PROS described the case as a "prototype of how sex workers are treated by the police and courts when they report rape and sexual assault."

The "Mitigating Violence Against Prostitutes" resolution demands that: those accused of coercion, extortion, battery, rape and other violent crimes against sex workers be arrested and vigorously prosecuted, and for the $7.6 million (1996 figure, $11.4 million in 2007) the city spends to enforce anti-prostitution laws be redirected into resources and services. Its implementation could mean that, for the first time, the police and courts would be truly obliged to prioritize protecting prostitute women from rape and other violence.

The resolution grew out of one of the most comprehensive community consultations on the issue of prostitution. The 1996 San Francisco Task Force on Prostitution of which US PROS was a key member, uniquely brought together representatives from Black, immigrant, youth, lesbian, bisexual, gay and transgender and women's groups, organizations on AIDS, health workers and lawyers together with the Mayor's office, the District Attorney, the public health department, the police and neighborhood residents. For the first time sex worker organizations were included and the police didn't dominate the agenda. Public concern over violence against sex workers was instrumental in making it happen.

After two years of active debate and careful considerations, the Task Force put forward groundbreaking recommendations reflecting the public sentiment that the City should move towards decriminalizing prostitution.

Recommendations included shifting police priorities by stopping the arrest and prosecution of sex workers and customers, vigorously enforce laws against rape and other violent crimes, redirect money currently spent on enforcement of the prostitution laws into services, support asylum and protection from violence and abuse for sex workers who are immigrant or refugee, support services for youth, lobby for the removal of prostitution-related offenses as grounds for deportation or denial of citizenship, recognize sex workers as workers with legal, civil and employment rights.

Decriminalization is supported by people from all walks of life because all the evidence shows that criminalization makes sex workers more vulnerable to violence. Prostitute women facing rape, sexual assault and murder are afraid to report violence for fear of arrest (especially if they have outstanding warrants) or deportation. So violent men feel they can hunt down hookers and get away with it.

Nia Jackson from the In Defense of Prostitute Women's Safety Project describes the problem:

A woman who wanted to press charges against a violent rapist was prevented from doing so because the police insisted that any outstanding warrants against her would be enforced, despite receiving a letter from the Office of Citizen Complaints. We later heard that the same man had attacked another woman.

Where a woman courageously persists and a case comes to court she is then subjected to what many women describe as the second rape. Sexism, hostility, indifference from the police and courts ensures that very few rape cases end in conviction, even less where the victim is a prostitute. Black, Latina or other women of color who face racism at every stage of the criminal justice process are even less likely to get protection or any form of redress against rape, racist sexual assault or other violence. Serial attackers often start with prostitute women (or with wives and other family members who suffer a similar lack of protection) and then go on to attack other women, proving our slogan that "when prostitute women aren't safe, no woman is safe."

Criminalization also traps women and young people in prostitution. One woman described it as "The conviction that ruined my life." She had tried for all kinds of jobs since getting a criminal record and had been rejected from all. When she was eventually employed her employer was able to pay her less because he knew she couldn't go elsewhere.

Extending criminalization in the form of Stay Out of Areas of Prostitution (SOAP) orders has had a devastating effect on the safety of people on the street. Introduced in the 90's, SOAPs ban people from an area under threat of a fine or prison sentence. They have encouraged abuse of power by the police and have fuelled a climate of hostility against children and young people, sex workers, Black people and immigrant people.

The Criminalization of Survival

When women working in Capp Street in San Francisco were asked what changes would enable them to get out of prostitution they almost unanimously answered: affordable housing and childcare. About 70 percent of prostitute women are mothers, mostly single mothers struggling to support families. There is little or no recognition for women as the primary caregivers in society. With women's wages still pitched at less than 76 percent of men's, and mothers among the lowest paid workers, most jobs available to women go nowhere near covering the costs of survival. Welfare "reform" has destroyed the safety net which saved many from destitution—over 11 million mainly women—headed families have lost their sole income.

And what of the thousands of homeless people who are forced to sell sex to survive? Why are they there? According to a 1991 Senate Judiciary hearing, nationally 50 percent of all homeless women and children are on the streets because of violence in the home. One third of San Francisco's homeless are women. Yet domestic violence is still treated as a low priority by San Francisco police.

As a result of pressure from homeless people, the District Attorney in San Francisco recently agreed to an amnesty which withdraws all pending warrants for so-called nuisance "crimes." This amnesty could easily be extended to sex workers facing charges of loitering and soliciting. It would help break the endless cycle where women are forced back on the streets to pay outstanding fines and, as mentioned above, would go a long way in enabling women to report violence.

With welfare cuts more women, especially mothers, have ended up in jail for "crimes of poverty." Those convicted of a drug-related felony are no longer entitled to welfare at any time in their life. What are women supposed to do to ensure that there is food on the table?

While women and children are refused the bare essentials of life and we are told there is no money for education, health care, housing and social security, the military budget continues to grow and $1.1 billion dollars a day is squandered on the wars in Iraq and Afghanistan.

Money and Resources for Women

The "Mitigating Violence against Prostitutes" resolution would free up much needed resources currently wasted on criminalization. The Task Force found that tax payers pay over $7 million a year on arrests, street sweeps, decoy operations, prosecutions and jailing of sex workers but "there is no evidence that it does any more than force street workers to move from one place to the next."

Currently, the vulnerability caused by criminalization and its resulting stigmatization, prevents most prostitute women from getting access to services, and saying what services are needed and how to make existing services accessible and relevant. How can services be effective if those of us who live and/or work on the streets are not involved in shaping them? Forcing women to accept services under threat of prosecution is not protection. It is judgmental, punitive and abusive.

We don't want to be corralled into hostels which are little better than prisons. Staff at one place told us that our children were better off without us. That's wrong seeing as I went on the streets in the first place to support my daughter after my violent ex left us with nothing.

Services including drug rehabilitation have to be voluntary and independent of the police and criminal justice system. We want the money for welfare benefits, affordable housing and childcare—all the resources that would enable women to leave prostitution if they want to. Community-based bodies which include sex workers could monitor the services to ensure that the principle of helping women is enforced.

Arresting Johns

What has not worked and must not be extended is the "Johns School" (First Offender Prostitution Program, FOPP). Under FOPP, men facing prostitution charges have the option of attending a course, for which they pay a $1,000 fee, instead of being prosecuted. Yet women report that arresting clients makes it even more dangerous to work on the streets. Established safety systems among women are broken up and negotiations with clients have to be done faster as there is less time to check men out. People out on the streets for reasons unrelated to prostitution, often people of color, get targeted in these police stings.

According to the public defender's office, there is no record of how much money is made from arresting men nightly, but fees paid are divided between the District Attorney office, the police and The SAGE Project, Inc. The SAGE Project runs FOPP and provides services—counseling, outreach for prostitute women and young people referred by the police and courts after arrest. Mothers are forced to attend SAGE to get their children back from Child Protective Services. SAGE opposes the decriminalization of prostitution, but their opposition has to be seen in the context of benefiting financially from people being arrested and referred to their programs—less arrests would mean less money and decriminalization would render them obsolete.

FOPP claims that its program can impact the issue of the trafficking of women. In fact the opposite is true as criminalizing sex workers and clients makes it harder for anyone to come forward to report violence and exploitation. Figures showing numbers of trafficked women, often put forward by organizations which have a vested interest in promoting trafficking as a burgeoning problem, are wildly exaggerated—no distinction is made between genuine victims and immigrant women working independently in the sex industry. Increasingly people understand that trafficking is not about prostitution but about immigration, women from poorer countries coming to the United States to improve their lives, and that anti-trafficking laws are being used primarily to target and deport those of us who are immigrant not to protect us.

Legalization versus Decriminalization

Other options that have at times being considered are the legalization of prostitution and/or zoning. This was rejected at the time of the Task Force and is vigorously opposed by the majority of prostitute women. Where legalization or zones exist, they are usually in isolated industrial areas, further segregating women from the rest of the community. Having to register with the police prevents women leaving prostitution and getting other jobs.

Women in the Netherlands describe the impact of legalization there:

A two-tier system has developed where premises can be licensed but street work, except in the few "tipplezones" remains illegal. Police use their powers to clamp down even harder on those who do not work in the legalised areas. . . . Administrative and legal controls have been intensified by the Dutch police in order to ban and deport illegals, in line with the overall stricter control of illegal migrants.—Gisela Dutting, Women's *Global Network for Reproductive Rights* newsletter, no. 3, 2000.

Those who proposed toleration zones have often been shown to be more interested in the potential revenue of an expanded sex industry than in protecting the rights of sex workers.

New Zealand decriminalized prostitution, including street work, over six years ago. The New Zealand Prostitutes Collective reports that: "Decriminalisation has made a big difference to whether women feel able to report rape and other violence. We have made substantial gains and in some cases have turned police and courts around. Women can now question police actions."

It is clear that the demand is intensifying in San Francisco and many other places for an end to criminalization of sex work and the violence and divisiveness it promotes. The Task Force recommendations can guide us and the implementation of Resolution 810-00 would be a significant step on the road to justice for all of us made vulnerable to violence and other degradation by poverty and lack of resources.

Source: "The Criminalization of Survival," produced by the US PROStitutes Collective, used with permission.

Appendix 3

Legal Documents and Commentary

THE MANN ACT OF 1910

The Mann Act of 1910, the U.S. federal law also called the White Slave Traffic Act, was passed in 1910 during a white slavery panic. It is a federal law, meaning that it is in force throughout the United States and its territory. This Act initially prohibited women and girls, but not men and boys, traveling across state lines for unspecified "immoral purposes" and for prostitution and debauchery, or inducement to become a prostitute or debauched. The Mann Act was passed in the name of protecting women from "white slavery," but the people prosecuted under the Mann Act were overwhelmingly women, many of whom were arrested for traveling to meet boyfriends and fiancés.

CHAP. 395 — An Act to further regulate interstate commerce and foreign commerce by prohibiting the transportation therein for immoral purposes of women and girls, and for other purposes.

Be it enacted by the Senate and House of Representatives of the United States of America in Congress assembled, That the term "interstate commerce," as used in this Act, shall include transportation from any State or Territory or the District of Columbia, and the term "foreign commerce," as used in this Act, shall include transportation from any State or Territory or the District of Columbia to any foreign country and from any foreign country to any State or Territory or the District of Columbia.

SEC. 2. That any person who shall knowingly transport or cause to be transported, or aid or assist in obtaining transportation for, or in transporting, in interstate or foreign commerce, or in any Territory or in the District of Columbia, any woman or girl for the purpose of prostitution or debauchery, or for any other immoral purpose, or with the intent and purpose to induce, entice, or compel such woman or girl to become a prostitute or to give herself up to debauchery, or to engage in any other immoral practice; or who shall knowingly procure or obtain, or cause to be procured or obtained, or aid or assist in procuring or obtaining, any ticket or tickets, or any form of transportation or evidence of the right thereto, to be used by any woman or girl in interstate or foreign commerce, or in any Territory or the District of Columbia, in going to any place for the purpose of prostitution or debauchery, or for any other immoral purpose, or with the intent or purpose on the part of such person to induce, entice, or compel her to give herself up to the practice of prostitution, or to give herself up to the practice of debauchery, or any other immoral practice, whereby any such woman or girl shall be transported in interstate or foreign commerce, or in any Territory or the District of Columbia, shall be deemed guilty of a felony, and upon conviction thereof shall be punished by a fine not exceeding five thousand dollars, or by imprisonment of not more than five years, or by both such fine and imprisonment, in the discretion of the court.

SEC. 3. That any person who shall knowingly persuade, induce, entice, or coerce, or cause to be persuaded, induced, enticed, or coerced, or aid or assist in persuading, inducing, enticing or coercing any woman or girl to go from one place to another in interstate or foreign commerce, or in any Territory or the District of Columbia, for the purpose of prostitution or debauchery, or for any other immoral purpose, or with the intent and purpose on the part of such person that such woman or girl shall engage in the practice of prostitution or debauchery, or any other immoral practice, whether with or without her consent, and who shall there by knowingly cause or aid or assist in causing such woman or girl to go and be carried or transported as a passenger upon the line or route of any common carrier or carriers in interstate or foreign commerce, or any Territory or the District of Columbia, shall be deemed guilty of a felony and on conviction thereof shall be punished by a fine of not more than five thousand dollars, or by imprisonment for a term not exceeding five years, or by both fine and imprisonment, in the discretion of the court.

SEC. 4. That any person who shall knowingly persuade, induce, entice or coerce any woman or girl under the age of eighteen years from any State or Territory or the District of Columbia to any other State or Territory or the District of Columbia, with the purpose and intent to induce or coerce her, or that she shall be induced or coerced to engage in prostitution or debauchery, or any other immoral practice, and shall in furtherance of such purpose knowingly induce or cause her to go and to be carried or transported as a passenger in interstate commerce upon the line or route of any common carrier or carriers, shall be deemed guilty of a felony, and in conviction there of shall be punished by a fine of not more than ten thousand dollars, or by imprisonment for a term not exceeding ten years, or by both such fine and imprisonment, in the discretion of the court.

SEC. 5. That any violation of any of the above sections two, three, and four shall be prosecuted in any court having jurisdiction of crimes within the district in which said violation was committed, or from, through, or into which any such woman or girl may have been carried or transported as a passenger in interstate or foreign commerce, or in any Territory or the District of Columbia, contrary to the provisions of any of said sections.

SEC. 6. That for the purpose of regulating and preventing the transportation in foreign commerce of alien women and girls for purposes of prostitution and debauchery, and in pursuance of and for the purpose of carrying out the terms of the agreement of project of arrangement for the suppression of the white-slave traffic, adopted July twenty-fifth, nineteen hundred and two, for submission to their respective governments by the delegates of various powers represented at the Paris conference and confirmed by a formal agreement signed at Paris on May eighteenth, nineteen hundred and four, and adhered to by the United States on June sixth, nineteen hundred and eight, as shown by the proclamation of the President of the United States, dated June fifteenth, nineteen hundred and eight, the Commissioner-General of Immigration is hereby designated as the authority of the United States to receive and centralize information concerning the procuration of alien women and girls with a view to their debauchery, and to exercise supervision over such alien women and girls, receive their declarations, establish their identity, and ascertain from them who induced them to leave their native countries, respectively; and it shall be the duty of said Commissioner-General of Immigration to receive and keep on file in his office the statements and declarations which may be made by such alien women and girls, and those which are hereinafter required pertaining to such alien women and girls engaged in prostitution and debauchery in this country, and to furnish receipts for such statements and declarations provided for in this act to the persons, respectively, making and filing them.

Every person who shall keep, maintain, control, support or harbor in any house or place for the purpose of prostitution, or for any other immoral purpose, any alien woman or girl within three years after she shall have entered the United States from any country, party to the said arrangement for the suppression of the white-slave traffic, shall file with the Commissioner-General of Immigration a statement in writing setting forth the name of such alien woman or girl, the place at which she is kept, and all facts as to the date of her entry into the United States, the port through which she entered, her age, nationality, and parentage, and concerning her procuration to come to this country within the knowledge of such person, and any person who shall fail within thirty days after such person shall commence to keep, maintain, control, support, or harbor in any house or place for the purpose of prostitution, or for any other immoral purpose, any alien woman or girl within three years after she shall have entered the United States from any of the countries, party to the said arrangement for the suppression of the white-slave traffic, to file such statement concerning such alien woman or girl with the Commissioner-General of Immigration, or who shall knowingly and willfully state falsely or fail to disclose in such statement any fact within his knowledge or belief with reference, to the age, nationality, or parentage of any such alien woman or girl, or concerning her procuration to come to this country, shall be deemed guilty of a misdemeanor, and on conviction shall be punished by a fine of not more than two thousand dollars, or by imprisonment for a term not exceeding two years, or by both such fine and imprisonment, in the discretion of the court.

In any prosecution brought under this section, if it appear that any such statement required is not on file in the office of the Commissioner-General of Immigration, the person whose duty it shall be to file such statement shall be presumed to have failed to file said statement, as herein required, unless such person or persons shall prove otherwise. No person shall be excused from furnishing the statement, as required by this section, on the ground or for the reason that the statement so required by him, or the information therein contained, might tend to criminate him or subject him to a penalty or forfeiture, but no person shall be prosecuted or subjected to any penalty or forfeiture under any law of the United States for or on account of any transaction, matter, or thing, concerning which he may truthfully report in such statement, as required by the provisions of this section.

SEC. 7. That the term "Territory," as used in this Act, shall include the district of Alaska, the insular possessions of the United States, and the Canal Zone. The word "person," as used in this Act, shall be construed to import both the plural and the singular, as the case demands, and shall include corporations, companies, societies, and associations. When construing and enforcing the provisions of this Act, the act, omission, or failure of any officer, agent, or other person, acting for or employed by any other person or by any corporation, company, society, or association, within the scope of his employment or office, shall in every case be also deemed to be the act, omission, or failure of such other person, or of such company, society, or association as well of that of the person himself.

SEC. 8. That this Act shall be known and referred to as the "White-slave traffic Act."

Approved, Sixty-First Congress, June 25, 1910.

The Mann Act was amended to apply only to acts that are criminal in the location in which they were committed:

18 USCS @ 2421 (1994) @ 2421.

*** THIS SECTION IS CURRENT THROUGH P.L. 103-321, APPROVED

8/26/94 ***

TITLE 18. CRIMES AND CRIMINAL PROCEDURE PART I. CRIMES

CHAPTER 117. TRANSPORTATION FOR ILLEGAL SEXUAL ACTIVITY AND

RELATED CRIMES @ 2421.

Transportation generally

Whoever knowingly transports any individual in interstate or foreign commerce, or in any Territory or Possession of the United States, with intent that such individual engage in prostitution, or in any sexual activity for which any person can be charged with a criminal offense, shall be fined under this title or imprisoned not more than five years, or both.

Source: Mann Act of 1910 (White Slave Traffic Act) (ch. 395, 36 Stat. 825; codified as amended at 18 U.S.C. § 2421–2424)

"THE USE OF RAIDS TO FIGHT TRAFFICKING IN PERSONS"

Below are selected excerpts from a report by Melissa Ditmore for the Sex Workers Project at the Urban Justice Center. These excerpts were chosen because they clarify U.S. anti-trafficking law, its enforcement, and its effects.

Trafficking in persons refers to the transportation and compulsion of an individual into any form of labor through use of force, threats of force, fraud, or coercion, or debt bondage. In 2000, the United States passed legislation recognizing "serious forms of trafficking" as "recruitment, harboring, transportation, provision, or obtaining of a person for labor or services, through the use of force, fraud, or coercion" in all forms of labor, including, but not limited to, sex work, bringing domestic legislation in line with international standards governing trafficking in persons.[1]

Enforcement of federal anti-trafficking legislation has taken place in large part through anti-trafficking raids, conducted by federal law enforcement agents, and vice raids targeting prostitution conducted by local law enforcement agencies. Notwithstanding the broader reach of the current legislative definition of trafficking, U.S. law enforcement agencies have been criticized for continuing to focus on trafficking into sex work to the exclusion of other widespread forms of trafficking.[2] Indeed the word "trafficking" primarily evokes images of women and children forced into sexual servitude in the popular imagination and, prior to 2000, anti-trafficking legislation focused exclusively on prostitution, based on the presumption that no woman would ever exchange sex for material gain without extreme coercion. In reality, trafficking occurs in a far broader range of sectors and types of work, including domestic work, agricultural labor, manufacturing and the service industries, and affects men as well as women and children.

This report summarizes the findings of a human rights documentation project conducted by the Sex Workers Project in 2007 and 2008 to explore the impacts and effectiveness of current anti-trafficking approaches in the United States from a variety of perspectives. It is among the first efforts since the passage of the Trafficking Victims Protection Reauthorization Act to give voice to the experiences and perspectives of trafficked persons and sex workers who have experienced anti-trafficking raids. A total of 46 people were interviewed for this report, including immigrant sex workers and trafficked persons who have experienced raids or otherwise had contact with law enforcement, service providers, attorneys, and law enforcement personnel.

The data collected from this small to medium-sized sample is extremely rich, and suggests that vice raids conducted by local law enforcement agencies are an ineffective means of locating and identifying trafficked persons. Our research also reveals that vice raids and federal anti-trafficking raids are all too frequently accompanied by violations of the human rights of trafficked persons and sex workers alike, and can therefore be counterproductive to the underlying goals of anti-trafficking initiatives. Our findings suggest that a rights-based and "victim-centered" approach to trafficking in persons requires the development and promotion of alternate methods of identifying and protecting the rights of trafficked persons which prioritize the needs, agency, and self-determination of trafficking survivors. They also indicate that preventative approaches, which address the circumstances that facilitate trafficking in persons, should be pursued over law enforcement-based responses.

Legal Framework

The passage of the Victims of Trafficking and Violence Protection Act (TVPA) in 2000 created a legal framework for the prosecution of the crime of "trafficking in persons," and provided for assistance to trafficked persons identified or "certified" as such by law enforcement or another government agency.

Under the TVPA there are two forms of temporary immigration relief available specifically to trafficking victims. Continued Presence (CP) is an interim status that can only be conferred by Immigration and Customs Enforcement (ICE) on non-citizens whom law enforcement believes may be trafficking victims, allowing them to stay in the United States pending criminal prosecution of their traffickers. This status is renewable after a year, and although it confers work authorization and certification for benefits by the Department of Health and Human Services (HHS), it does not lead to permanent immigration status. In contrast, the T Visa is a four-year temporary visa, which not only grants work authorization and certification for benefits, but also makes recipients eligible to apply for adjustment to permanent residency status after three years. T visa recipients can also apply to have their close family members join them in the United States. Certified trafficking victims are eligible for the same benefits and services as refugees and asylum seekers, and thus service programs are largely provided through HHS refugee resettlement programs.

Law enforcement raids have served as the U.S. government's primary means of identifying victims of trafficking in persons.[3] While there have been some successes, law enforcement based approaches to trafficking have led to the identification of very few trafficked persons.[4] According to recently released federal regulations, as of December 2008, only 787 T visas total have been granted to trafficked persons since they became available—nowhere near the 5,000 visas available for trafficked persons annually. Meanwhile, in 2008 alone it appears that 483 people—more than half of the total number of T-visas issued to date—were placed in immigration proceedings following anti-trafficking raids.[5]

The failure of law enforcement raids to successfully locate, identify, and refer large numbers of trafficked persons to supportive services may result from the fact that they are driven by and sometimes indistinguishable from efforts to curb prostitution and other forms of sex work. Government funding streams reflect this conflation of trafficking with prostitution. Funding made available under the Trafficking Victims Protection Reauthorization Act (TVPRA) of 2005 focuses on "grants to state and local law enforcement to investigate and prosecute buyers of commercial sex."[6] As a result, local law enforcement agencies have sought federal funding for "anti-trafficking task forces," which, in theory, are made up of local and federal law enforcement personnel alongside social and legal service providers, but which in reality can simply be vice squads by another name. One study found that "some local task forces have focused exclusively on prostitution, making no distinction between prostitution and sex trafficking and not pursuing labor trafficking cases."[7] Not only does this approach severely limit the possibility of locating and identifying individuals trafficked into domestic, agricultural, and service sectors, but approaching situations where trafficked individuals may be found from a perspective that prioritizes policing of prostitution undermines the identification of trafficked persons.

Scholars and advocates suggest that another reason only a relatively small number of trafficking visas have been issued to date may be that most immigrants are unaware of the existence of the services and assistance made available under TVPA, let alone how to access them.[8] Additionally, the current anti-immigrant climate and intensified immigration enforcement efforts may have rendered many trafficked persons fearful of coming forward to access such services even if they are aware of them.

In Their Own Voices

Marta

Marta, who never believed that she had been forced or coerced into prostitution, described what happened during her only interaction with law enforcement, a federal anti-trafficking raid, as follows:

"They were men [government agents] dressed in regular clothing, but their cars had lights, so I knew they were law enforcement . . . I was going in a van, and it was nighttime. We passed this car that was just sitting there, wasn't moving. It was a police car. Once we passed it, the lights went on, and another set of police came in front of the van, trapping the van between the two police cars. I don't know if they were waiting for the van specifically. They put a spotlight on the van, maybe it was flashlights, because there were many women in the van. There were six or seven of us. They approached the driver and asked for his ID and documents and asked for the door to the back to be opened (where most of the people were sitting.) Then they asked us if we had papers or if we were illegal. We all answered that we did not have papers. They cuffed the driver and the woman sitting in front with him. I didn't know at the time if it was federal agents or local police. Now, I think they were federal agents. They asked general questions to the group. One of the police got into the driver's part of the car and drove them. They drove us to a place with a lot of computers and they took our fingerprints and our pictures.

"They asked me for the money I was carrying at the time and took my cell phone and jewelry (watch and earrings) from me. I thought that this is it— they will send me back, but this is not the way it worked!

"After taking our things, they had us go separately one by one to a separate room to check to see that we did not have money in our bra or in our pants. Two women did the checking. So once they took off our jewelry, and took our pictures and fingerprints, they put us all in a room together and told us they were not going to take us to a jail. They were going to take us to a hotel instead and ask us a few questions.

"They had us there [in the first place] all night long, for about 10 hours, and I arrived at the hotel. There were 50 more of us brought for questioning there at the hotel. I don't know where the other women came from. I was there for a week. I think the questioners were federal agents because one man was from Washington.

"The place was not a jail. It was a hotel, but in the hotel, we were closed in for a week, and couldn't leave . . . we couldn't do anything. Then I went to a shelter for women. After about a week. . . . I was worried about myself—my future, what was going to happen. . . . [I felt] bad. Very stressful. I had headaches. It's kind of difficult to talk about, because I felt a lot of stress. I had a lot of headaches. It made me feel like I wanted to cry. I didn't want to eat.

"When were in the hotel being interviewed, there were insults. I had to tell them how I got here, that I had come here on foot, and explain again, once I'd already done it, and they didn't believe me. Then after all that began the insults. Then they started to generalize, saying that you guys come to this country *muertas de hambre* [pitifully poor people, literally 'dying of hunger']—it is a term that in Mexico is not a pretty thing to say about someone. It means that we come to take something that this country has. They were angry in their tone, demanding a lot of things. [One particular agent] stands out because he was the one yelling at us most. All of them though, there was a doubt or demand when they spoke to us. They wanted me to tell the story, but every time I did, they said it was lies.

"I was scared to go to the interview room, because they told us that if we did not answer things well, they were going to haul us off to jail or punish us. Yeah, [I did believe them]—they had me in the hotel, so I figured in the moment that was a distinct possibility, or something that could happen. I was afraid of going to jail."

About the policing of sex work, Marta said, "Prostitution is something that is the decision of the person who's in it, until they decide to leave it. If someone wants to stop working, all they have to do is not go to work, but if someone wants to continue to work, you should be able to. Each person should be able to come to that decision." She added, "I would say to listen to the women, because some people do it out of necessity—some people are forced to work in prostitution, but there are others who are not. When I say for necessity, I mean that here are those of us who have nothing in our country, and we do it to get a little house, or buy a piece of land, and it can be the easiest way to achieve that."

Jin

Jin was looking for inexpensive accommodation, was offered a cheap place and accepted. But when she arrived, she was forced into prostitution. After a few days, the premises were raided by local police and Jin was arrested. She served several months in jail for prostitution, despite the fact that she had been forced into it. She was identified as trafficked only after her criminal defense attorney took the time to learn more about her, and brought in a service provider who specialized in trafficking cases. Jin describes the raid as follows:

"There were so many policemen, the whole house was filled with maybe fifteen officers. I was in 'the boss' house.' I didn't know anything. I saw the auntie run so I ran too and as I was running a police officer struck me in the back of the head with the back of a gun and I fell to the floor and I passed out. At the time I didn't know what was going on. There was someone in the house and he was wearing plainclothes and it wasn't until later that we realized he was a police officer. When I saw the auntie run I started running. It was after that I discovered that they were police. I had no idea they were police when they all broke in. The ones that came in were not wearing uniforms. When I woke up, then I saw people with uniforms. I was passed out for less than a minute. I was struck in the head really hard. I woke up because someone was picking me up. It was a female officer and she opened up my skirt and revealed my undergarments in front of everyone to see if I was hiding anything on me. I was scared, I didn't even know what they wanted to do, at that point I would do whatever they said I was so frightened.

"They took me to the police station. The whole time I was shaken and I was in shock. I didn't know how far away it was because I was in shock. They took us in a small car, they put us each in different cars. It looks like a regular car.

"At the police station, I was asked a few questions. They were saying things to me but I didn't understand. All I did was say my name and I handed over my documents. They kept saying things to me that I didn't understand. Later on I fainted and they called a medical person to take a look at me. I was locked up by myself. They asked me questions first and then later on I was locked up. There was a telephone interpreter. I understood the person on the phone. He said, 'This person is so-and-so, and he wants to ask you some questions.' I don't remember what they asked. They asked me who I was, how did I get here, my family members, I think.

"Later on it was immigration agents (after I was out of jail). When they asked me questions, they asked me what I was doing here and how I came to the U.S. I begged them not to send me back. They came that day. I think they were there when the raid happened. Immigration [agents] came and asked me questions such as do you recognize this person. They asked if I recognized certain men who came into the house, but I couldn't remember the differences between anyone at that point.

"I wasn't allowed to make a phone call on the first night, but from jail I could make phone calls but I had to sign up for it, and could only make phone calls to a home phone, not to a cell phone. The first night I was in a police precinct. The second night I was in jail and I was there for a week to 10 days. My lawyer came to see me and a social worker, but not the immigration agents. Then I was bailed out and was free for a week. Then I went to court and was locked up for about a month. After I was out, then the immigration agents interviewed me. I was given a sentence of a few months of parole, then I was taken to an immigration holding cell. I had been in for three months. I was only in the immigration holding cell for an hour waiting for the agents to pick me up. The first time when I saw the judge after being bailed out for a week, at court, I thought that I would make bail from the immigration agents at that time, but unfortunately the judge sentenced me to six months, but then it turned out to be only served three months and then three months on parole. I didn't think the immigration agents were going to come back to get me, I had given up all hope.

"The agent took me to the immigration office and that's when the social worker came to get me and took me to the shelter. I was told that it was better to stay with the social worker at the shelter. I think [the agent] wanted me to stay there, I don't remember. The shelter was pretty nice. They would give you money to spend. You could come and go as you please. They let you use the phone. I didn't think it was a shelter and they just said, 'We're going to take you to another place.' I didn't know if it was another jail or what. Once I got there I understood it was a shelter. They gave me a telephone card and allowed me to make calls. And I was free to come and go and do whatever I wanted. At first I was really afraid, thinking 'the boss' [the trafficker] could [find me and] just walk in. But eventually I started to get the hang of how it was there. They really valued safety because there were many types of residents. So they would tell us not to bring strangers or anyone to the shelter. They might be our friends but they might be enemies of others. It made me feel safe and like it was a home where you have to be careful and guard the vicinity and watch out for each other.

"Later on when I met people from immigration I thought they were pretty nice. I didn't go straight to see the immigration agents. I was taken in a truck or bus to an immigration holding cell. The agent and the social worker came to pick me up. She told me not to be afraid. During immigration interviews while in the shelter, they were asking me to point out [the person who forced me into prostitution] and at the time I had just gotten out and when I was arrested in the police station they had given me photos and asked me to identify people. I saw pictures of [the trafficker] but didn't identify anyone. I said that I wanted to take the blame and say I willingly did this and get this over with. When I was free the first time for a week, [the person who forced me into prostitution] said I shouldn't tell the police anything and not go back to court because she knew a lot of people in the police and only bad things would happen to me. She asked if I had told on her and I said 'no' and she asked if I had pointed out her husband and I said I hadn't. I said I didn't point out anyone and asked her to help me get this case over with. She warned me not to tell on her. So when I showed up for court it was just like [the trafficker] said, that I would be in trouble and it was true. So while I was locked up for those few months I felt a lot of anger and stress and I was really upset, why was I the only one in trouble and not her? So when I met with the agents they said, 'well we helped you, so now we want you to help us.' So when they pulled out pictures of [the trafficker] and her husband I pointed them out. They also wanted me to be a witness and help them for their case."

With respect to the use of raids to address trafficking, Jin said:

"A better way to help leave my situation would be anything that didn't involve the police. Because [the person who forced me into prostitution] had told me that she knew the police and that they would keep me and I would be in trouble. I thought the way I was going to leave was her taking me to the bus station. When [the raid] happened I thought it was my punishment, and that she was really powerful. With the police you can't tell them anything, you have to beg for them to send you home, you have to take the fall for anything. I think the police could have not hit me. It was not necessary, the whole house was surrounded. They could have caught me easily and they didn't need to hit me.

"Well, that day when I was ready to leave she said I only had to do another two days. So if I only had to stay for another two days to do that work for her I would take that over being arrested. The whole time I kept thinking about my children and was worried that they would know. If I just stayed there like [the person who forced me into prostitution] promised and then she let me go that would have been better."

NOTES

1. United Nations Optional Protocol to Prevent Suppress and Punish Trafficking in Persons, Especially Women and Children, 2000; Victims of Trafficking and Violence Protection Act, 2000.

2. Global Alliance Against Traffic in Women. *Collateral Damage: The Impact of Anti-Trafficking Measures on Human Rights around the World* (Bangkok, Thailand, 2007), 239–41; Women's Commission for Refugee Women and Children, *The US Response to Human Trafficking: An Unbalanced Approach* (New York: Women's Commission for Refugee Women and Children, 2007).

3. Human Trafficking Better Data Strategy and Reporting Needed to Enhance U.S. Antitrafficking Efforts Abroad (United States Government Accounting Office, 2006), http://www.gao.gov/new.items/d06825.pdf.

4. P. Meyer, "Three Paths to Dallas: How Three South Korean Women Made It to Dallas Spas," *The Dallas Morning News,* May 7, 2006.

5. U.S. Department of Homeland Security, Press Release, December 18, 2008, http://www.dhs.gov/xnews/releases/pr_1229609413187.shtm (accessed December 11, 2009).

6. Global Alliance Against Traffic in Women, 2007, 236–37; Women's Commission for Refugee Women and Children, 2007, 14.

7. Women's Commission for Refugee Women and Children, 2007, 14.

8. M. G. Paz and D. Fry, *Bringing the Global to the Local: Using Participatory Research to Address Sexual Violence with Immigrant Communities in NYC* (New York: New York City Alliance Against Sexual Assault, 2008); Women's Commission for Refugee Women and Children, 2007, 12.

Source: Ditmore, Melissa. *The Use of Raids to Fight Trafficking in Persons* (New York: Sex Workers Project of the Urban Justice Center, 2009), http://www.sexworkersproject.org/publications/reports/raids-and-trafficking/. Used with permission.

Online Resources about Prostitution in the United States

TEXT RESOURCES

Bound, Not Gagged
  Blog written by sex workers and allies across the country.
  http://deepthroated.wordpress.com/

ProCon.org: Prostitution
  Comprehensive information about prostitution, including a discussion of whether prostitution should be legal and a historical timeline of prostitution across the globe.
  http://prostitution.procon.org/viewtopic.asp

Prostitutes Education Network
  Information and resources about prostitution and sex worker activism.
  http://www.bayswan.org

Prostitution Research and Education
  Organization dedicated to research about prostitution and trafficking, founded by abolitionist Melissa Farley.
  http://www.prostitutionresearch.com/about.html

Sex Work 101
  Information about sex work and sex worker activism.
  http://www.sexwork101.com/

$pread Magazine Online
  Includes a blog and articles from back issues of *$pread*, a print magazine by and for sex workers.
  http://spreadmagazine.org/

SWOP-East Blog
Sex work-related news blog written by members of SWOP-East.
http://swopeast.blogspot.com/

Yes On Prop K
Website promoting support for Proposition K, the November 2008 ballot initiative to decriminalize prostitution in San Francisco.
http://yesonpropk.org/

AUDIO RESOURCES

Jazeera Iman and Shira Hassan of Young Women's Empowerment Project Interviewed on Chicago Public Radio
http://www.chicagopublicradio.org/Content.aspx?audioID=37026

Proposition K Advocates Interviewed on National Public Radio
http://www.npr.org/templates/story/story.php?storyId=96536498

Sex Workers Project Podcasts
Interviews with street-based sex workers in New York.
http://www.sexworkersproject.org/multimedia/podcasts/

Sex Worker Internet Radio Library (SWIRL)
Audio library of interviews, discussions, and art by sex workers.
http://www.jeweltone16.org/swirl/

VIDEO RESOURCES

Commentary by Audacia Ray on the Spitzer Scandal, from CNN Headline News.
http://www.sexworkawareness.org/audacia-ray-on-cnn/

Videos made during the National March for Sex Worker Rights in Washington, D.C.
http://www.redlightdistrictchicago.com/?p=51

Red Light District Chicago
Videos about sex worker issues made by activists in Chicago.
http://www.redlightdistrictchicago.com/

Sex Workers Present
Videos made by sex workers from around the world.
http://sexworkerspresent.blip.tv/

Taking the Pledge
A 13-minute film featuring sex workers from around the world describing problems created by the "anti-prostitution pledge" required to receive U.S. Agency for International Development (USAID) and President's Emergency Plan for AIDS Relief (PEPFAR) funds.
http://sexworkerspresent.blip.tv/file/181155/

Tired of the Private Show: Taking Sex Work out of the Shadows and into Public
Consciousness
Videos and information about sex worker activism, art, and literature.
http://www.nyc24.org/2006/issue3/story03/index.html

Yes on Prop. K
Margaret Prescod of the Black Coalition Fighting Back Serial Murders talks about
Proposition K as an anti-racist measure.
http://www.youtube.com/watch?v=solujyC8SIM

ADVOCACY AND OUTREACH ORGANIZATIONS

Desiree Alliance
National coalition of sex workers and allies working to build leadership in the sex
worker community and advocate for sex worker rights.
http://www.desireealliance.org/

Different Avenues
Outreach organization providing services for sex workers in Washington, D.C.
http://differentavenues.org/

HIPS (Helping Individual Prostitutes Survive)
Outreach organization providing services to sex workers in Washington, D.C.
http://www.hips.org/

International Sex Worker Foundation for Art, Culture and Education
Resource pages, including a video about the organization that was aired on VH1
in 1998.
http://www.iswface.org

Global Network of Sex Work Projects (NSWP)
International alliance of organizations that provide services to sex workers.
http://www.nswp.org/

Project Safe
Outreach organization providing services to sex workers in Philadelphia, Penn.
http://www.safephila.org/

Sex Work Awareness
New York-based sex worker advocacy organization.
http://www.sexworkawareness.org/

Sex Workers Outreach Project (SWOP-USA)
National social justice network dedicated to the human rights of sex workers, with
links to chapters across the United States.
http://www.swopusa.org/

Sex Workers Project
  New York organization providing legal services and training and engaging in
    documentation and policy advocacy for sex workers.
  http://sexworkersproject.org/

St. James Infirmary
  Health clinic in San Francisco run by and for sex workers.
  http://stjamesinfirmary.org/

Young Women's Empowerment Project (YWEP)
  Organization providing services for young women and girls involved in the sex
    trade and street economy in Chicago.
  http://youarepriceless.org/

ARTICLES AND BLOG POSTS

*Criminalizing Sex Work to Combat Trafficking: Rhode Island Considers the Wrong
    Solution to the Wrong Problem*
  Andrea Ritchie on RH Reality Check
  September 3, 2009
  http://www.rhrealitycheck.org/blog/2009/09/02/criminalizing-sex-work-combat
    -prostitution-rhode-island-poised

*Looking Beneath the Surface: A Response to the Washington Post's Attack on the Anti-
    Trafficking Movement in the U.S.*
  Donna M. Hughes on National Review Online
  October 1, 2007
  http://article.nationalreview.com/?q=ZTk0OTFjYzQ1MmFjNTA1YmU0YjkxZ
    DYxMTZkMjBlY2Y=

Police Arrest Prostitutes Because They Carry Condoms: New York Law
  Laura Agustín on Border Thinking on Migration, Trafficking, and Commercial Sex
  November 26, 2009
  http://www.nodo50.org/Laura_Agustin/police-arrest-prostitutes-because-they
    -carry-condoms-new-york-law

Sex Work, Trafficking: Understanding the Difference
  Melissa Ditmore on RH Reality Check
  May 6, 2008
  http://www.rhrealitycheck.org/blog/2008/05/05/sex-work-trafficking
    -understanding-difference

SF's Proposition K: Changing the Landscape for Sex Workers
  Sienna Baskin and Melissa Ditmore on RH Reality Check
  October 28, 2008
  http://www.rhrealitycheck.org/blog/2008/10/27/san-franciscos-proposition-k
    -starts-conversation-about-policing-sex-work

The Craigslist Sex Panic: How Shutting Down Its "Erotic Services" Section Hurts Prostitutes and Cops
Melissa Gira Grant on Slate
May 27, 2009
http://www.slate.com/id/2219167/

The Crusade Against Sex Trafficking and *Beyond Rescue*
Noy Thrupkaew on The Nation
September 16 and October 8, 2009
http://www.thenation.com/doc/20091005/thrupkaew
http://www.thenation.com/doc/20091026/thrupkaew

Who's Trafficked?
Melissa Ditmore on RH Reality Check
May 19, 2008
http://www.rhrealitycheck.org/blog/2008/05/16/whos-trafficked

Wilberforce Can Free Again: Protecting Trafficking Victims
Donna M. Hughes on National Review Online
March 12, 2008
http://article.nationalreview.com/?q=M2UyZWJjN2E2MTQ3ZDQ3MGFm
NTkyMWMyNDEwOGQzMWY=

RESEARCH AND REPORTS

Melissa Ditmore
The Use of Raids to Fight Trafficking in Persons (New York: Sex Workers Project at the Urban Justice Center, 2009)
http://www.sexworkersproject.org/publications/reports/raids-and-trafficking/

Global Alliance Against Traffic in Women
Collateral Damage: The Impact of Anti-Trafficking Measures on Human Rights Around the World (Bangkok, Thailand: Global Alliance Against Traffic in Women, 2007),
http://www.soros.org/initiatives/health/focus/sharp/articles_publications/
publications/collateraldamage_20070927.

Kate Hausbeck and Barb Brents
State-Sanctioned Prostitution: Negotiating Formal and Informal Regulatory Practices in Nevada Brothels, 2001
faculty.unlv.edu/brents/research/socpersp.pdf

Janice G. Raymond and Donna M. Hughes
Sex Trafficking of Women in the United States (2001)
http://www.uri.edu/artsci/wms/hughes/sex_traff_us.pdf

Sex Workers Project at the Urban Justice Center
Sex Work and Human Rights Media Toolkit (New York: Sex Workers Project, 2007)
http://sexworkersproject.org/media-toolkit/

St. James Infirmary Publications and Presentations
http://stjamesinfirmary.org/?page_id=30

SWEAT Shorts: A Blog about the Sex Worker Environmental Assessment Team Research Project
University of California, San Francisco, and St. James Infirmary, 2006–2007
http://sweat-shorts.blogspot.com/

Juhu Thukral and Melissa Ditmore
Revolving Door: An Analysis of Street-based Prostitution in New York City (New York: Sex Workers Project at the Urban Justice Center, 2003)
http://www.sexworkersproject.org/publications/reports/revolving-door/

Juhu Thukral, Melissa Ditmore, and Alexandra Murphy
Behind Closed Doors: An Analysis of Indoor Sex Work in New York City (Sex Workers Project at the Urban Justice Center, 2005)
http://www.sexworkersproject.org/publications/reports/behind-closed-doors/

Young Women's Empowerment Project
Girls Do What They Have to Do to Survive: Methods Used by Girls in the Sex Trade and Street Economy to Fight Back and Heal (Chicago: Young Women's Empowerment Project, 2009)
http://youarepriceless.org/node/190

BOOKS AND REPORTS IN THE PUBLIC DOMAIN

William Burgess and Harry Olson
The World's Social Evil: A Historical Review and Study of the Problems Relating to the Subject (Chicago: Saul Brothers, 1914)
http://books.google.com/books?id=uy8KAAAAIAAJ&printsec=frontcover&dq=social+evil&lr=&as_drrb_is=b&as_minm_is=1&as_miny_is=1700&as_maxm_is=1&as_maxy_is=1923&as_brr=0#v=onepage&q=&f=false

Committee of Fifteen
The Social Evil: With Special Reference to Conditions Existing in the City of New York (1900)
http://books.google.com/books?id=7O4TAAAAIAAJ&printsec=frontcover&dq=the+social+evil#v=onepage&q=&f=false

Committee of Fourteen
The Social Evil in New York City: A Study of Law Enforcement (1910)
http://books.google.com/books?id=_c3C8qftAfgC&printsec=frontcover&dq=the+social+evil#v=onepage&q=&f=false

Andrew F. Currier

The Unrestricted Evil of Prostitution (The Philanthropist, 1891)

http://books.google.com/books?id=X4NUwLDUrJsC&printsec=frontcover&dq
=prostitution&lr=&as_drrb_is=b&as_minm_is=1&as_miny_is=1700&as_maxm
_is=1&as_maxy_is=1923&as_brr=0#v=onepage&q=&f=false

Albert W. Elliott

The Cause of the Social Evil and the Remedy. (Atlanta: Webb and Vary Co. Printers, 1914)

http://books.google.com/books?id=YqMYAAAAYAAJ&printsec=frontcover
&dq=the+social+evil&lr=#v=onepage&q=&f=false

William Packard Hatch and John B. Hammond

Prostitution and Sex Education (San Francisco, 1910)

http://books.google.com/books?id=qTpDAAAAIAAJ&printsec=frontcover&dq
=prostitution&lr=&as_drrb_is=b&as_minm_is=1&as_miny_is=1700&as_maxm
_is=1&as_maxy_is=1923&as_brr=0#v=onepage&q=&f=false

Honolulu Social Survey

Report of Committee on the Social Evil (Honolulu Star-Bulletin, 1914)

http://books.google.com/books?id=l3nJAAAAMAAJ&pg=PA1&dq=social+evil
+honolulu&lr=&as_drrb_is=b&as_minm_is=1&as_miny_is=1700&as_maxm
_is=1&as_maxy_is=1923&as_brr=0&source=gbs_selected_pages&cad=2#v
=onepage&q=&f=false

George J. Kneeland

Commercialized Prostitution in New York City: Publication of the Bureau of Social Hygiene (New York: The Century Co., 1913)

http://books.google.com/books?id=Qn9DAAAAIAAJ&printsec=frontcover&dq
=prostitution&lr=&as_drrb_is=b&as_minm_is=1&as_miny_is=1700&as_maxm
_is=1&as_maxy_is=1923&as_brr=0#v=onepage&q=&f=false

Maude E. Miner

Slavery of Prostitution: A Plea for Emancipation (New York: The Macmillan Company, 1916)

http://books.google.com/books?id=RTVZJSuGJucC&printsec=frontcover&dq
=related:LCCN13011647#v=onepage&q=&f=false

William W. Sanger

The History of Prostitution: It's Extent, Causes, and Effects Throughout the World (New York: The Medical Publishing Co., 1897)

http://books.google.com/books?id=5wS_loZhkoQC&printsec=frontcover&dq
=related:LCCN13011647#v=onepage&q=&f=false

William T. Stead

If Christ Came to Chicago! A Plea for the Union of All Who Love in the Service of All Who Suffer (Chicago, IL: Laird & Lee, 1894)

http://books.google.com/books?id=olqCOpl4SWoC&printsec=frontcover&dq
=if+christ+came+to+Chicago&client=firefox-a&cd=1#v=onepage&q=&f=false

Syracuse Moral Survey Committee
The Social Evil in Syracuse (1913)
http://books.google.com/books?id=zA3UAAAAMAAJ&printsec=frontcover
&dq=the+social+evil&lr=#v=onepage&q=&f=false

Vice Commission of Chicago
The Social Evil in Chicago (1912)
http://books.google.com/books?id=AhXaAAAAMAAJ&printsec=frontcover
&dq=the+social+evil#v=onepage&q=&f=false

Howard Brown Woolston
Prostitution in the United States (New York: The Century Co., 1921)
http://books.google.com/books?id=3gVS1mAX3kEC&printsec=frontcover
&dq=howard+brown+woolston&lr=#v=onepage&q=&f=false

Selected Bibliography

Abbott, Karen. *Sin in the Second City: Madams, Ministers, Playboys, and the Battle for America's Soul.* New York: Random House, 2007.

Agustín, Laura María. *Sex at the Margins: Migration, Labour Markets and the Rescue Industry.* London: Zed Books, 2007.

Albert, Alexa E. *Brothel.* New York: Random House, 2001.

Amnesty International. *Stonewalled: Police Abuse and Misconduct against Lesbian, Gay and Transgender People in the U.S.* New York: Amnesty International, 2005. http://www.amnestyusa.org/lgbt-human-rights/stonewalled-a-report/page.do?id=1106610 (accessed November 2, 2009).

Andersen, Peggy. The Associated Press. "Sister's 1983 Murder Still Fuels Brother's Rage at Ridgway." *The News Tribune*, December 24, 2003. http://www.thenewstribune.com/news/projects/gary_ridgway/story/366375.html (accessed December 8, 2009).

Anonymous. *Madeleine: An Autobiography.* Persea Books, 1986 (1919).

Anonymous. *Put's Golden Songster: Containing the Largest and Most Popular Collection of California Songs Ever Published by John A. Stone.* San Francisco: D. E. Appleton & Co., 1858.

Asia Watch Women's Rights Project. *A Modern Form of Slavery Trafficking of Burmese Women and Girls into Brothels in Thailand.* New York, Washington, Los Angeles and London: Human Rights Watch, 1993.

Associated Press. "Suspect in Ohio Killings Was Arrested Last Year." *The New York Times*, November 13, 2009.

Associated Press. "German Prostitutes May Get Benefits"; and *Province*, Friday, August 6, 1999, A38, "Rights for hookers" via News Services.

Bailey, Beth, and David Farmer. "Prostitutes on Strike: The Women of Hotel Street during World War II." In *Women's America Refocusing the Past*, edited by Linda K. Kerber and Jane Sherron De Hart. New York and Oxford: Oxford University Press, 1995.

Baker, Elizabeth. *Technology and Women's Work*, 91–96. New York: Columbia University Press, 1964.

Bard, M. *The Rape Victim: Challenge to the Helping System*. Research Utilization Briefs, v. 1, n. 2, 1976.

Barnhart, Jacqueline Baker. *The Fair but Frail*. Reno, NV: University of Nevada Press, 1986.

Bell, Laurie, ed. *Good Girls/Bad Girls*. Seattle: Seal Press, 1987.

Belza, M. J. "Risk of HIV Infection among Male Sex Workers in Spain." *Sexually Transmitted Infections* 81, no. 1 (2005), 85–88.

Bindman, Jo, with Jo Doezema. "Redefining Prostitution as Sex Work on the International Agenda." www.walnet.org/csis/papers/redefining.html (accessed June 10, 1999).

Blair, Jayson. "3 Officers at Jail Accused of Sex Acts with Prisoner." *The New York Times*, September 16, 1999.

Block, Jennifer. "Sex Trafficking: Why the Faith Trade Is Interested in the Sex Trade." *Conscience*, Summer/Autumn 2004.

Boseley, Sarah, and Suzanne Goldenberg. "Brazil Spurns U.S. Terms for AIDS Help." *The Guardian*. http://www.guardian.co.uk/aids/story/0,7369,1475965,00.html (accessed February 2, 2010).

Brown, David. "U.S. Backs Off Stipulation on AIDS Funds." *The Washington Post*. http://www.washingtonpost.com (accessed May 18, 2005).

Burgess, Ann Wolbert, and Linda Lytle Holmstrom. "Rape Trauma Syndrome." *American Journal of Psychiatry* 131 (1974): 981–86.

Butler, Anne M. *Daughters of Joy, Sisters of Misery: Prostitutes in the American West 1865–90*. Urbana and Chicago: University of Illinois Press, 1985.

Canadian Criminal Code sections 210 and 211.

Carmen, Arlene, and Howard Moody. *Working Women: The Subterranean World of Street Prostitution*. New York: Harper and Row, 1985.

Carter, David. *Stonewall*. New York: St. Martin's Press, 2004.

Chancer, Lynn. *Reconcilable Differences*. Berkeley: University of California Press, 1998.

Chapkis, Wendy. *Live Sex Acts*. New York: Routledge, 1997.

Cho, Grace M. *Haunting the Korean Diaspora: Shame, Secrecy and the Forgotten War*. Minneapolis, MN: University of Minnesota Press, 2008.

Clark, Sue Ainslie, and Edith Wyatt. *Making Both Ends Meet: The Income and Outlay of New York Working Girls*. New York: Macmillan, 1911.

Clements-Nolle, K., R. Marx, R. Guzman, and M. Katz. "HIV Prevalence, Risk Behaviors, Health Care Use, and Mental Health Status of Transgender Persons: Implications for Public Health Intervention." *American Journal of Public Health* 91 (2001): 915–21.

CNN AMFix. "RI Closes Loopholes on Minors Stripping, Indoor Prostitution." November 2, 2009. http://amfix.blogs.cnn.com/2009/11/02/ri-closes-loopholes -on-minors-stripping-indoor-prostitution/ (accessed November 2, 2009).

Connell, Noreen, and Cassandra Wilson, ed. *Rape: The First Sourcebook for Women*. New York: Plume, 1974.

Connolly, Mark Thomas. *The Response to Prostitution in the Progressive Era*. Chapel Hill: University of North Carolina, 1980.

Crago, Anna-Louise. *Our Lives Matter Sex Workers United for Health and Rights*. New York: Open Society Institute Public Health Program, 2008.

Crago, Anna-Louise. "Unholy Alliance." Alternet. http://www.alternet.org/story/ 15947/ (accessed May 23, 2005).

Crary, David. Associated Press. "Missing Prostitutes Worry Vancouver." July 24, 1999.

Curtis, Ric, Karen Terry, Meredith Dank, Kirk Dombrowski, and Bilal Khan. *The Commercial Sexual Exploitation in New York City Executive Summary*, 4. New York: The center for court Innovation, 2008. http://www.ncjrs.gov/App/publications/ Abstract.aspx?id=247061 (accessed November 14, 2009).

Delacoste, Frédérique, and Priscilla Alexander, eds. *Sex Work*. Seattle: Cleis, 1987.

D'Emilio, John, and Estelle M. Freedman. *Intimate Matters: A History of Sexuality in America*. Chicago: University of Chicago Press, 1988.

Desiree Alliance. http://www.desireealliance.org/ (accessed November 1, 2009).

Ditmore, Melissa. "Contemporary Anti-Trafficking Legislation in the U.S." Network of Sex Work Projects, 2002. http://www.nswp.org (accessed May 17, 2005).

Ditmore, Melissa Hope, ed. "The Impact of New International Anti-trafficking Law in Asia." In *Shifting the Debate*, edited by Kamala Kempadoo, Bandana Pattanaik, and Jyothi Sanghera. Boulder, CO: Paradigm Press, 2005.

Ditmore, Melissa. *The Use of Raids to Fight Trafficking in Persons*. New York: Sex Workers Project, 2009. http://www.sexworkersproject.org/publications/reports/ raids-and-trafficking/ (accessed November 2, 2009).

Ditmore, Melissa H. *Encyclopedia of Prostitution and Sex Work*. Westport, CT: Greenwood, 2006.

Donovan, Pamela. "Crime Legends in Old and New Media." Graduate Center of the City University of New York dissertation, 2001.

Dowd, Allan. Associated Press. "Missing 31 Women in Canada Fan Serial Killer Fears." July 27, 1999.

Dworkin, Andrea. *Pornography*. New York: Perigee, 1981.

Elifson, Kirk W., Jacqueline Boles, Ellen Posey, Mike Sweat, William Darrow, and William Elsea. "Male Transvestite Prostitutes and HIV Risk." *American Journal of Public Health* 832 (1993): 260–62.

End Demand for Sex Trafficking Act of 2005.

Epstein, Emily Landau. " 'Spectacular Wickedness': New Orleans, Prostitution, and the Politics of Sex, 1897–1917." Ph.D. diss., Yale University, 2005.

Farley, Melisssa, Isin Baral, Merab Kiremire, and Ufuk Sezgin. "Prostitution in Five Countries." *Feminism & Psychology* 8, no. 4 (1998): 405–26.

Federal Register. May 24, 2005 (Volume 70, Number 99) (Notices) (Page 29759–29760). From the Federal Register Online via GPO Access (wais.access.gpo.gov) (DOCID:fr24my05-62).

Fisher, Helen. *Anatomy of Love*. London: Simon and Schuster, 1992.

Fitzgerald, Francis Scott. *Tender Is the Night*. New York: Scribner, 1934.

Fitzgerald, Francis Scott. *This Side of Paradise*. New York: Scribner, 1920.

Frazier, Amy. Associated Press. "Federal judge Throws Out Alabama's Sex Toy Ban." March 30, 1999.

Freedman, Estelle B. *Their Sisters' Keepers: Women's Prison Reform in America, 1830–1930*. Ann Arbor, MI: University of Michigan Press, 1981.

Freeman, Jo. "From Protection to Equal Opportunity: The Revolution in Women's Legal Status." In *Women, Politics and Change*, edited by Louise Tilly and Patricia Gurin, 457–81. New York: Russell Sage, 1990.

French, Dolores. *Working: My Life as a Prostitute*. New York, E. P. Dutton, 1988.

Friedman, Mack. *Strapped for Cash: A History of American Hustler Culture*. Los Angeles: Alyson Publications, 2003.

Fusco, Coco. "Hustling for Dollars: Jineterismo in Cuba." In *Global Sex Workers*, *edited by* Kempadoo and Doezema, 151–66. New York: Routledge, 1998.

Galli, M., R. Esposito, S. Antinori, M. Cernuschi, M. Moroni, F. Giannelli, et al. "HIV-1 Infection, Tuberculosis, and Syphilis in Male Transsexual Prostitutes in Milan, Italy." *Journal of Acquired Immune Deficiency Syndrome* 410 (1991): 1006–7.

Gang, Bill. "Metro Officer to Be Tried in Sexual Extortion—Court Views Video Showing Activity with Prostitute." *Las Vegas Sun*, February 28, 1997.

Gattari, P., L. Spizzichino, C. Valenzi, M. Zaccarelli, and G. Rezza. "Behavioural Patterns and HIV Infection among Drug Using Transvestites Practising Prostitution in Rome." *AIDS Care* 41 (1992): 83–87.

Geffert, James A. "Anti-Prostitution Activity and Public Health." Abstract of paper to be presented at Answers to Action, Grant MacEwan Community College, Edmonton, AB, Canada, May 4–6, 2000.

Gilfoyle, Timothy. *City of Eros*. New York and London: Norton, 1994.

Global Alliance Against Traffic in Women. *Collateral Damage: The Impact of Anti-Trafficking Measures on Human Rights around the World*, 239–41. Bangkok, Thailand, 2007.

Global Rights, International Organization for Adolescents, Lawyers Committee for Civil Rights, The Door, Urban Justice Center. "Comments on Bill to End Demand for Sex Trafficking Act of 2005." April 22, 2005.

Goldman, Marion S. *Gold Diggers and Silver Miners*. Ann Arbor, MI: University of Michigan Press, 1981.

Goodson, Teri. "A Prostitute Joins NOW." In *Whores and Other Feminists*, edited by Jill Nagle. New York: Routledge, 1997.

Grandi, J. L., A. C. Ferriera, and A. Kalichman. "HIV and Syphilis Infection among Transvestites in Sao Paulo City." IX International Conference on AIDS, Berlin, June 6–11, 1993.

Gras, M. J., T. van der Helm, R. Schenk, G. J. van Doornum, R. A. Coutinho, and J. A. van den Hoek. "HIV Infection and Risk Behaviour among Prostitutes in the Amsterdam Streetwalkers' District: Indications of Raised Prevalence of HIV among Transvestites/Transsexuals." *Nederlands tijdschrift voor geneeskunde* 14125 (1997): 1238–41 (Abstract in English on Medline.)

Grittner, Frederick K. *White Slavery: Myth, Ideology, and American Law.* New York: Garland, 1990.

Gutierrez, Maite, Pilar Tajada, Amparo Alvarez, Rosa De Julian, Margarita Baquero, Vincent Soriano, and Africa Holguin. "Prevalence of HIV-1 Non-B Subtypes, Syphilis, HTLV, and Hepatitis B and C Viruses among Immigrant Sex Workers in Madrid, Spain." *Journal of Medical Virology* 744 (2004): 521–27.

Hegarty, Marilyn E. *Victory Girls, Khaki-wackies, and Patriotutes: The Regulation of Female Sexuality during World War II.* New York and London: New York University Press, 2008.

Henderson, Mike. *Reno Gazette-Journal.* August 8, 1999.

Hobson, Barbara Meil. *Uneasy Virtue: The Politics of Prostitution and the American Reform Tradition.* New York: Basic Books, 1987.

Hollander, Xaviera, with Robin Moore and Yvonne Dunleavy. *The Happy Hooker,* 186. New York: Dell, 1972.

Human Rights Watch. "Ravaging the Vulnerable: Abuses against Persons at High Risk of HIV Infection in Bangladesh." August 2003, 15: 6c.

Inciardi, J. A., and H. L. Surratt. "Male Transvestite Sex Workers and HIV in Rio de Janeiro, Brazil." *Journal of Drug Issues* 271 (1997): 135–39.

International Committee for Prostitutes' Rights. "World Charter for Prostitutes' Rights." In *A Vindication of the Rights of Whores,* edited by Gail Pheterson, 40–42. Seattle: Seal Press, 1989.

Jacobson, Jodi. "DOJ Drops Appeal of 'Prostitution Pledge' Injunction." *RHReality-Check.* July 21, 2009. http://www.rhrealitycheck.org/blog/2009/07/21/department-justice-withdraws-appeal-injunction-against-prostitution-pledge (accessed February 2, 2010).

Jeffers, Joseph. "Paresis Hall." In *Encyclopedia of Prostitution and Sex Work,* edited by Melissa Ditmore. Vol. 2, 343–44. Westport, CT: Greenwood Press, 2006.

Jenkins, Carol. "Sex Work and HIV/AIDS." UNAIDS Technical Update. UNAIDS Best Practice Collection, 2002.

Jenness, Valerie. *Making It Work: The Prostitutes' Rights Movement in Perspective.* Hawthorne, NY: Aldine de Gruyter, 1993.

Kaplan, Esther. "Just Say Não." *The Nation,* May 30, 2005.

Kim, Rose. "Alleging Brutality." *New York Newsday,* March 23, 1998, A3.

Kneeland, George. *Commercialized Prostitution in New York City.* New York: The Century Company, 1913.

Koken, Juline A., Blair W. Morris, Kevicha H. Echols, and Jeffrey T. Parsons. "My Fair Lady of the Evening: Cultural Capital among Independent Escorts." Presented at the Annual meeting of the Society for the Scientific Study of Sexuality, San Juan, PR. November 2008.

Kramer, Kate. "Chamberlain-Kahn Act." In *Encyclopedia of Prostitution and Sex Work*, edited by Melissa Ditmore. Vol. 1, 93–94. Westport, CT: Greenwood Press, 2006.

Kuo, Lenore. "Licensed Prostitution, Nevada." In *Encyclopedia of Prostitution and Sex Work*, edited by Melissa H. Ditmore. Vol. 1, 252–54. Westport, CT: Greenwood, 2006.

Kwong, Peter. *Forbidden Workers*. New York: New Press, 1997.

Langum, David J. *Crossing Over the Line: Legislating Morality and the Mann Act.* Chicago: University of Chicago, 1994.

Leigh, Carol. *Unrepentant Whore: Collected Works of Scarlot Harlot.* San Francisco: Last Gasp, 2004.

Leigh, Carol, a.k.a. Scarlot Harlot. "In Defense of Prostitution." *Gauntlet* 1, no. 7 (December 1993).

Leuridan, Elke, K. Wouters, M. Stalpaert, and P. Van Damme. "Male Sex Workers in Antwerp, Belgium: A Descriptive Study." *International Journal of STD & AIDS* 1611 (2005): 744–48.

Lim, Lin Lean, ed. *The Sex Sector.* Geneva: ILO Publications, 1998.

Lombroso, Cesare, and William Ferrero. *The Female Offender.* New York: D. Appleton, 1895.

Mayor's Task Force Report on Adult Oriented Businesses, New York, 1994.

Meillón, Cynthia, ed., in collaboration with Charlotte Bunch. *Holding on to the Promise: Women's Human Rights and the Beijing + 5 Review.* New Brunswick: Rutgers, 2001.

Meyer, P. "Three Paths to Dallas: How Three South Korean Women Made It to Dallas Spas." *The Dallas Morning News*, May 7, 2006. http://extrablog.dallasnews .com/ (accessed May 7, 2006).

Miller, Heather. "Prostitution." In *Encyclopedia of U.S. and Working Class History*, edited by Eric Arneson. Vol. 3. New York, NY and Oxon, UK: Routledge, 2006.

Millett, Kate. *The Prostitution Papers: A Quartet for Female Voice.* New York: Ballantine Books, 1971.

Modan, B., R. Goldschmidt, E. Rubinstein, A. Vonsover, M. Zinn, R. Golan, A. Chetrit, and T. Gottlieb-Stematzky. "Prevalence of HIV Antibodies in Transsexual and Female Prostitutes." *American Journal of Public Health* 824 (1992): 590–92.

Moon, Katherine. *Sex among Allies: Military Prostitution in U.S.-Korea Relations.* New York: Columbia University Press, 1997.

Murphy, Dean. *Los Angeles Times*, July 15, 1999. Taken from the UN Wire, July 15.

Nemoto, T., D. Operario, J. Keatley, and D. Villegas. "Social Context of HIV Risk Behaviours among Male-to-Female Transgenders of Color." *AIDS Care* 16, no. 6 (2004): 724–35.

Nevada State Law NRS 244.342.

Norris, Jimmy, and Hwang Hae-rym. "Soldiers Warned about Prostitution Crackdown Near Yongsan Garrison." *Stars and Stripes*, Pacific edition, September 11,

2008. http://www.stripes.com/article.asp?section=104&article=64513&archive =true (accessed November 24, 2008).

Nye County v. Plankinton 94 Nev. 739, 1978.

O'Connell, Peter. "A Former Policeman Who Used His Job to Get Sex Will Serve 45 Days in Jail and Be Put on a Sex Offenders' List." *Las Vegas Review-Journal*, August 11, 1999.

Paz, M. G., and D. Fry. *Bringing the Global to the Local: Using Participatory Research to Address Sexual Violence with Immigrant Communities in NYC*. New York: New York City Alliance Against Sexual Assault, 2008.

Pearson, Michael. *The £5 Virgins*. New York: Saturday Review Press, 1972.

Peiss, Kathy. " 'Charity Girls' and City Pleasures: Historical Notes on Working-Class Sexuality, 1880–1920." In *Powers of Desire*, edited by Ann Snitow, Christine Stansell, and Sharon Thompson, 74–87. New York: Monthly Review Press, 1983.

Pheterson, Gail, ed. *A Vindication of the Rights of Whores*. Seattle: Seal Press, 1989.

Pisani, Elizabeth, P. Girault, M. Gultom, N. Sukartini, J. Kumalawati, S. Jazan, et al. "HIV, Syphilis Infection, and Sexual Practices among Transgenders, Male Sex Workers, and Other Men Who Have Sex with Men in Jakarta, Indonesia." *Sexually Transmitted Infections* 806 (2004): 536–40.

Potterat, John J., Devon D. Brewer, Stephen Q. Muth, Richard B. Rothenberg, Donald E. Woodhouse, John B. Muth, Heather K. Stites, and Stuart Brody. "Mortality in a Long-term Open Cohort of Prostitute Women." *American Journal of Epidemiology* 159 (2004), 778–85. http://aje.oxfordjournals.org/cgi/ content/full/159/8/778 (accessed November 19, 2009).

Prostitutes of New York. *PONY X-Press*, n. 2, 1991.

Prus, Robert, and Styllianoss Irini. *Hookers, Rounders, and Desk Clerks*. Salem, WI: Sheffield, 1980.

Quan, Tracy. "The Name of the Pose: A Sex Worker by Any Other Name." In *Prostitution and Pornography: Philosophical Debate about the Sex Industry*, edited by Jessica Spector, 341–48. Stanford, CA: Stanford University Press, 2006.

Reuters. July 24, 1999. "Police Swoop on Century-Old Bangladeshi Brothel."

Ross, Mirha-Soleil. "Dear John" performance piece excerpted from "Yapping Out Loud: Contagious Thoughts from an Unrepentant Whore." 2002. Published *in eXXXpressions: Forum XXX Proceedings*, Stella, April 2006. http://cybersolidaires .typepad.com/ameriques/2006/05/dear_john.html (accessed December 6, 2009).

Russi, Jose C., Margarita Serra, Jose Vinoles, M. T. Perez, D. Ruchansky, G. Alonso, Jose L. Sanchez, Kevin L. Russell, Silvia M. Montano, Monica Negrete, and Mercedes Weissenbacher. "Sexual Transmission of Hepatitis B Virus, Hepatitis C Virus, and Human Immunodeficiency Virus Type 1 Infections among Male Transvestite Commercial Sex Workers in Montevideo, Uruguay." *American Journal of Tropical Medicine and Hygiene* 68, no. 6 (2003): 716–20.

Sante, Luc. *Low Life: Lures and Snares of Old New York*. New York: Vintage, 1991.

Screaming Queens. Film, 2005.

Self, Helen J. *Prostitution, Women and Misuse of the Law: The Fallen Daughters of Eve.* London: Head, Frank Cass, 2003.

Sex Workers Project. http://www.sexworkersproject.org (accessed November 1, 2009).

Simon, P., C. J. Reback, and C. Bemis. "HIV Prevalence and Incidence among Male-to-Female Transsexuals Receiving HIV Prevention Services in Los Angeles County." *AIDS* 1418 (2000): 2953–55.

Sonner, Scott. "Mustang Ranch Closure Nevada County Officials Say They Will Miss Legal Brothel—For Its License Revenue." *National Post*, August 5, 1999, A14. Associated Press.

Spizzichino, Laura, Mauro Zaccarelli, Giovanni Rezza, Giuseppe Ippolito, Andrea Antinori, and Pietro Gattari. "HIV Infection among Foreign Transsexual Sex Workers in Rome: Prevalence, Behavior Patterns, and Seroconversion Rates." *Sexually Transmitted Diseases* 287 (2001): 405–11.

Sprinkle, Annie. *Post Porn Modernist: My 25 Years as a Multi-Media Whore.* San Francisco: Cleis, 1998.

Sprinkle, Annie. "Stopping the Terror: A Day to End Violence against Prostitutes." *On the Issues.* Fall 2008. http://www.ontheissuesmagazine.com/cafe2.php?id=21 (accessed November 20, 2009).

St. James Infirmary. http://stjamesinfirmary.org (accessed November 1, 2009).

Stansell, Christine. *City of Women: Sex and Class in New York, 1789–1860.* Urbana and Chicago, IL: University of Illinois Press, 1987.

Stead, William T. *If Christ Came to Chicago.* Chicago: Laird & Lee, 1894.

Sterry, David Henry, ed. *Hos, Hookers, Call Girls and Rent Boys: Professionals Writing on Life, Love, Money, and Sex*, 23. Brooklyn, NY: Soft Skull Press, 2009.

Straight for the Money, video, 1994.

Suleiman, J., G. Suleiman, and P. A. Galvao. "Seroprevalence of HIV among Transvestites in the City of Sao Paolo." V International Conference on AIDS, Montreal, June 4–9, 1989.

SWOP-USA. http://www.swop-usa.org (accessed November 1, 2009).

Talji, Silja J. A. "The Truth about the Green River Killer." *Alternet*, November 12, 2003. http://www.alternet.org/story/17171/ (accessed November 20, 2009).

Thukral, Juhu, and Melissa Ditmore. *Revolving Door: An Analysis of Street Prostitution in New York City.* New York: Sex Workers Project, 2003. http://sexworkersproject.org/publications/reports/revolving-door (accessed November 2, 2009).

Thukral, Juhu, Melissa Ditmore, and Alexandra Murphy. *Behind Closed Doors: An Analysis of Indoor Prostitution in New York City.* New York: Sex Workers Project, 2005. http://sexworkersproject.org/publications/BehindClosedDoors.html (accessed November 2, 2009).

Tong, Benson. *Unsubmissive Women: Chinese Prostitutes in Nineteenth-Century San Francisco.* Norman, OK: University of Oklahoma Press, 1994.

Trafficking Victims Protection Act of 2000.

Trafficking Victims Protection Reauthorization Act of 2003. http://www.state.gov/documents/organization/28225.pdf (accessed May 23, 2003).

United Nations Optional Protocol to Prevent Suppress and Punish Trafficking in Persons, Especially Women and Children, 2000.

United States Government Accounting Office. *Human Trafficking Better Data Strategy and Reporting Needed to Enhance US Antitrafficking Efforts Abroad.* 2006. http://www.gao.gov/new.items/d06825.pdf (accessed December 11, 2009).

United States President's Emergency Plan for AIDS Relief. 2003. http://www.pepfar.gov/about/index.htm (accessed February 2, 2010).

U.S. Department of Homeland Security, Press Release, December 18, 2008. http://www.dhs.gov/xnews/releases/pr_1229609413187.shtm (accessed December 11, 2009).

USAID. "Trafficking in Persons: The USAID Strategy for Response." February 2003.

Vance, Carole, Anne Snitow, and Ellen Willis, eds. *Pleasure and Danger.* Boston: Routledge & K. Paul, 1984.

Verster, Annette, Marina Davoli, Antonella Camposeragna, C. Valeri, and Carlo A. Perucci. "Prevalence of HIV Infection and Risk Behaviour among Street Prostitutes in Rome, 1997–1998." *AIDS Care* 133 (2001): 367–72.

Weitzer, Ronald John. "Community Groups vs. Prostitutes." *Gauntlet* 1, no. 7 (1994): 121–24.

Weitzer, Ronald John. "Flawed Theory and Method in Studies of Prostitution." *Violence Against Women* 11, no. 7 (July 2005): 934–49. http://www.gwu.edu/~soc/faculty/weitzer.cfm (accessed December 12, 2009).

Wiessing, Lucas G., Marielle S. van Roosmalen, Paula Koedijk, Bert Bieleman, and Hans Houweling. "Silicone, Hormones, and HIV in Transgender Street Prostitutes." *AIDS* 13, no. 16 (1999): 2315–17.

Wijers, Marjan, and Lin Lap-Chew. *Trafficking in Women: Forced Labour and Slavery-like Practices in Marriage, Domestic Labour and Prostitution.* Utrecht: Foundation Against Trafficking in Women (STV), 1997.

Women's Commission for Refugee Women and Children. *The US Response to Human Trafficking: An Unbalanced Approach.* New York: Women's Commission for Refugee Women and Children, 2007.

Woolston, Howard B. *Prostitution in the United States.* New York: Century, 1921.

World Health Assembly WHA45.35.

Yellin, Emily. *Our Mother's War: American Women at Home and at the Front during World War II.* New York: Simon and Schuster, 2004.

Young Women's Empowerment Project. *Girls Do What They Have to Do to Survive: Illuminating Methods Used by Girls in the Sex Trade and Street Economy to Fight Back and Heal.* Chicago: Young Women's Empowerment Project, 2009. http://youarepriceless.org/node/190 (accessed November 14, 2009).

Index